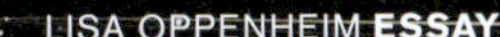

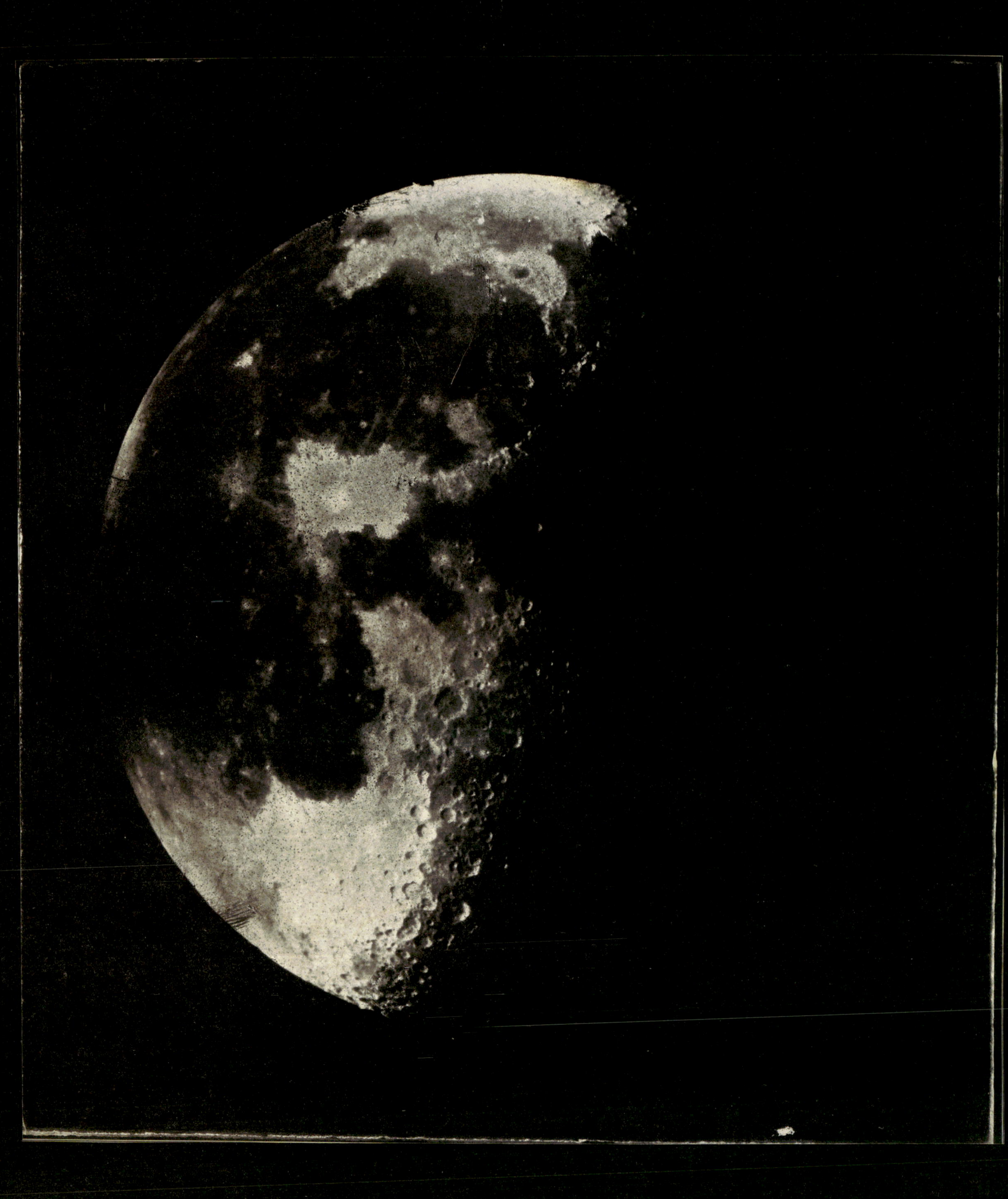

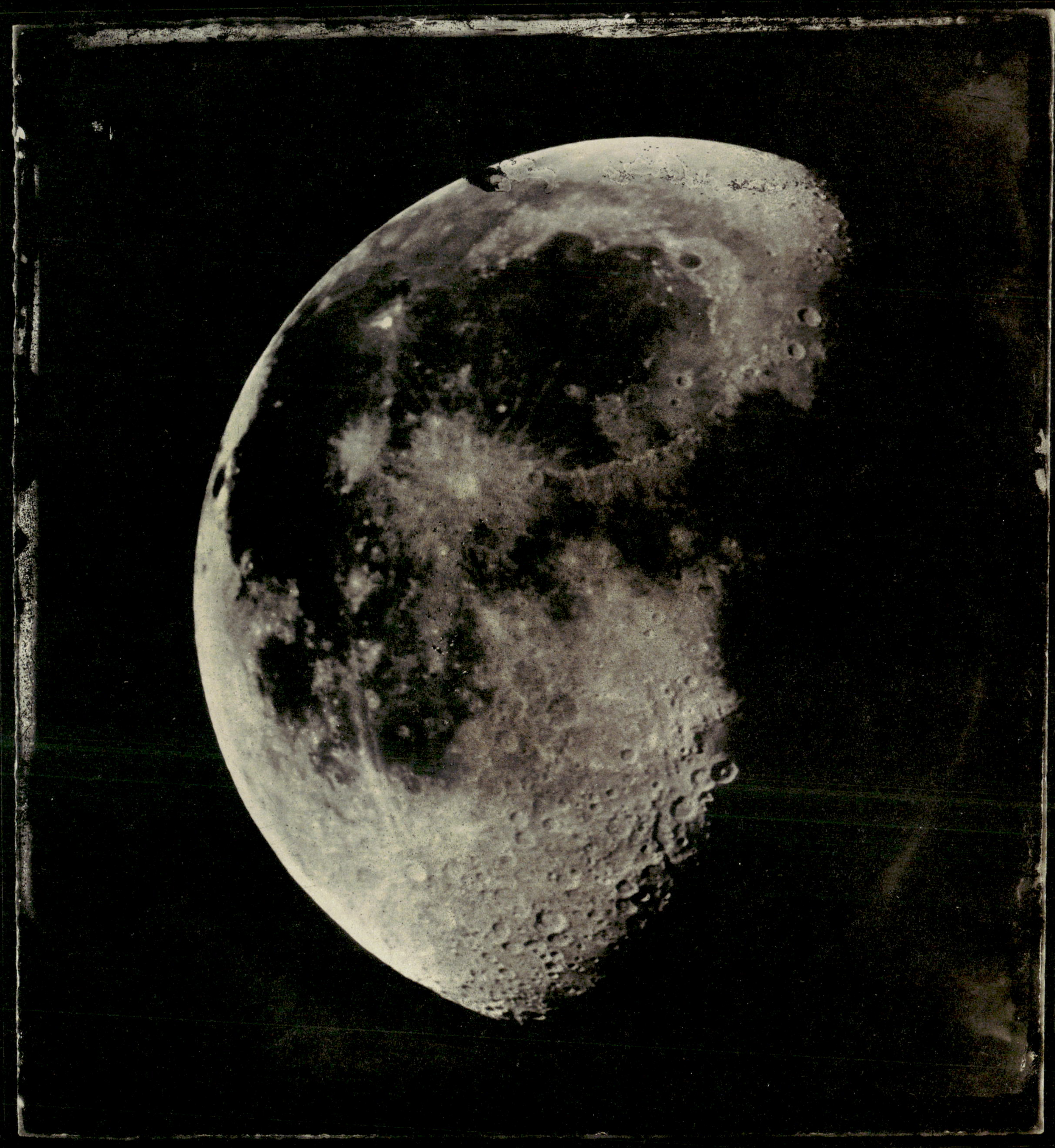

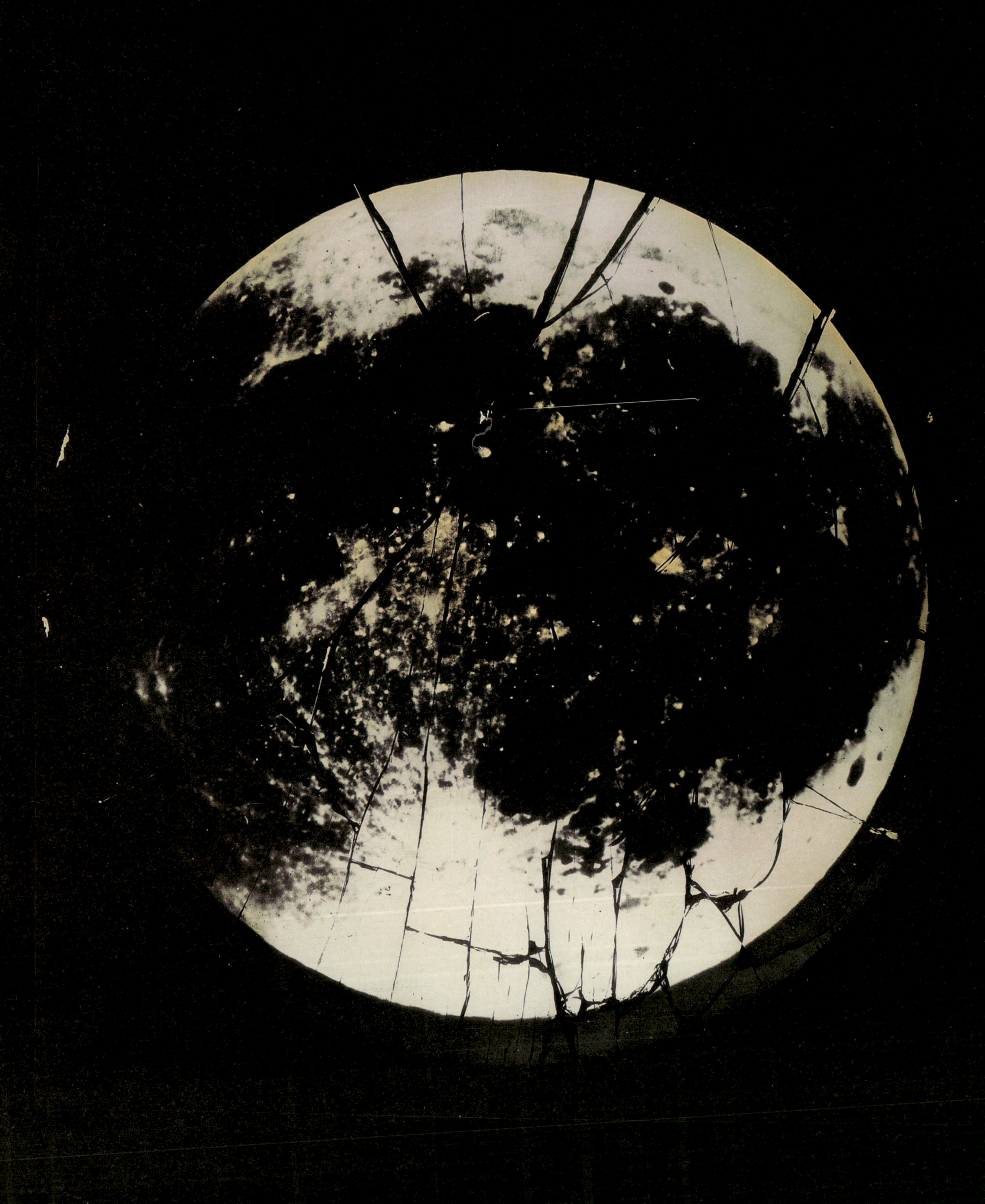

Lunagrams
LISA OPPENHEIM
by Christian Rattemeyer

The library and archives of New York University are not only a treasure trove for a great number of documents that can invoke times past both distant and near - their Downtown Collection is an invaluable source for the documentation of the 1980s New York Underground scene - but they can also provide inspiration for artists to create new works from old. New York-based artist Lisa Oppenheim was drawn to a holding of glass-plate negatives of 19th century photographs of the moon, which were taken by John William Draper and his son Henry. In 1840, Draper took the first ever image of the moon and over the next twenty years continued to record and study the heavenly body, while advancing the emulsive technology of photography (Draper was a professor of chemistry at New York University). These early examples of photographs of celestial objects reveal the moon as a protagonist with different faces, cratered and luminous, and ever changing across its path and phases. To photograph the moon in the nineteenth century not only had the obvious advantage of choosing an object of relative stillness required for the long exposure times of early photography but also served the desire to reveal something invisible to the human eye through technological means, a scientific and mystical magic, aesthetic and esoteric.

True to her long-standing interest in the intersections of the technological and the conceptual in the representational logic of photography, Oppenheim mines a particularly rich and fascinating aspect of these images for her own practice: drawing on the swings between negative-less daguerreotypes and glass negatives that already in the mid-nineteenth century represented the two faces of photography - the unique impression and the reproducible template - she subjects the images to a series of translations and reversals that draw out the paradoxes and potential of the image itself. Starting with Draper's glass-plate negatives, Oppenheim makes large-format copy negatives of the original glass-plates and places them on photographic paper. Exposing the paper to the light of the moon at the time of the lunar phase depicted in the original glass-plate, she creates a photogram of the moon by the moon, a self-image

where the moon shows and makes itself as and through its particular characteristics of each lunar phase. At the same time, as the moonlight of 2010 produces an image of the moon in 1851, Oppenheim is contracting the time between the original and the second photograph, or, rather, she marks its passing. As a final touch, Oppenheim silver-tones her 'lunagrams' before fixing, turning the white parts of the image silver.

Oppenheim's practice is always finely attuned to the possibilities of meaning that are revealed when the technical history of the medium is read against itself, opening fissures between the formal and the ideological. She has made works using additive color mixing about the moment when Crayola crayons began to reflect non-white skin tones in their collections and she has re-photographed the missing punch dot in "killed" negatives by Walker Evans. In those works, as in these, the formal means and their effects become both object and subject of their meaning.

In the *Lunagrams*, Oppenheim goes a third way between the photogram and the negative by creating, in effect, a direct contact print from a much enlarged inter-negative. Pointing to the essential battle between daguerreotype and the negative/positive technology of the 1840s, as well as the experiments with photograms in the 1910s and 1920s, Oppenheim produces an object of a paradoxical, conflicted status within the advancement of technology and the experimental order of the avant-garde. The silver toning furthers this unhinging from a linear progressive history by situating it within an outdated order of vintage or fine-art photography, while simultaneously referencing a whole corona of metaphors between the color, the element, and the moon - from its silver light to more alchemistic and ancient symbolic interchangeabilities. In the end, the *Lunagrams* are above all stunning images - highly reflective, surprisingly detailed, subtly nostalgic, oddly magical and ethereal. They appear as if disjointed from time, and allow one to begin to grasp the true magic these images must have had in 1840, when the visible world was so much more mysterious.

All images Untitled, Lunagrams, 1851-2010 © *the artist, courtesy Harris Lieberman, New York and Galerie Klosterfelde, Berlin*

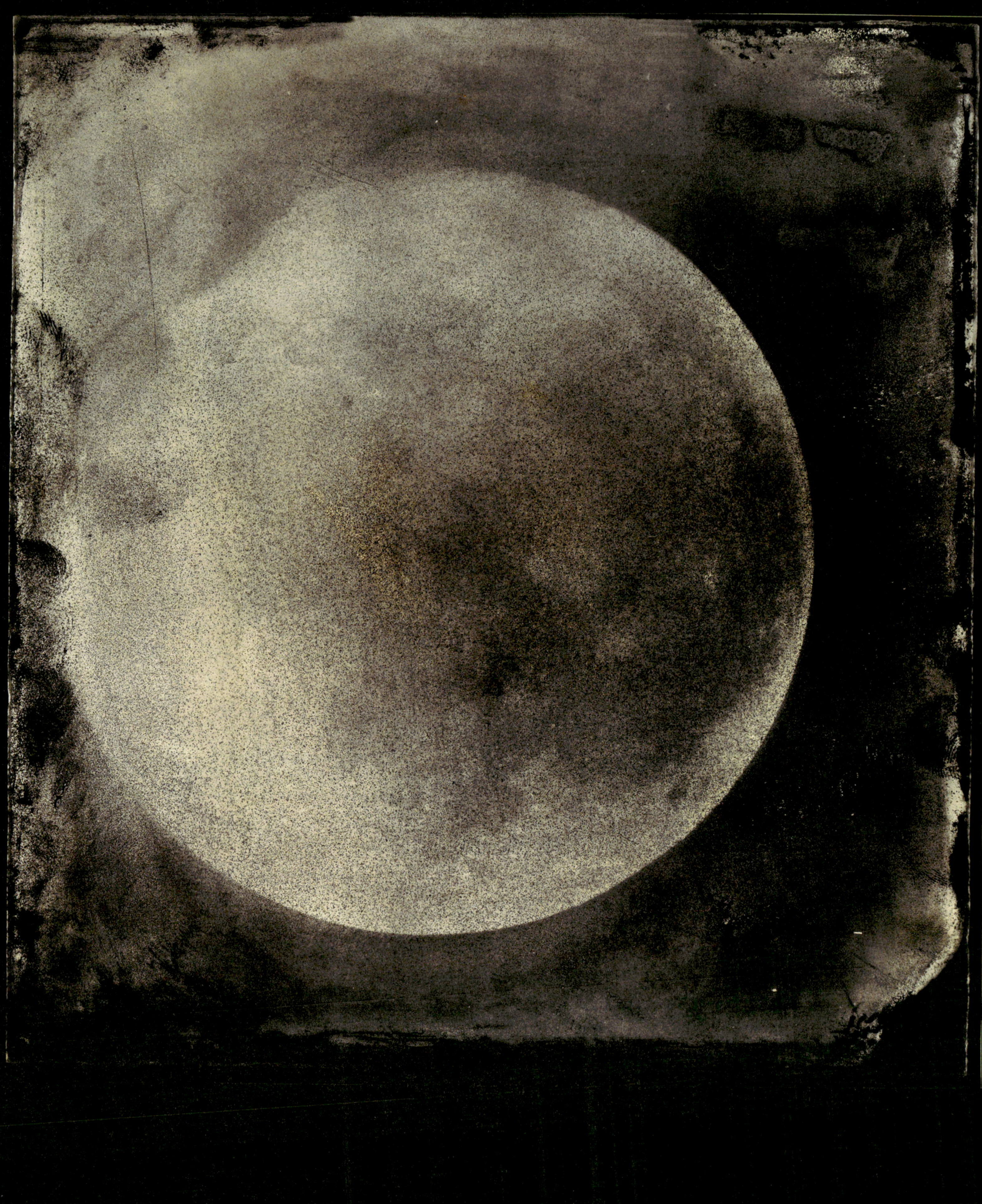

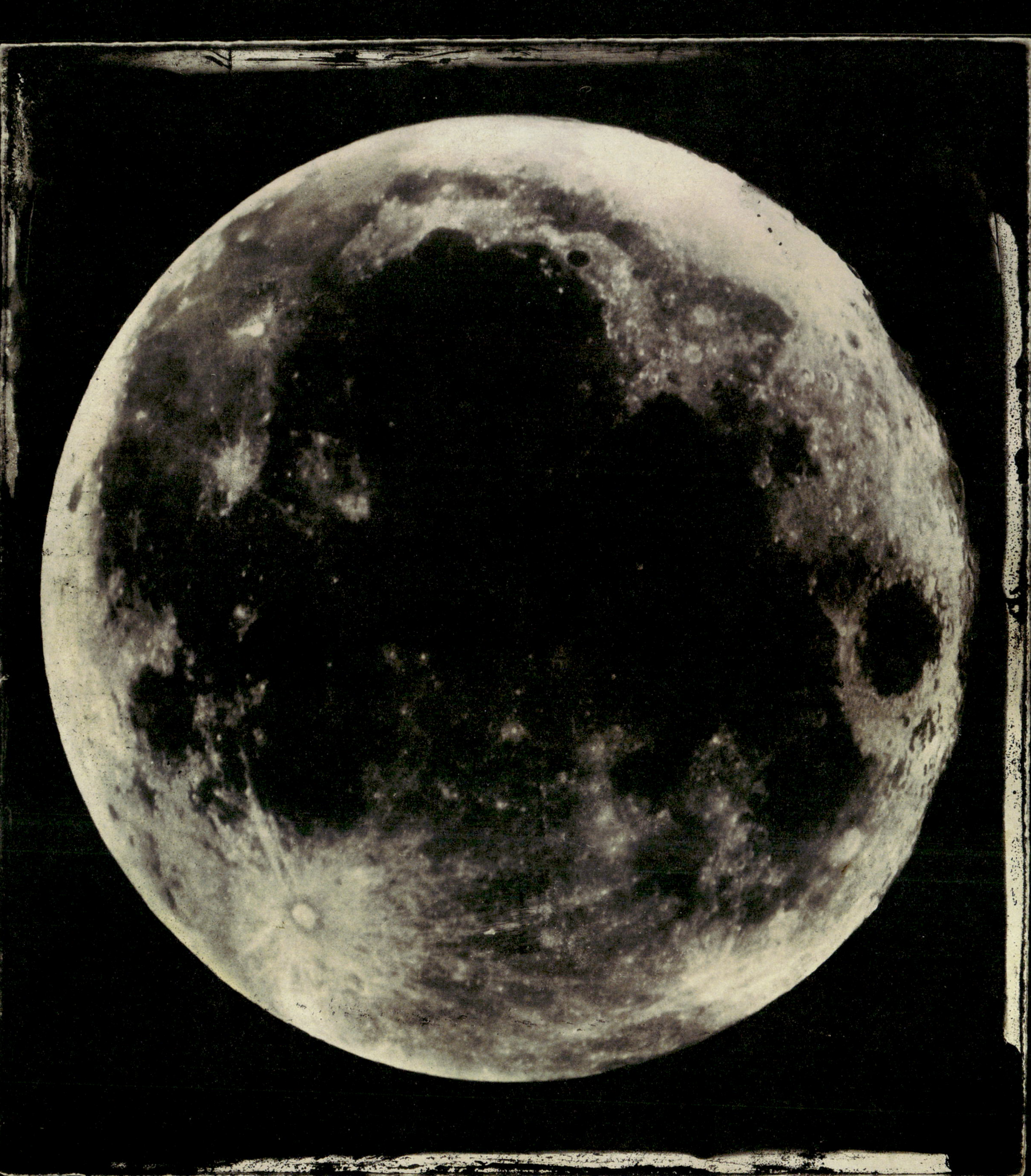

YUMIKO UTSU Her work is a mix of performance, sculpture, photography, Pop and Surrealism. Her process usually starts when she finds beautiful bugs in her garden or things like vegetables, flowers and other organic materials at the market. These are the basic subjects for the installations she prepares and then photographs. "I take pictures of my sets because of my desire to see the scene and every detail in a much larger scale. I want to be 'inside of it', literally… Another reason is preservation. I am fascinated by the texture of the living things. They will be dead soon, but can look fresh forever on a photograph". And what about the balance she always finds between life and death? "In my view, death and decay are not dark, desperate elements. Death is part of the natural cycle and all living things will go back to the ground. So, joy, death and decay are not something I need to balance. They are all aspects of life, equal elements in my photography". – Yumiko Utsu was born in 1978 in Tokyo, where she currently lives. Her work gained high reputation on the occasion of Paris Photo 2008. Utsu's first monograph, *Out of the Ark*, has just been released by Artbeat Publishers.

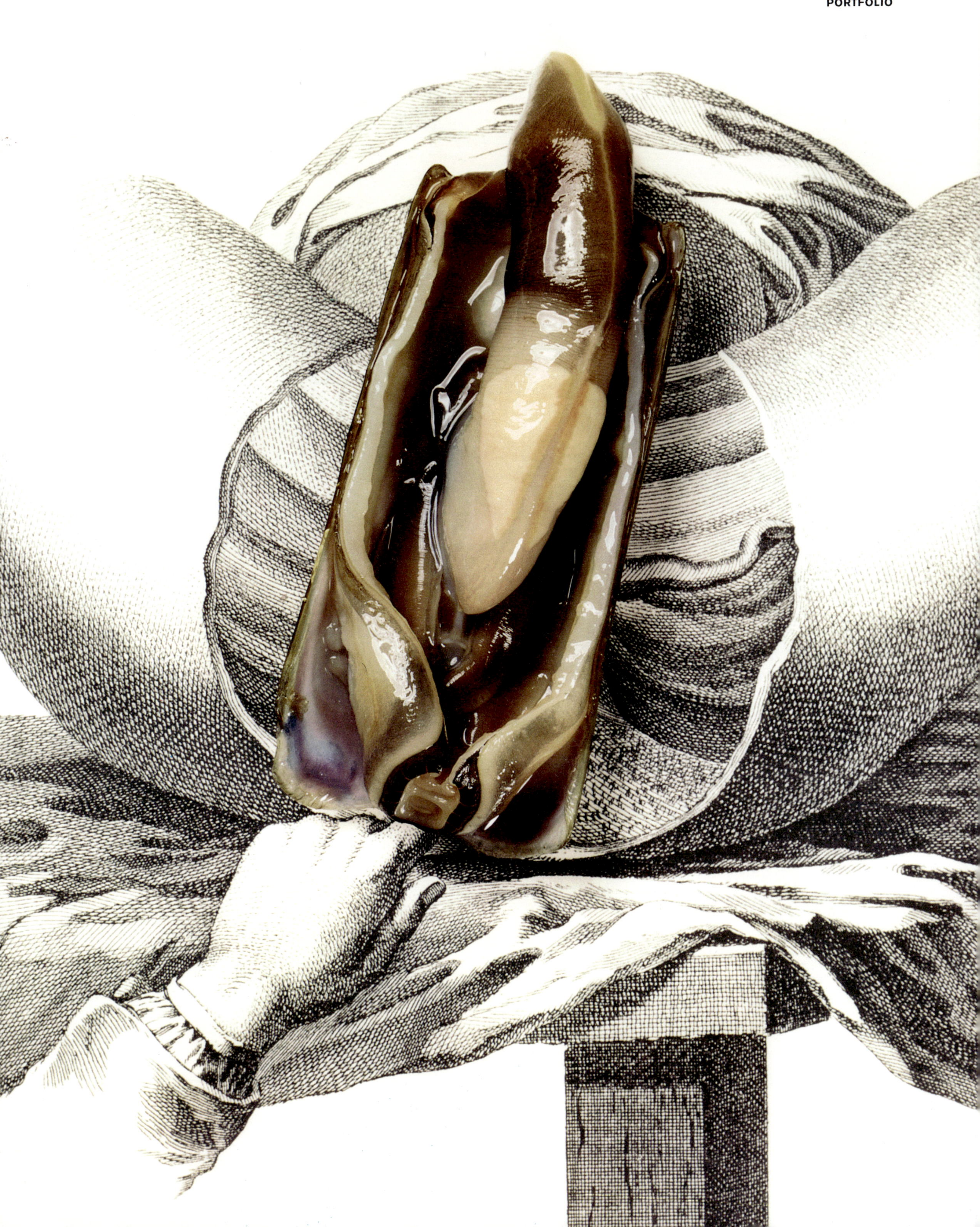

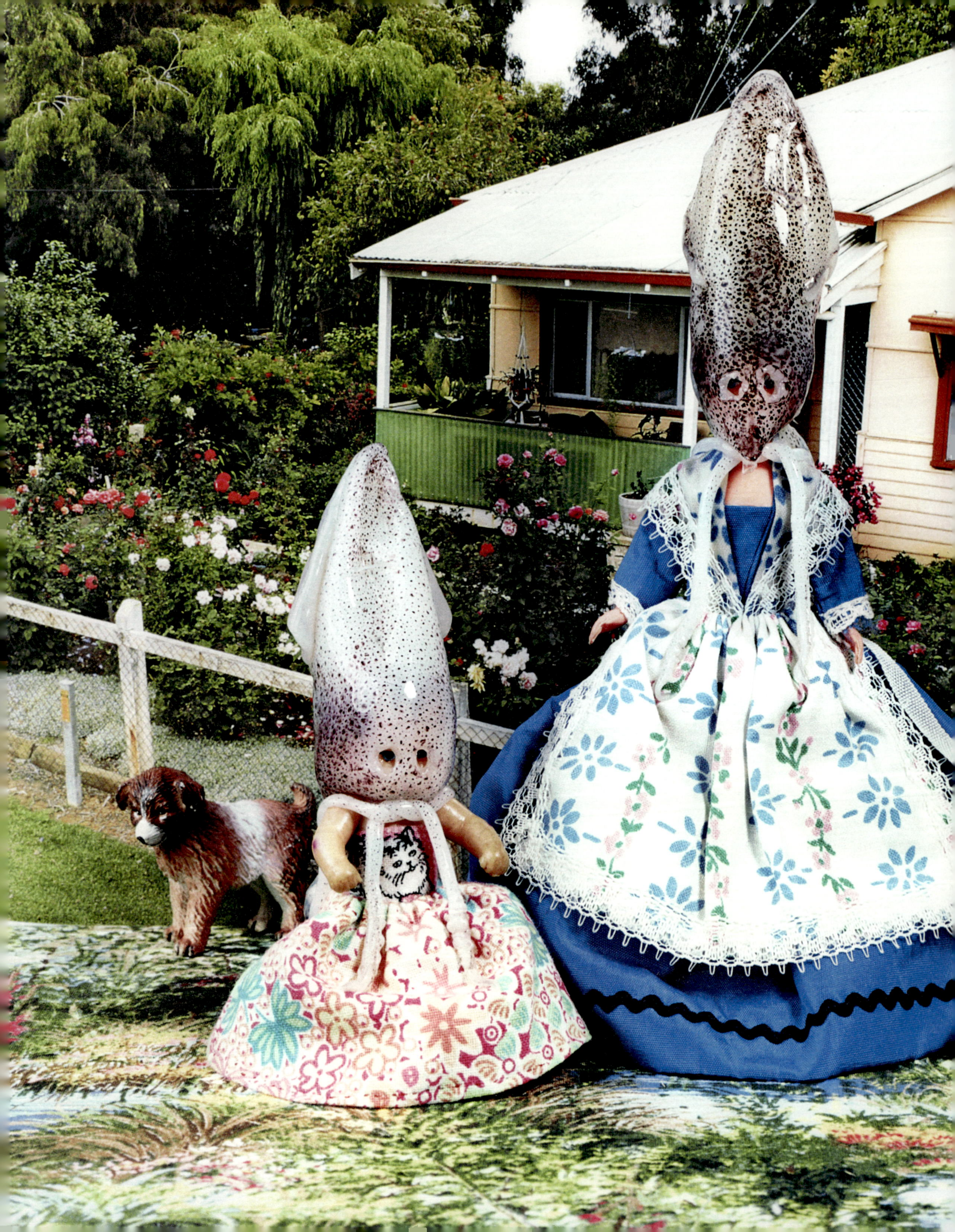

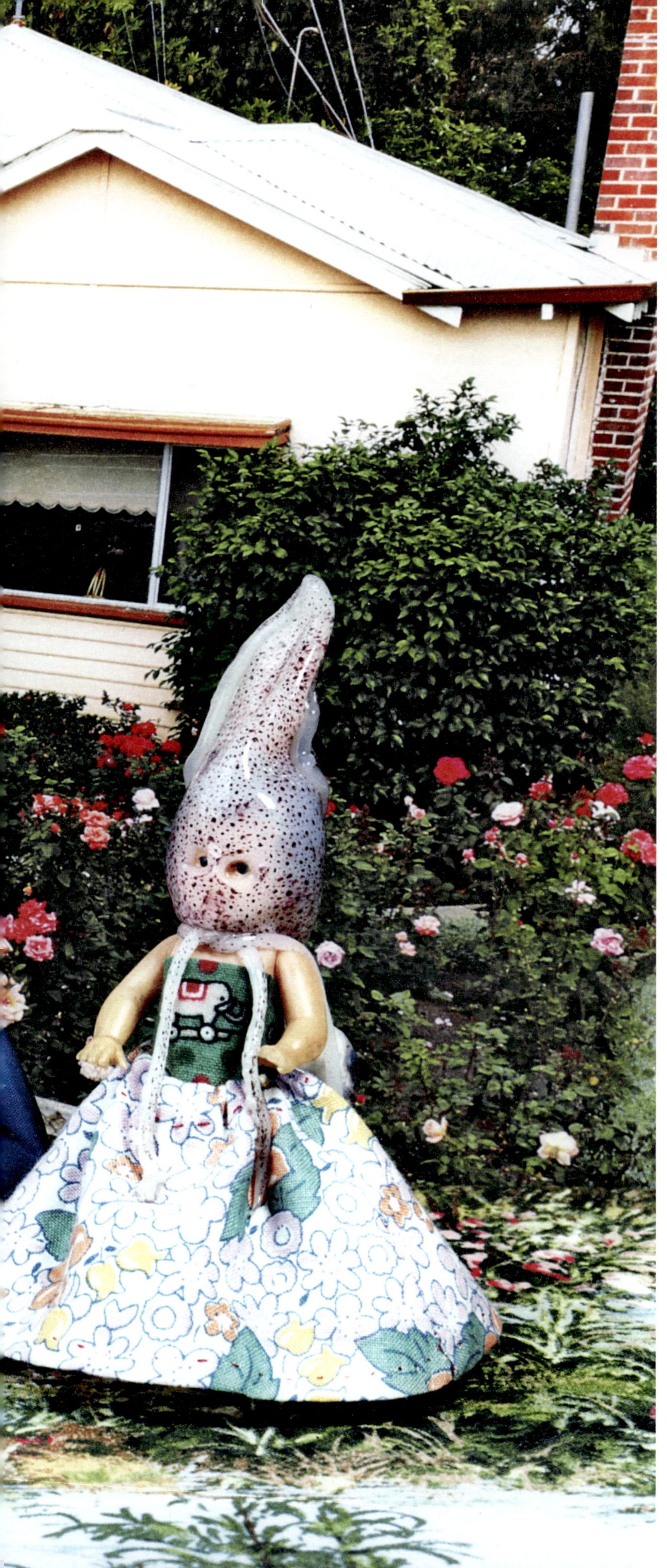

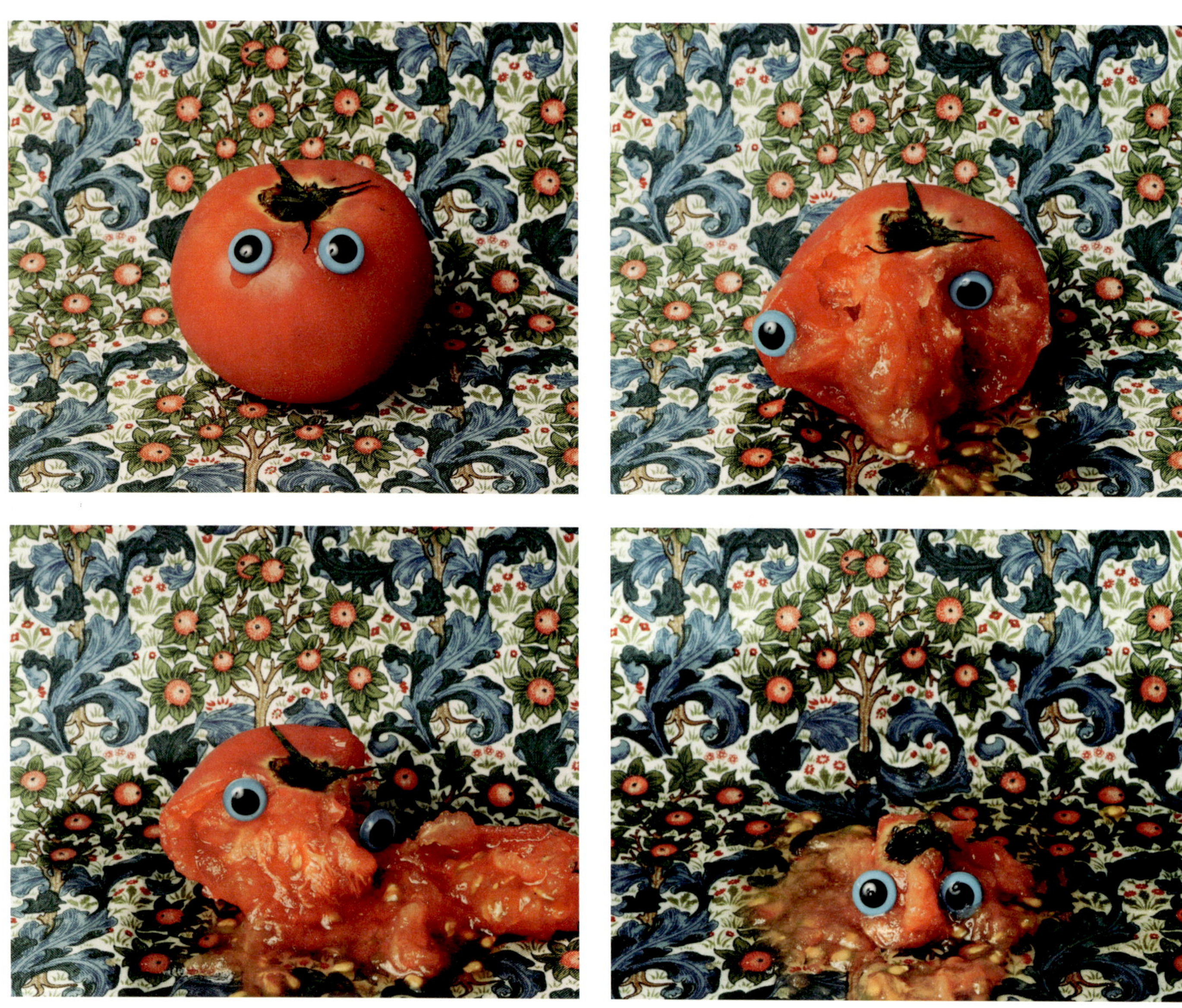

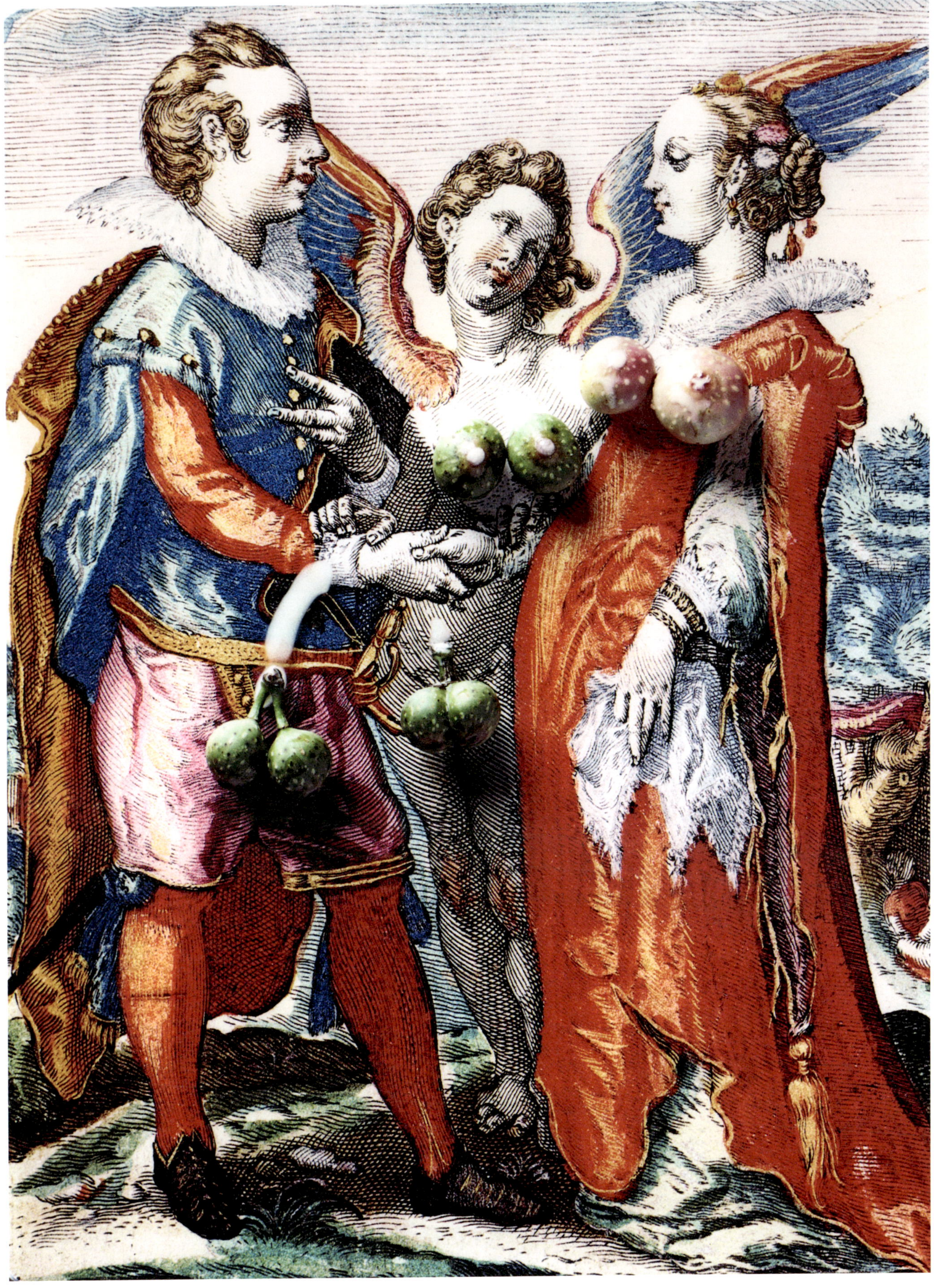

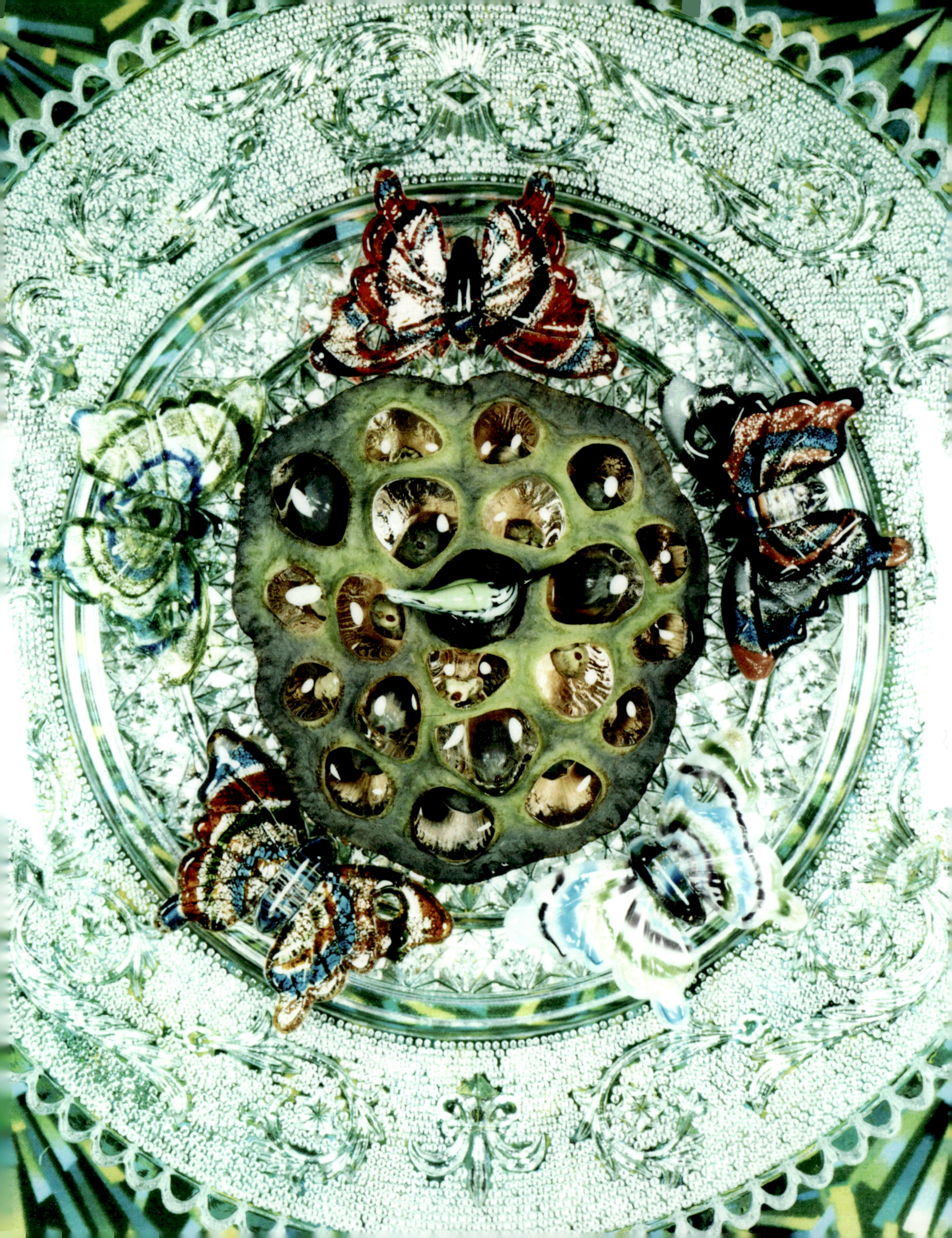

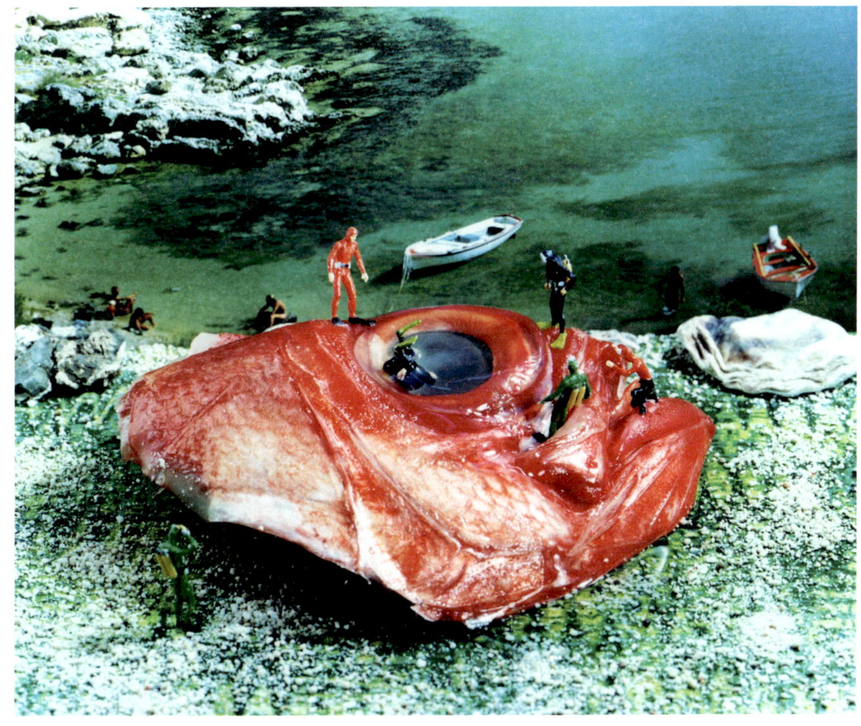

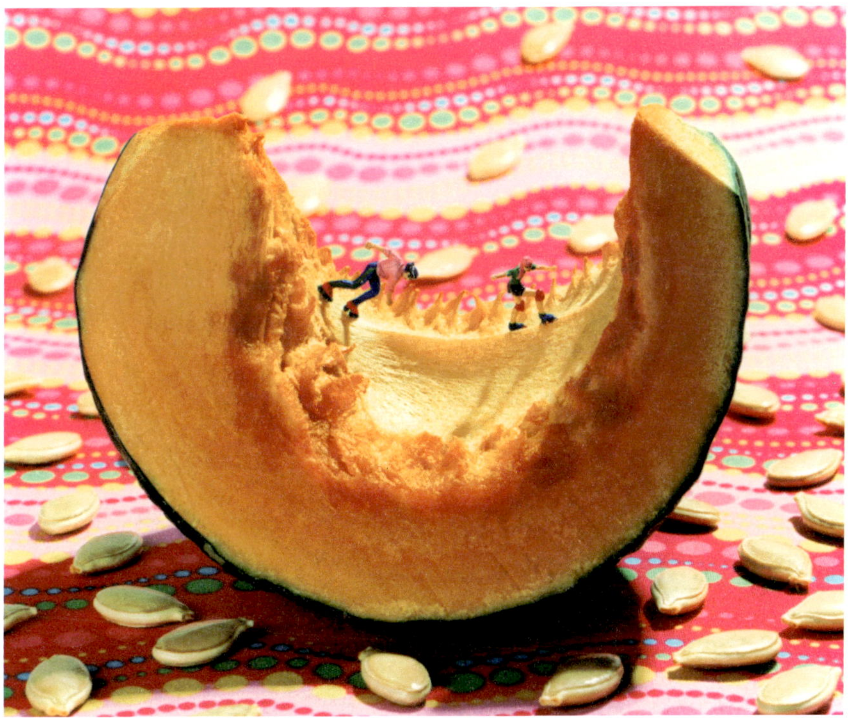

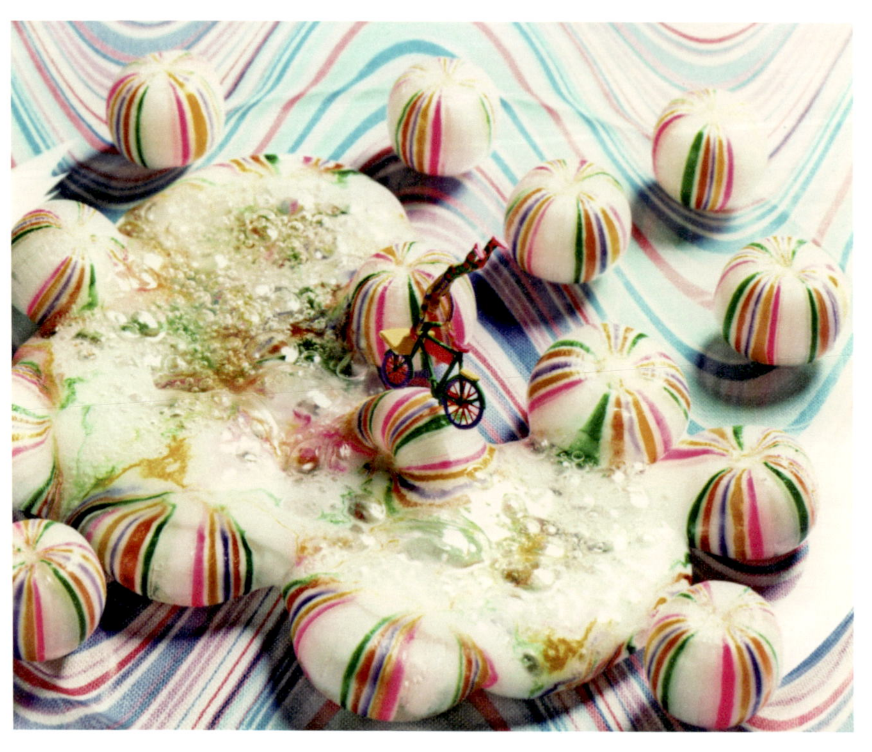

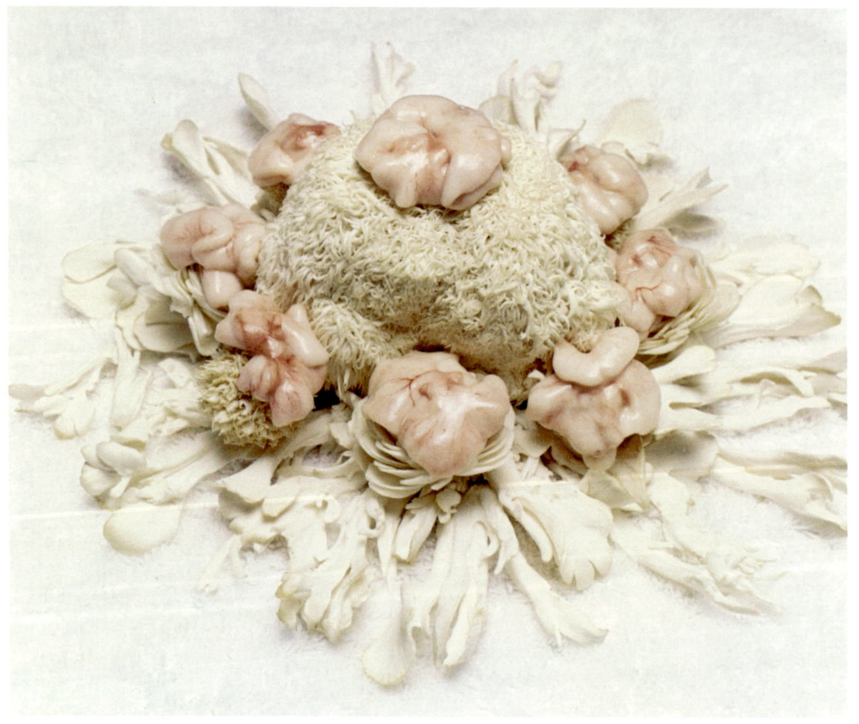

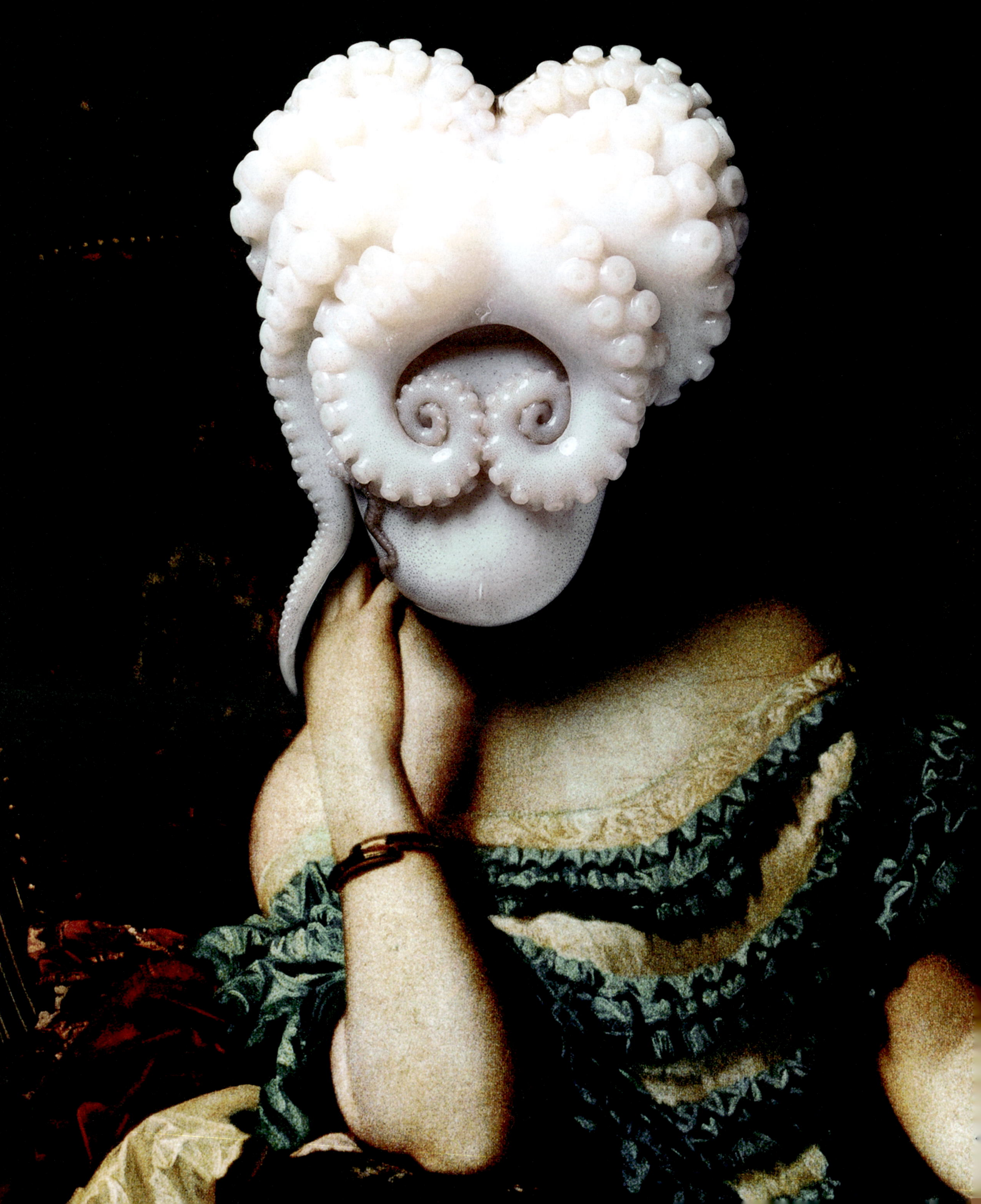

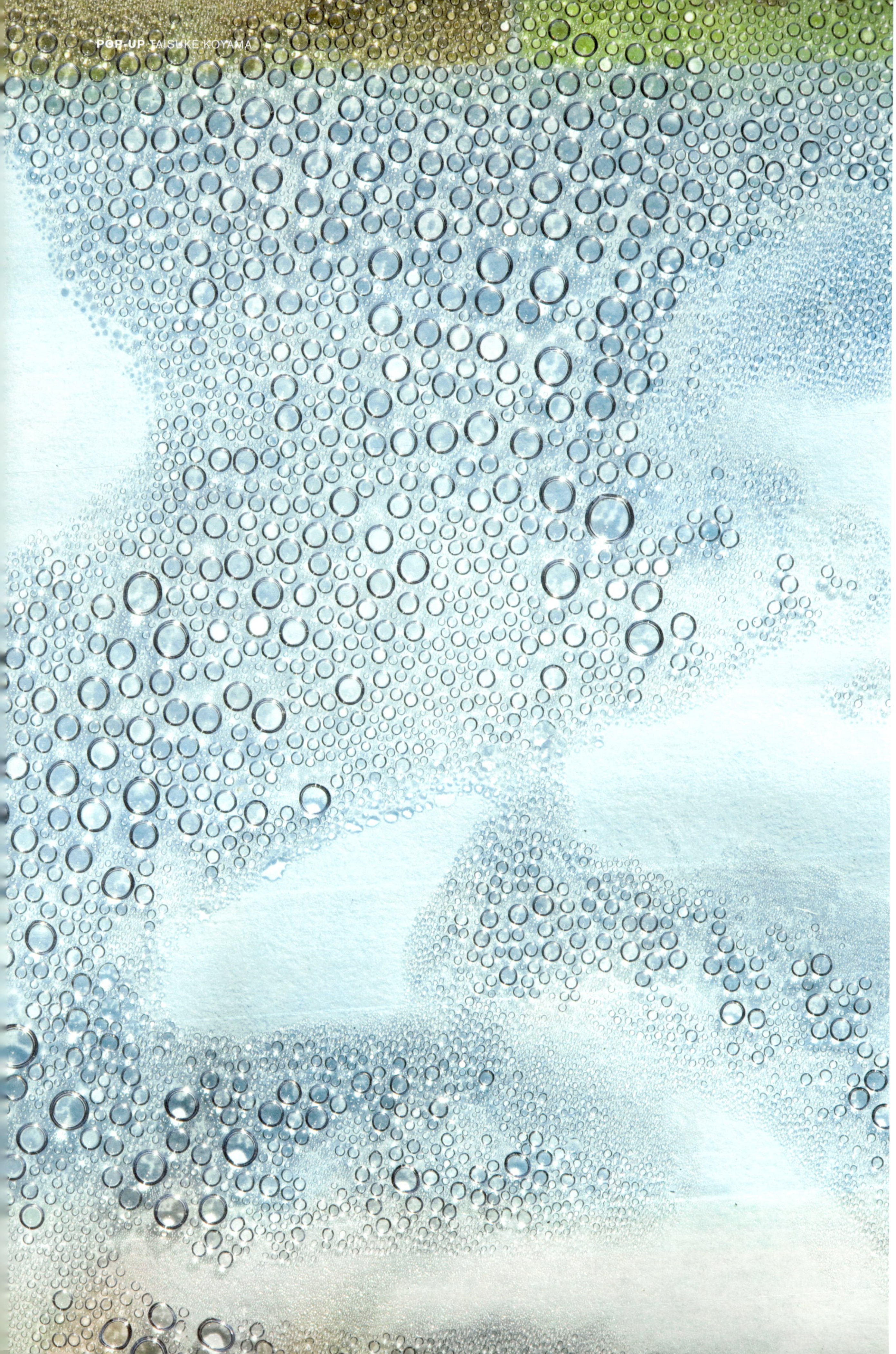

Untitled (Numerous Shadow) 2008

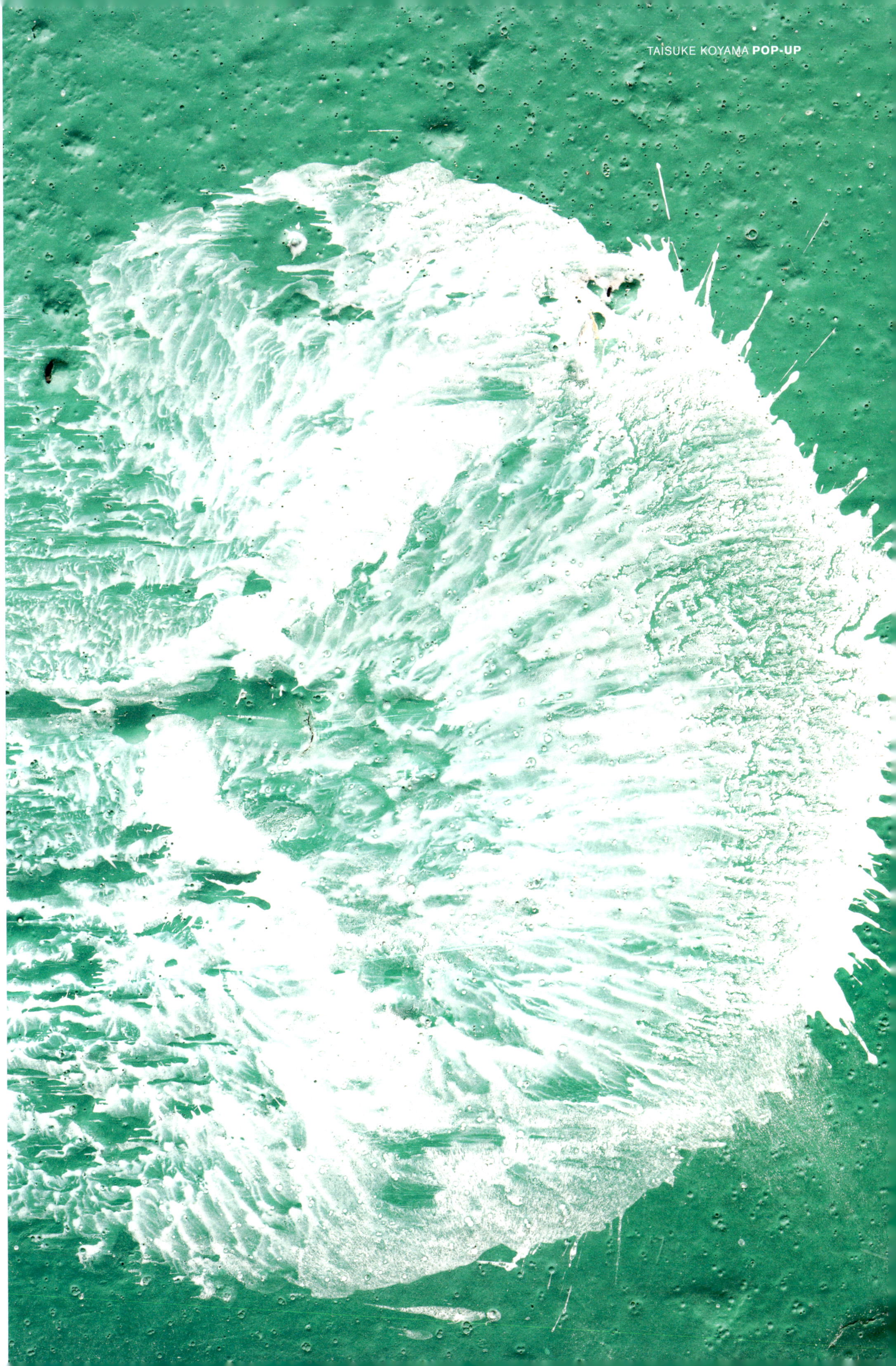

Untitled (Thousand Impacts 3) 2009

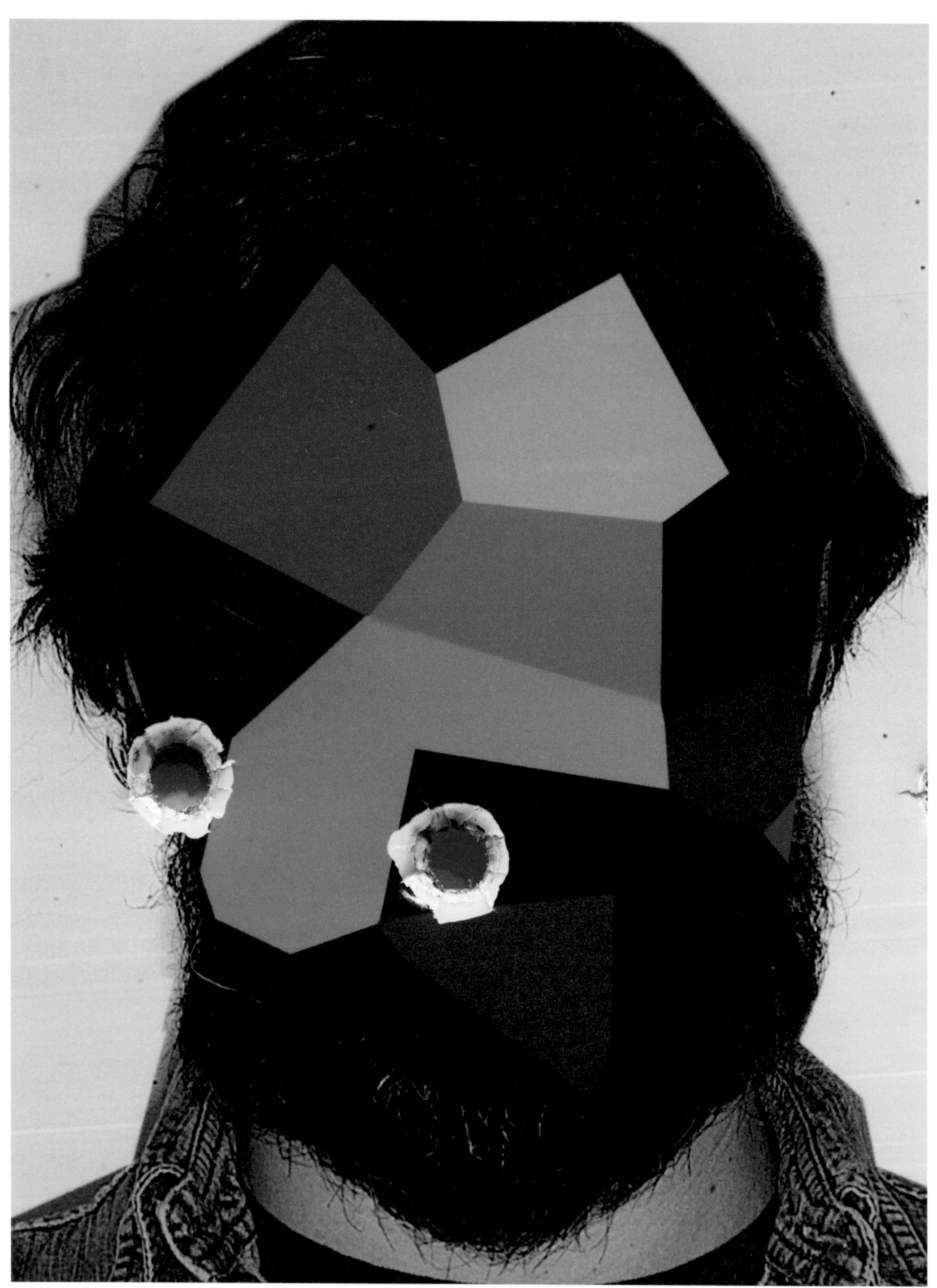

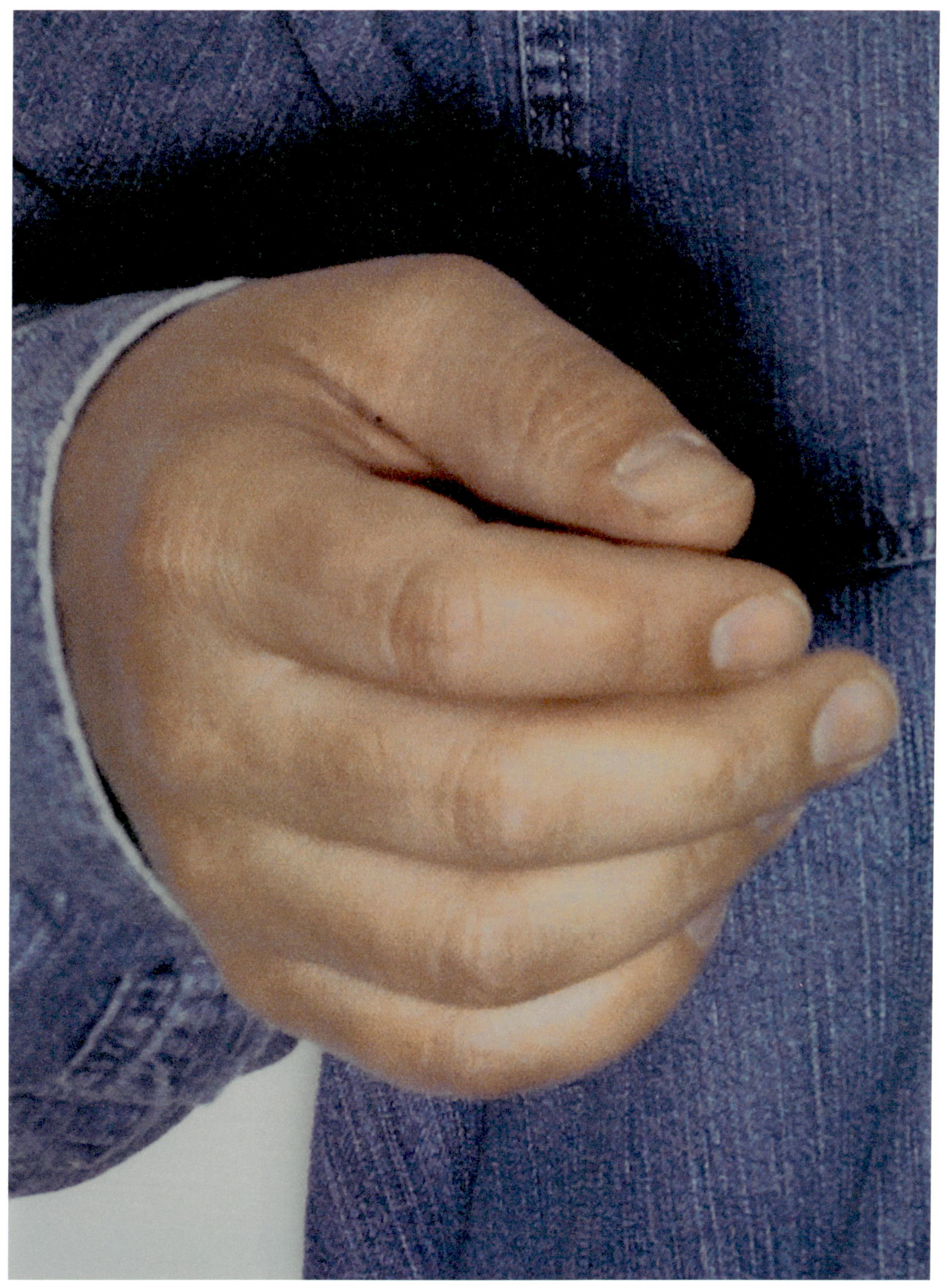

The Big Manual, Alec Soth meets
LESTER B. MORRISON

A number of years ago I became fascinated by the story of the Olympic Park Bomber, Eric Rudolph. While his bombings were of course despicable (along with Olympic Park he bombed an abortion clinic and a gay nightclub), I'm oddly enchanted by Rudolph's tale of life on the lam. For five years he evaded the authorities while living in the Appalachian wilderness. They knew he was there, but they couldn't find him. In 2006 I went to North Carolina to see where Rudolph hid out. Along the way I stopped by the Gethsemane Monastery in Kentucky where Thomas Merton lived for twenty-seven years. Looking at dozens of Merton's publications at the Monastery bookstore, I realized that the appeal of Merton isn't so different than that of Rudolph. Both stories ignite a fantasy of retreat. After returning home from these two pilgrimages, I met another hermit: Lester B. Morrison. Unlike Rudolph and Merton, Morrison isn't a celebrity with a political or spiritual ax to grind. Nor does Lester consider himself an artist. He simply hopes to escape. For years Morrison has been assembling a massive document he calls his "Big Manual". He describes it as a guidebook for men to escape their humdrum lives, but the collection is much more than a set of instructions. Poems, drawings and collages play as much of a role as his writing. In hopes of exposing this work to a broader public, my company (Little Brown Mushroom) is publishing a series of booklets from the larger manual. And ever since the Rudolf/Merton trip, I've been photographing around the country to help illustrate some of Morrison's ideas. Steidl will publish a book of this work later this year. On the eve of all of this attention, I met with Morrison to talk about *The Big Manual* and his feeling about putting it out into the world.

ALEC SOTH *So Les, it's finally all happening. All of this work you've done is going to see the light of day. Are you excited?*

LESTER B. MORRISON No.

Really? I don't believe you.

Unlike you, my ambition isn't about being recognized and celebrated. Just the opposite; I want to be invisible. Underground. I want to be left alone.

So then why make a manual? Presumably such a thing is made in order to help other people?

Just because I want to be alone doesn't mean I dislike other people. I know there are a lot of broken men out there like me that need help, or hope, or something. And God forbid they fall into the clutches of God and his bloody book.

C'mon, Les, you don't believe that. I know for a fact that you've gotten a lot of inspiration from religious thinkers. I remember that you were really excited when I told you I'd gotten special access to photograph Merton's cabin in the woods at Gethsemane. And in your booklet, Library for Broken Men, *we published a page from the* Elder Paisios of Mount Athos.

When it comes to the literature of retreat, I'm an omnivore.

I want to talk about the passage that you highlight from Elder Paisios. *It is entitled 'Good Use of the Cell.' It says: "Apart from contacts with people, try as much as you can to avoid every human consolation if you want to feel the divine one, which cannot be compared with anything human. Therefore, love your cell, your hive, for it will help you in your concentration". How do you feel about "the divine one"?*

Well, one of the things I like about that passage is that he isn't specific about the divine one. For Ted Kaczynski it was a self-invented being he called "The Grandfather Rabbit". For me, I'd say it's less about God than God's heteropalindrome. You know, forgive me Fido for I have sinned [laughter].

Can you tell me about your cell?

You mean my doghouse. There's the temporary cell I have

now and then there's the place I'm working on for my great escape. I prefer not to divulge any details about my current location. I'd rather focus on the future. And *The Big Manual* is the blueprint for this future. It's all in there.

Lost Boy Mountain?

Yeah, a treehouse, a cave, water. All of it well above sea level. All that.

What about women?

What about them?

Well, first of all, this book is directly addressed to men. Presumably you think that only men have the need for escape, not women.

It's just a fact. Women might fantasize about leaving, but this fantasy always includes entering another social environment. Or at least having a "Thelma & Louise" type partner. This is very different than what I'm talking about. There are men out there that can't function in our society. They're lost and broken and I want to help them find a way out.

But what about sex? Don't you need women for that?

That's what you photographers are for [laughter]. Seriously though, women are indeed a major obstacle for the retreater.

In Step 13 of The Big Manual *you talk about masturbation. What are your feelings on this subject?*

In Peter Damian's *Liber Gomorrhianus* he tells the story of a hermit who was tricked by the devil into thinking that semen was the same as any other bodily fluid. Just as you reach for a tissue when you have a stuffy nose, this hermit would reach in his pants when he felt desire. After the hermit died, of course, he is seized by demons and condemned to live in hell forever. So what you've got is all of these hermits walking around in the woods with the sexual equivalent of desperately stuffy noses. And if they happen to stumble across anything with an ass in the woods, watch out!

Just as you don't have religious convictions, you don't seem to have traditionally defined political convictions. You aren't left or right.

Most true retreaters aren't binary automatons. That is the culture we're trying to escape.

When I was out making pictures for The Big Manual, *I'd often encounter these people I'd call "Hippies With Guns". Their ideologies seemed chock full of contradictions.*

They are only contradictions when viewed in the brain dead context of consumer culture. When you strip away consumerism for the equation, everything changes.

If the goal of consumer culture is to possess the world, what is the goal of the lifestyle you're proposing?

Well, if I say survival, then you'll label me a survivalist and think I'm some sort of wing nut. Anyway, my goal isn't to just survive. My goal is to create a new life. "If you have built castles in the air", said Thoreau, "your work need not be lost; that is where they should be".

What exactly is the role of creativity in your escape? Why all of the drawings and poems?

When you are on your own in the world, you need to create a community in your mind. As children, many of us had pretend friends. As retreaters, we need the same thing. I use my imagination to create my universe. Pencils only help me describe that universe on the cave wall.

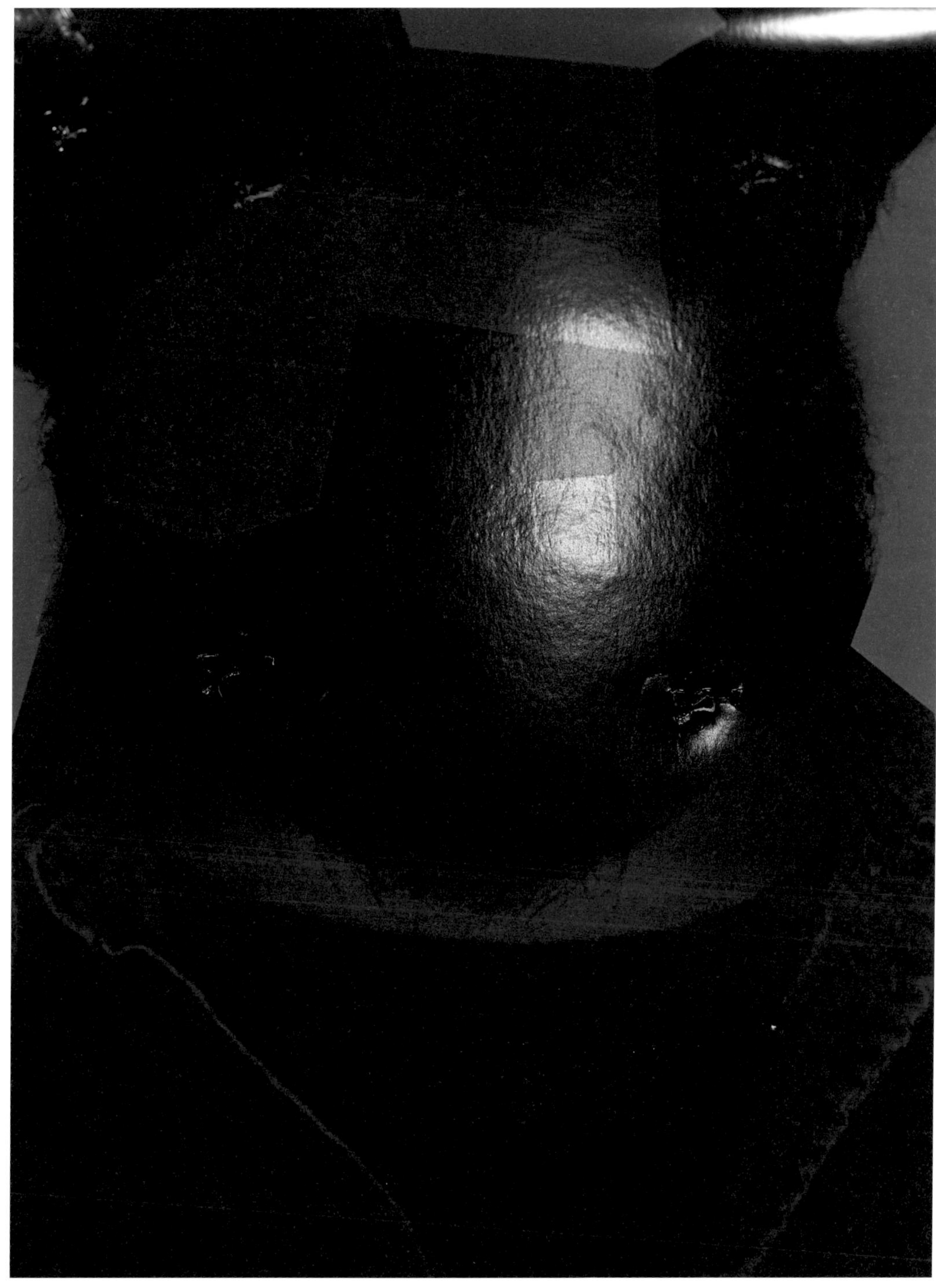

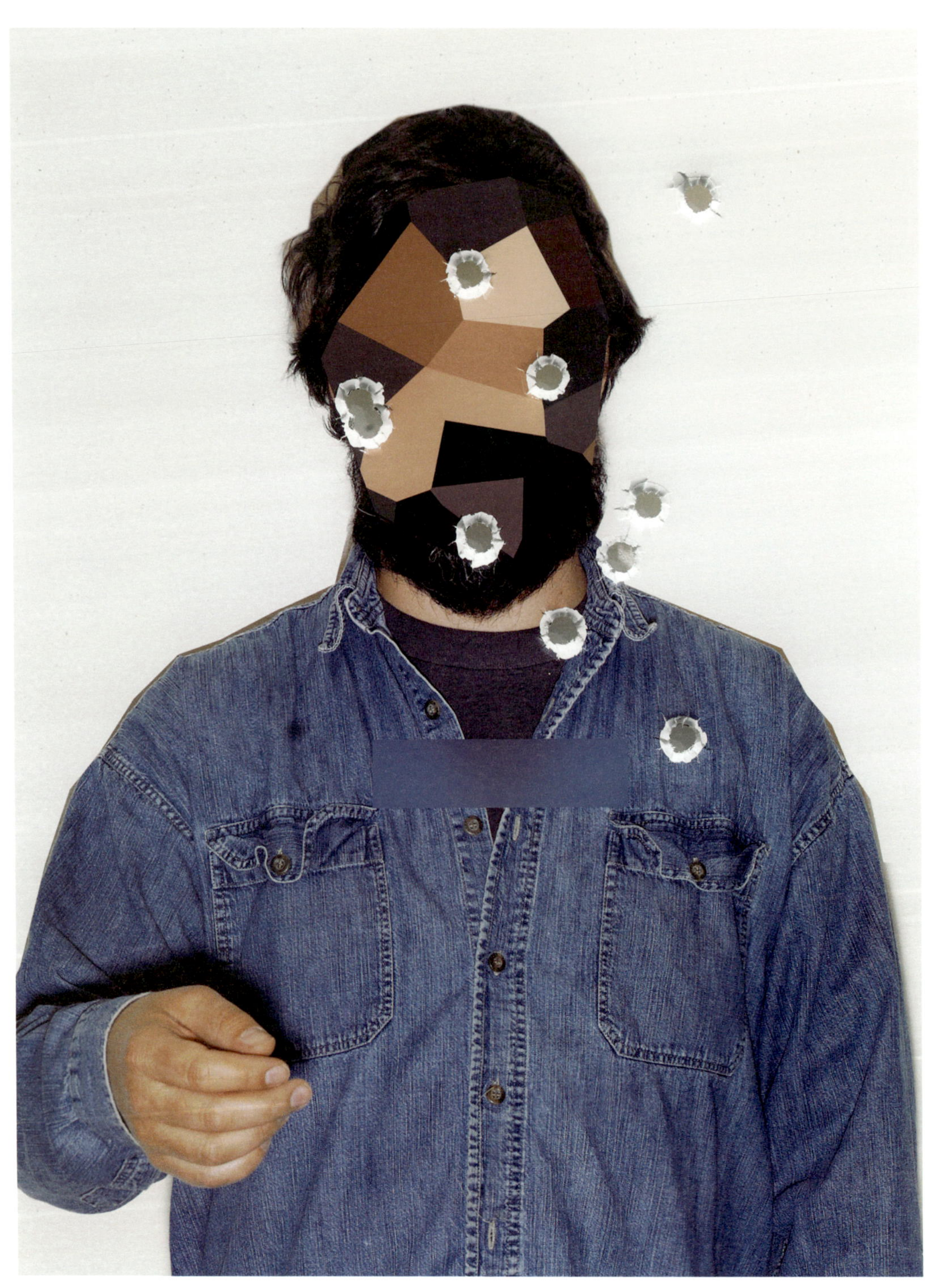

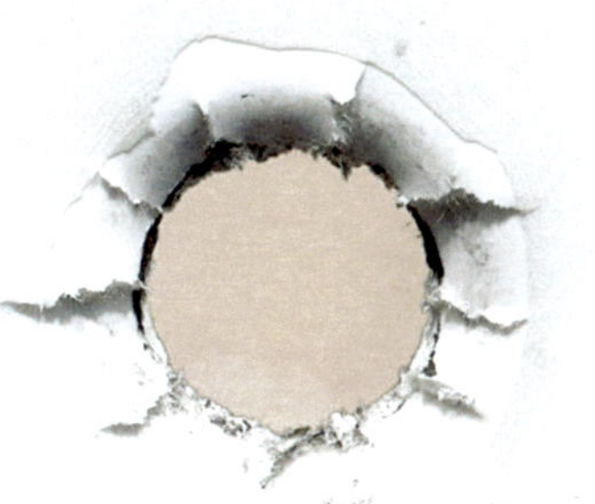

ON TOOLS AND BIKINIS OR,
THE VOYAGE OF LIZ COHEN
introduced by her gallerist
Fabienne Stephan

Liz Cohen once documented the lives of transgender prostitutes in the Panama Canal area. She now heads the photography department at Cranbrook Academy of Art and works next door, at Kustom Creation, a Detroit bodyshop, on the Trabantimino…

"I started thinking an interesting way for me to push my documentary practice would be to become part of what I was looking at. I started to think about things I'm just not supposed to be a part of and how I could become a part of it during the process of photographing it. I keyed in on building a car and becoming a lowrider". Many artists have ventured into the car building world, but Liz has fully entered it since 2003, when she found a Trabant in Berlin and decided to learn how to morph it into another discontinued car, an El Camino. The car of the people vs. the car of the cowboy… the mini, practical, cheap family car vs. the ultimate 'guy' car… turned into a muscle car in an improbable low rider mash up, jumping hydraulics included. Liz has installed a V8 motor into the tiny East German car, placed Dual acting hydraulics in the chassis, as well as added a four times telescopic drive shaft stretching the Trabant into the length of an El Camino - and the car runs well.

To introduce Liz's work, I picked 2 series of photographs, one taken at the beginning of this 7 year project and another, shot last summer. The car will be finished in August 2010 before which Liz plans to do at least one more shoot.

The 5 P's (Proper Planning Prevents Poor Performance) 2005. This series of 150 photographs were shot at Elwood Bodyworks in Arizona, where Liz started working on the car. Her mentor, Bill Cherry, let her use all the tools from his toolbox, the collection of objects amassed throughout his life as a mechanic. Bill Cherry, when Liz met him, was on the verge of retiring and had amassed 30 years worth of tools! When she left Arizona to move to Detroit she wanted to honor Bill's practice as a car body man and took pictures of his tools in a style reminiscent of Walker Evans' *Beauties of the Common Tool* (shot for *Fortune* magazine in 1955, with Robert Frank helping for the lighting!). While she only realized the similarities between her photographs and Evans's project later, Liz loved the connection and it became another way to document both her process as an apprentice bodyworker and the Trabantimino project as a whole. They trace a moment in the project, marking what she's learnt, used or touched. For me, the tools represent the key to Liz's project. As she gave herself the goal of becoming a legitimate part of the car bodywork community, she had to earn her 'creds' by practicing and the tools represent the route to her transformation toward being a skilled mechanic. She likes the image of a journeyman, a worker that had to go through a journey of experiences to become an experienced tradesperson. And the series of pin-up photographs she has taken of herself in the various places she worked on the car mirror this process - we see Liz change as the project advances.

Zwickau Routine 2009 is the latest in a series of photographs using the trope of the pin-up bikini models, self-portraits engaging with the car and its surroundings. In 2005, Liz shot herself as a coy, bikini car show model, and then as a 'chica' in an Arizona bodyshop. In *Zwickau Routine*, she poses in seventies style pin-up gear at the old Trabant factory in Zwickau, Germany. It is said that "3 million cars were produced by 30,000 workers in 30 years". And now it is empty, much like the Ford and GM factories in Detroit where Liz lives. She wondered how to photograph herself in the birthplace of the car she had been transforming for 6 years. She thought of Tina Modotti's still lifes of the tools of the Revolution and images she had seen as a child of Nadia Comaneci at the Olympics. It was important for her to have the tools present in the shape of a hammer and sickle, a metaphor for the years and experiences she had just gone through and she chose to pose in the style of the still images she found of Comaneci competing at the Olympics, where West and East competed during the Cold War. She didn't work on the car at the Trabant factory, yet she felt like entering this space and documenting the way it looks now, though she had trouble finding it in Zwickau, as people seemed to have forgotten the address of the factory. Soon she will shoot at a Chevrolet factory in Detroit.

Right from the series Zwickau Routine, 2010: Black Execution. *Next spread top* Yellow Inward Turn*; bottom* Yellow Push Up Arch. *Pages 34 and 35 from the series* Proper Planning Prevents Poor Performance, 2007. *Page 36 and 37 from the series* Zwickau Routine, 2010 *top* Red Cossack *bottom* White Optionals. *All images © the artist, courtesy Salon 94, New York*

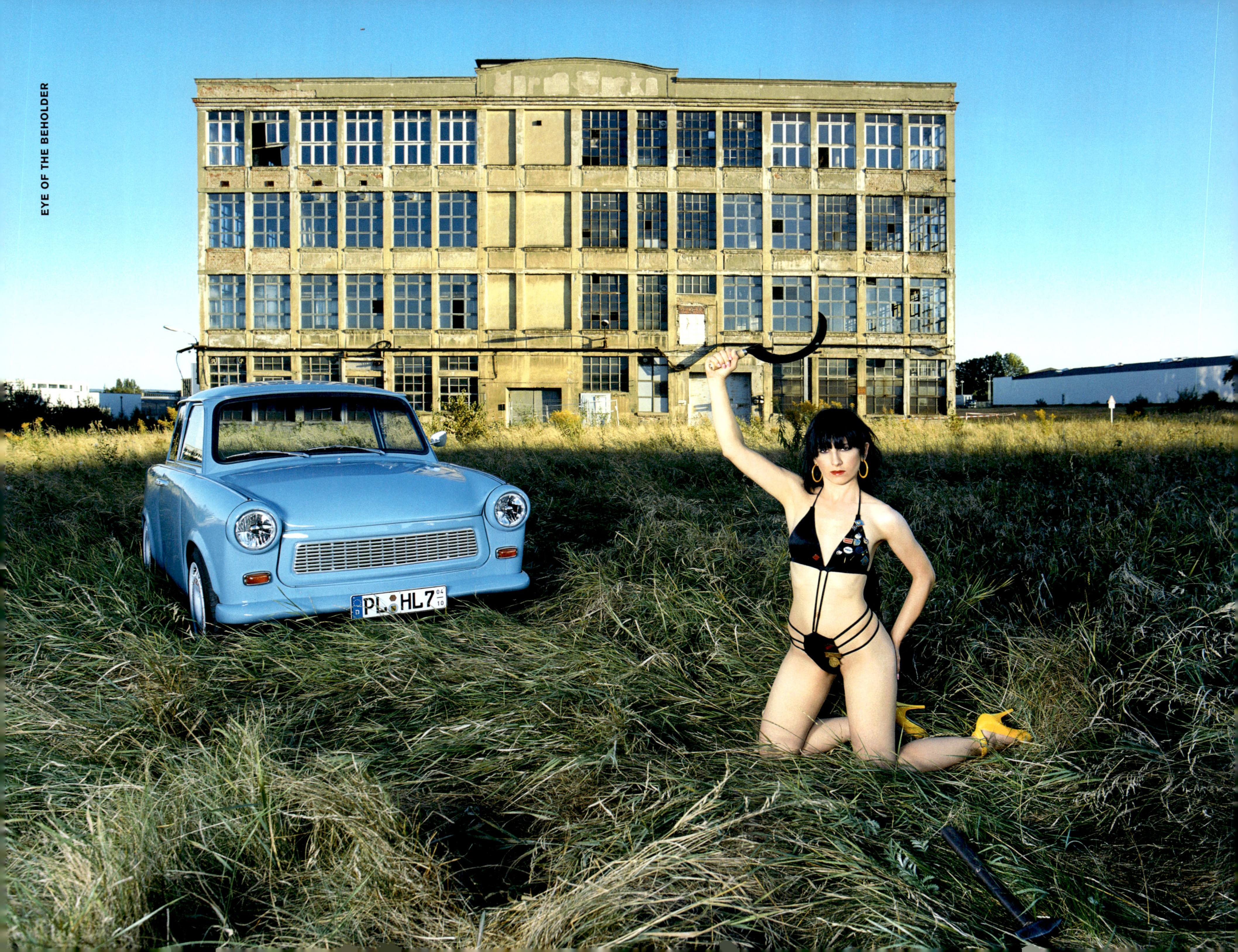

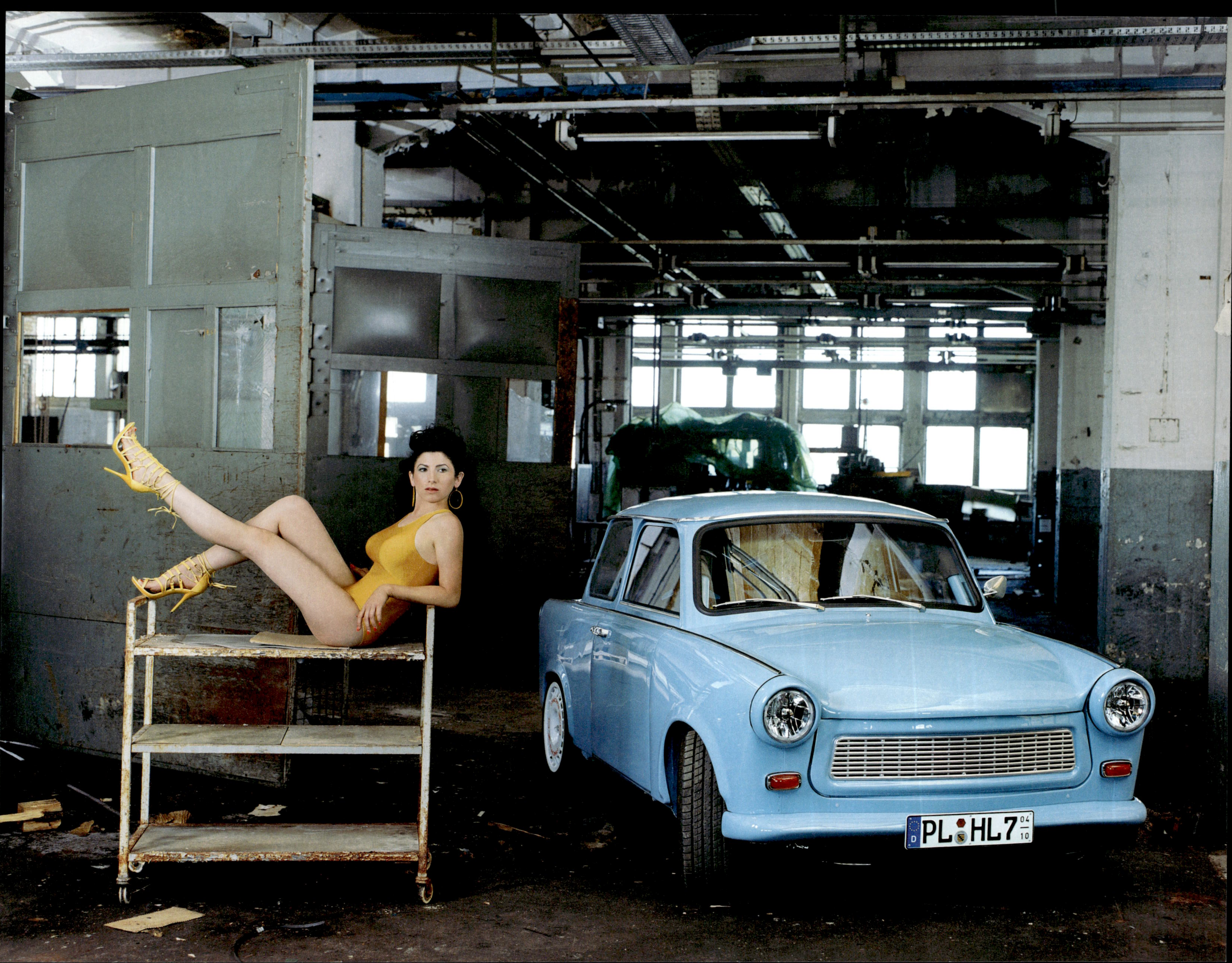

D PL HL 7

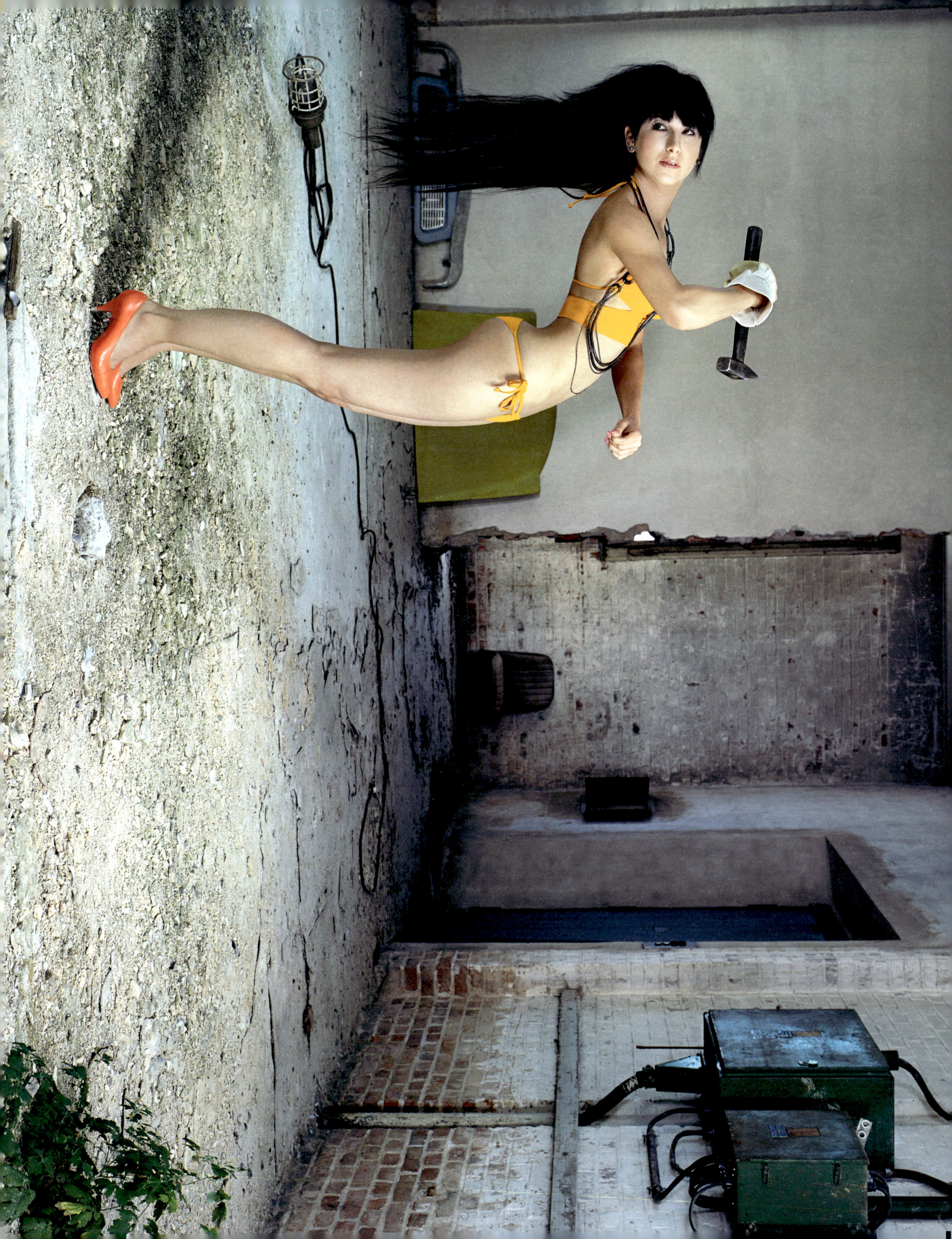

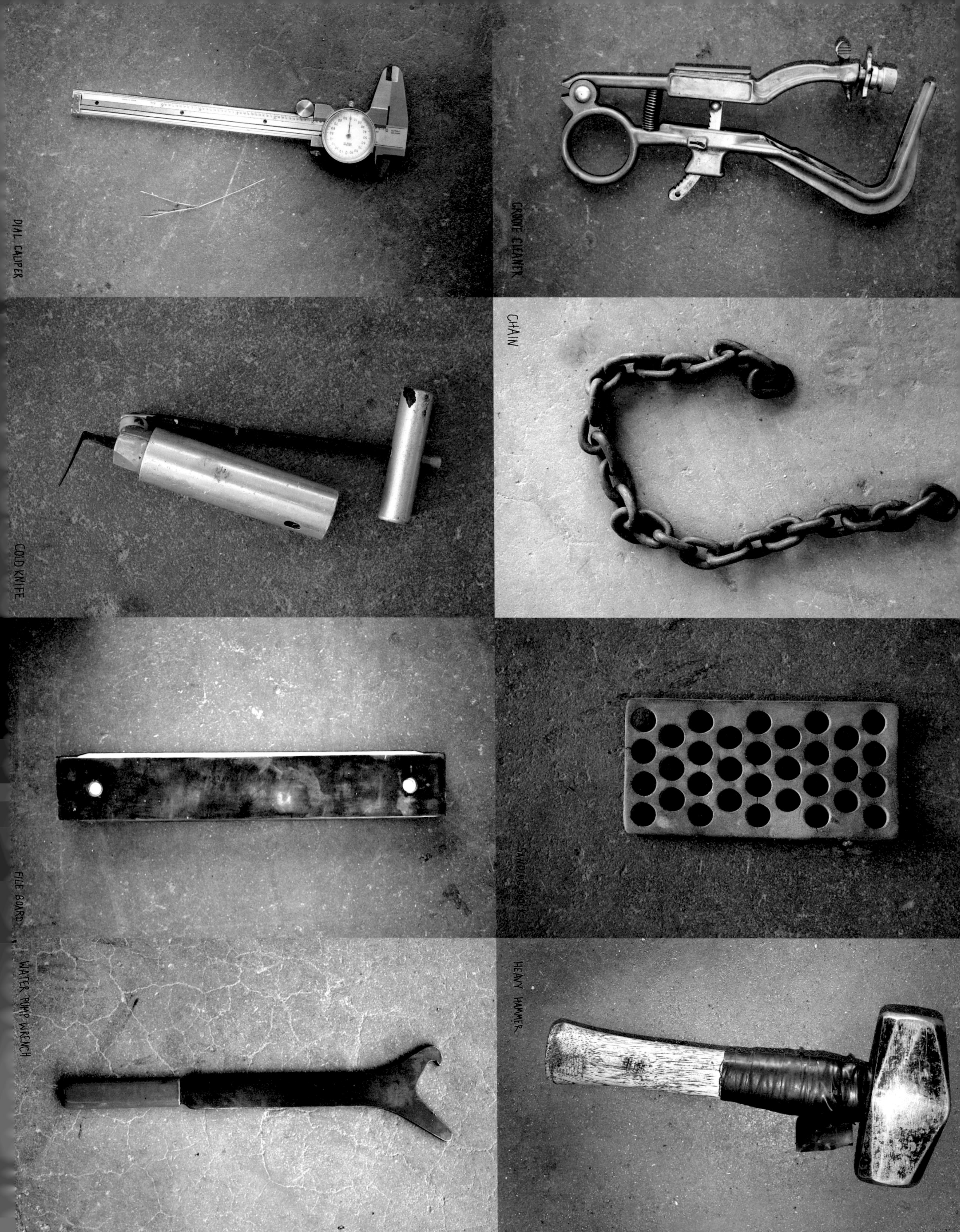
DIAL CALIPER
GROOVE CLEANER
CHAIN
COLD KNIFE
FILE BOARD
SANDING BLOCK
WATER PUMP WRENCH
HEAVY HAMMER

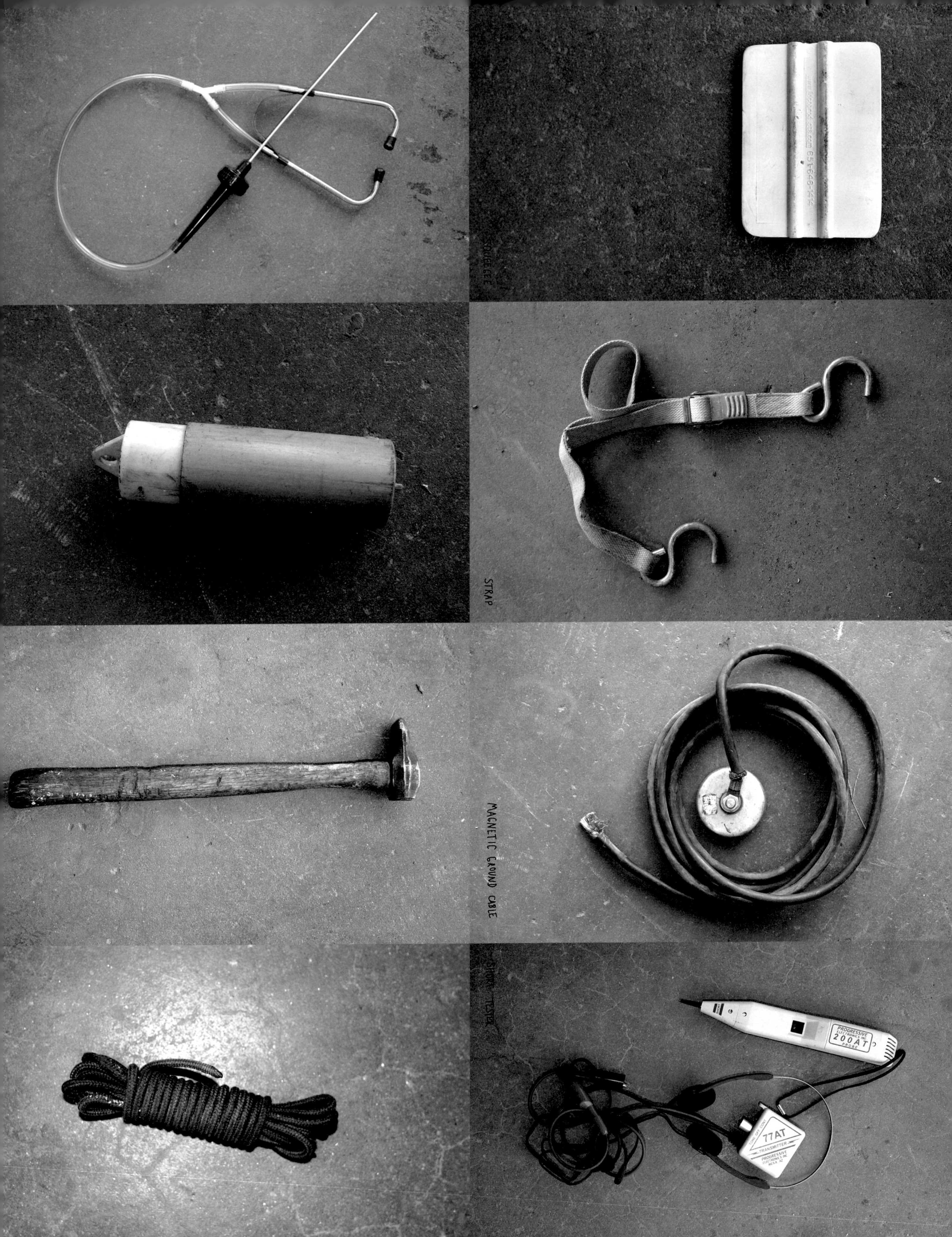
SQUEEGEE
STRAP
MAGNETIC GROUND CABLE
SHORT TESTER
200AT
TRANSMITTER
77AT

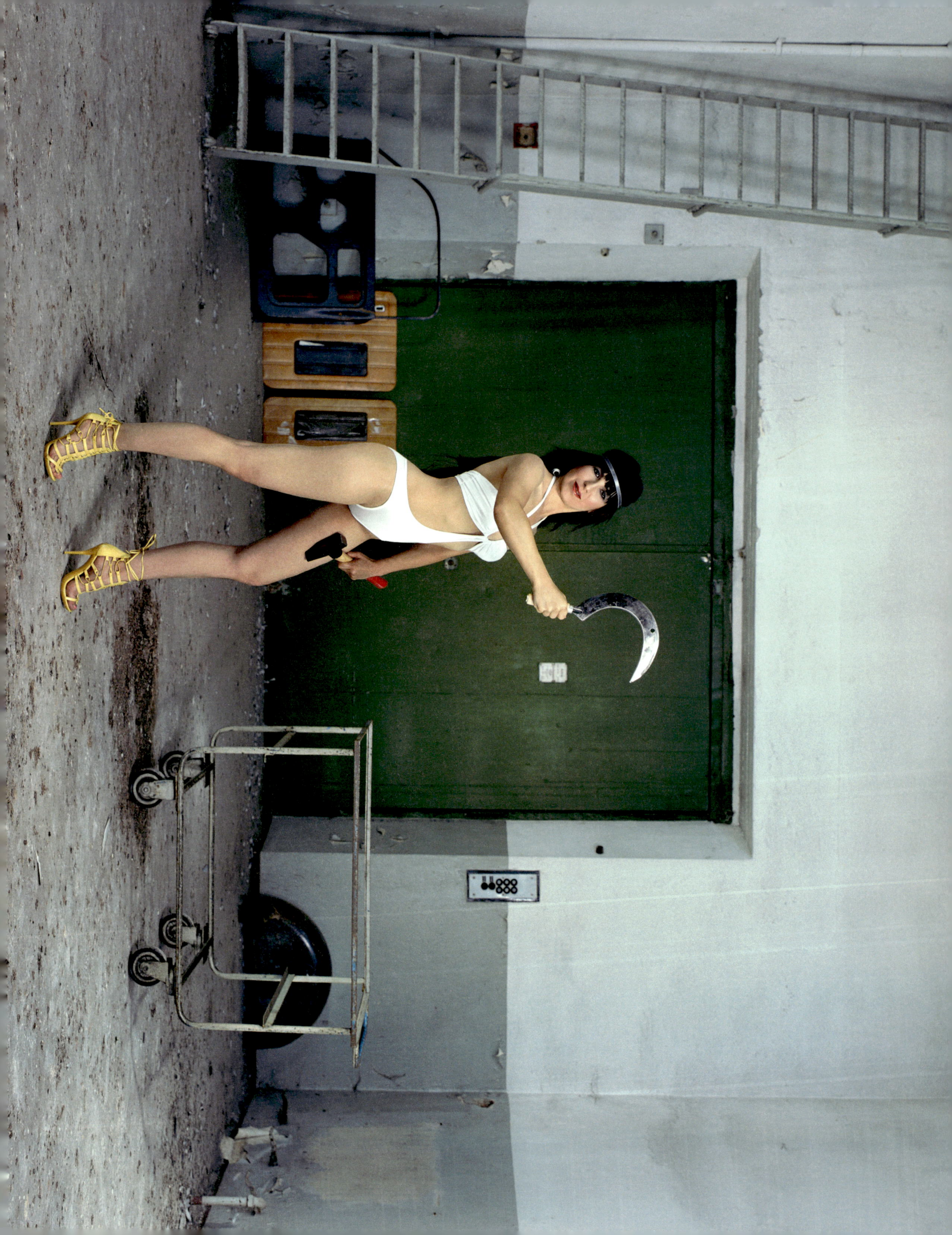

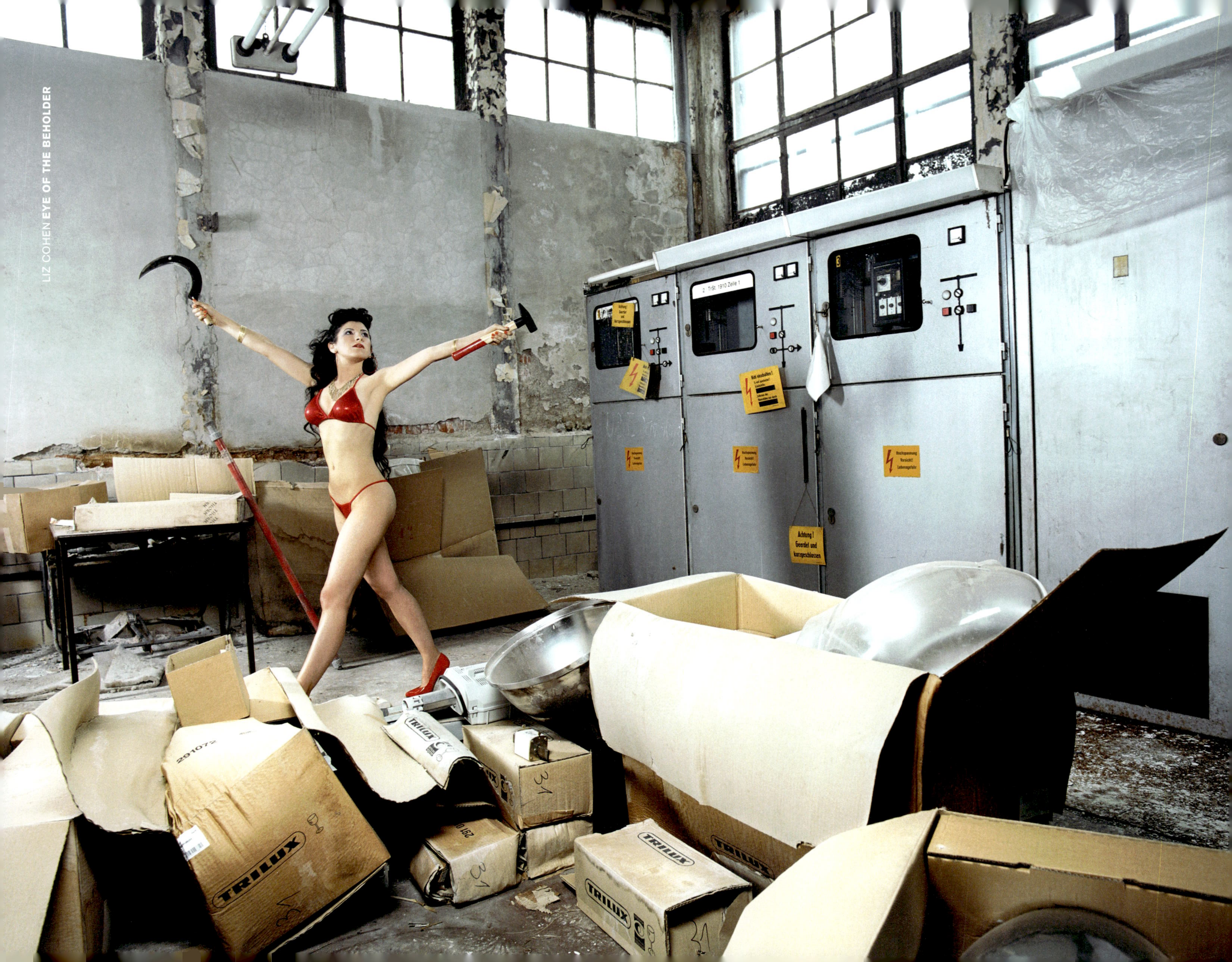

Bazooka® Bubble Gum

DIMENSIONS: 1½" L × 1"W × ¼" D

PACKAGE: Waxed paper, printed in three colors.

ORIGINATOR: Unknown

DATE OF ORIGIN: Circa 1949

INGREDIENTS: Dextrose, sugar, corn syrup, gum base, softeners, natural and artificial flavors, artificial colors, BHT (to maintain freshness).

MAKER: Topps Chewing Gum, Brooklyn, New York

SLOGAN: "Young America's Favorite"

NOTES: Bubble gum must be flexible enough so that the tongue can push it forward to enable air to be blown into the pocket created. Brands vary and formulas are closely guarded secrets.

The size of the biggest bubble ever blown is not certain, since bubble gum blowing contests abound. (There is even a set of rules available from the Bazooka company.) Records are not often kept, but one documented big bubble was 18¼" in diameter, blown at the Joe Garagiola/Bazooka Big League Bubble Gum Blowing Championship in 1975. Children are the primary users of bubble gum, often buying 25 to 50 pieces at a time, but 25% of the 68 million dollar bubble gum market belongs to adults, including some congressmen and movie stars.

Shown: Miss Anna Marta using the watermelon flavor.

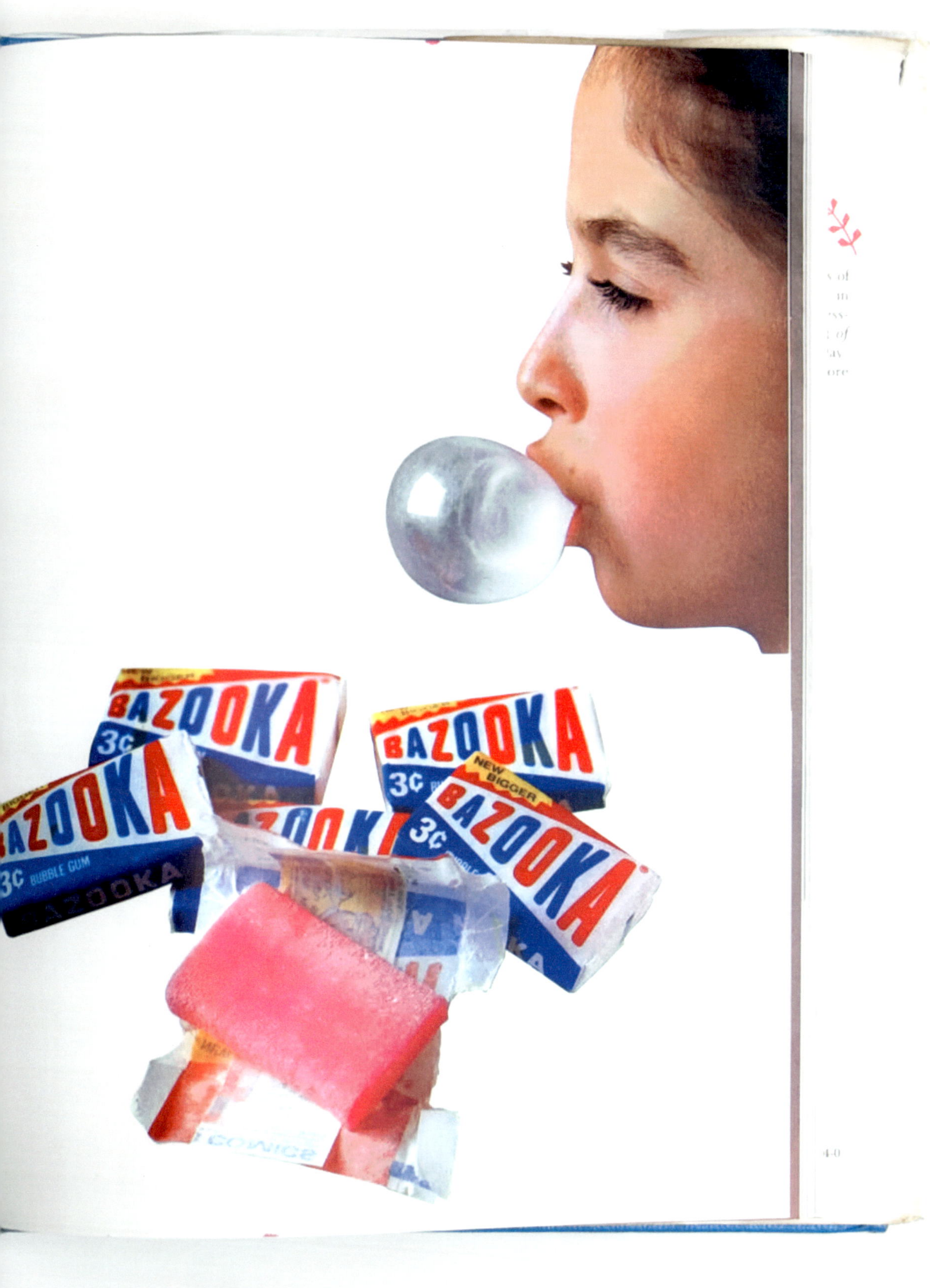

Aunt Jemima® Syrup

DIMENSIONS: 12 oz. jar: 8½" H × 3½" W at base × 1⁵⁄₁₆" D
PACKAGE: Plastic, printed in four colors. Plastic cap.
ORIGINATOR: The Quaker Oats Company
DATE OF ORIGIN: 1964
INGREDIENTS: Corn syrup (75.2%), sugar syrup (20.8%), maple sugar syrup (2.0%), corn syrup solids, cellulose gum, natural and artificial flavors, sodium benzoate and sorbic acid (preservatives), caramel color.
MAKER: The Quaker Oats Company, Chicago, Illinois
NOTES: Sugarcane has been cultivated in Asia since prehistoric times. Arab traders taught the Chinese how to refine sugar in the 16th century. During the Middle Ages, sugar, called the "Indian honeybearing seed", came to Europe where it was sold as a medicine or a luxury.

Maple syrup was first made by American Indians from the sap of sugar maple and black maple trees. It was the staple sweetener of the early settlers.

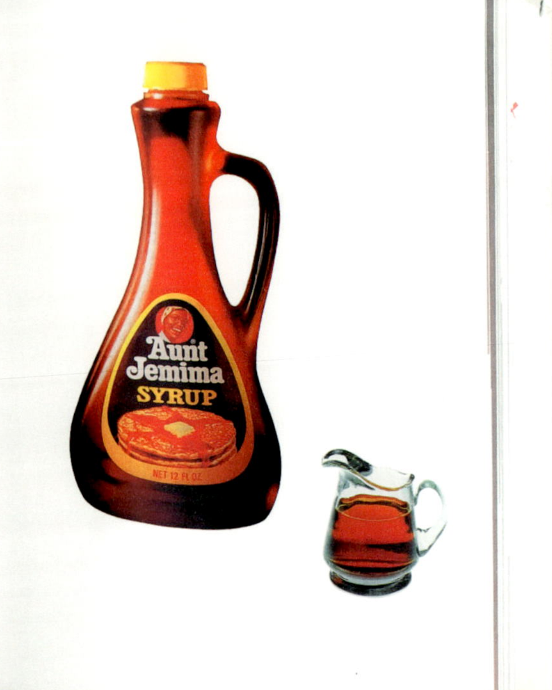

Jiffy Pop® Popcorn

DIMENSIONS: 5 oz. pan: 12" L incl. handle × 7" Diam. × 1⁵⁄₁₆" D
PACKAGE: Aluminum and aluminum foil, double polyboard, printed five-color offset lithography.
ORIGINATOR: Fred Mennen
DATE OF ORIGIN: Circa 1958
INGREDIENTS: Popcorn, partially hydrogenated vegetable oil shortening (contains one or more of the following: soybean oil, cottonseed oil, palm oil), salt.
MAKER: American Home Foods, New York, New York
SLOGAN: "Jiffy Pop Popcorn—Simple to Make, Tasty to Eat"
NOTES: Archaeological evidence of popcorn has been found in Central America dating back 7,000 years. A native American grain, the popcorn plant is somewhat smaller than the rest of the corn family and is thought to be the first corn to have been eaten.

Popcorn contains 13.5% moisture. When it is heated to 400°F the moisture changes into steam, building up pressure inside the hard kernel until finally the kernel bursts and the white insides pop out.

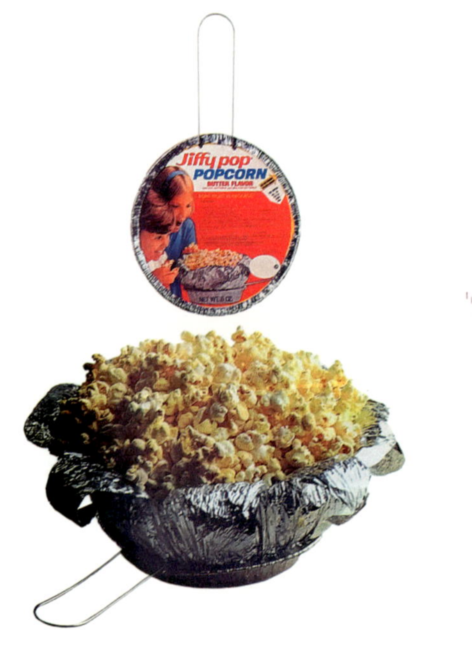

AMERICA'S FAVORITES
sampled by Emma Reeves

In the winter of 2007, not long after I arrived as a recent émigré to New York from London, I came across an obscure bookshop housed in the ground floor of what felt like someone's home. The books on offer were for the most part first edition copies of highly prized recipe and cookery manuals. Despite its illustrated cover that featured graphic renderings of a beefburger and an ice cream cone, the book that I bought contained not one single recipe; *America's Favorites* published in 1980 by Kay and Marshall Lee is a celebration of "75 of the most popular and enduring food, confections, and beverages of America in our time".

The Lee's introductory text claims that the 75 products featured in the book have been recorded with the same "high standards of reproduction and documentation as works of art and other classic artifacts". Across the pages the photographic treatment of these foodstuffs varies. The photographs are oddly compelling. In some cases the hyper-real shadowless objects seemingly hover on a white page. Others products, such as Jiffy Popcorn and Bazooka, are a more bizarre juxtaposition of different scale images reminiscent of pop art collage. Any fixation with graphic identity of U.S. brands obviously echos Warhol's obsessive multiples but somehow all the images in the book seem weirdly artless, an amateurish attempt at investing those everyday products with the status of icons.

The documentation that accompanies each of the images mimics museum cataloguing and further serves the attempted iconography of the products. It also lends a less than subtle jingoistic tone to the venture; French's Idaho Mashed Potatoes claims to be "the first instant mashed potato in the world for retail sale" and we are told that "billions of packages" of Lifesavers were supplied to the Armed forces during World War II.

Read from start to finish, the captions throughout the book become a much condensed history of the United States of America and filtered through the screen of a Howard Zinn mind-set how loaded the history of the Aunt Jemima syrup becomes: "Maple syrup was first made by American Indians from the sap of sugar maple and black maple trees. It was the staple sweetener of the early settlers". The laughing face of Aunt Jemima, presumably a slave or descendent of slaves, seen on the label adds a further rather tragic twist to the story.

To anyone well-versed in American history, the publication date of the book instantly conjures the Reagan presidential campaign. Domestic concerns were in the forefront of his bid for election. *America's Favorites* could not be more in keeping with his rallying cry for what became known as the Reagan Revolution.

All images from the book America's Favorites *edited by Kay & Marshall Lee, G. P. Putnam's Sons, New York*

French's Idaho® Mashed Potatoes

DIMENSIONS: 13⅜ oz. box: 7″ H × 5⅛″ W × 1⅞″ D

PACKAGE: Cardboard carton and paper/foil laminated inner pouches, printed four-color offset lithography, designed by Ed C. Kozlowski Designs.

ORIGINATOR: Dr. John Fogelberg invented the flexible innerpack and nitrogen packing system.

DATE OF ORIGIN: October 1946

INGREDIENTS: Dehydrated Idaho® potatoes 99%, vegetable monoglyceride, sodium phosphate, sodium sulfite, BHA and BHT added to preserve quality.

MAKER: The R. T. French Company, Rochester, New York

SLOGAN: "Tastes Like Idaho"

NOTES: Potatoes were grown by the Incas in Peru and brought to Europe by Spanish explorers. Mashed potatoes (also called purée) are a favorite form, but take a lot of work. Instant mashed potatoes need no peeling, mashing, or cooking. French's was the first instant mashed potato in the world for retail sale.

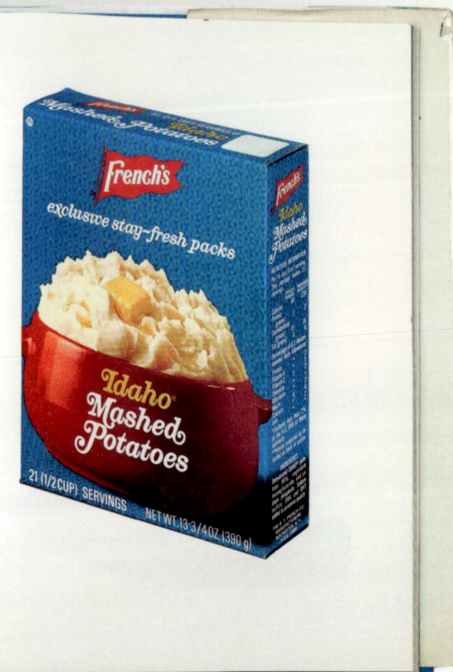

Skippy® Peanut Butter

DIMENSIONS: 18 oz. size: 5¼″ H × 3¼″ Diam.

PACKAGE: Glass, metal cap. Paper label, printed offset lithography, designed by Rosefield Packing Corp.

ORIGINATOR: Rosefield Packing Corp.

DATE OF ORIGIN: 1923

INGREDIENTS: U.S. grade no. 1 peanuts, dextrose, partially hydrogenated vegetable oil, salt, sugar.

MAKER: CPC International, Englewood Cliffs, New Jersey

SLOGAN: "It's Hard to Beat Skippy"

NOTES: Over 650,000,000 pounds of peanut butter are consumed by Americans each year, mainly in peanut butter sandwiches. There are many peanut butter recipes used in other countries, including an Ecuadorian dish of potatoes, lettuce, eggs, and peanut butter called *yapingacho*.

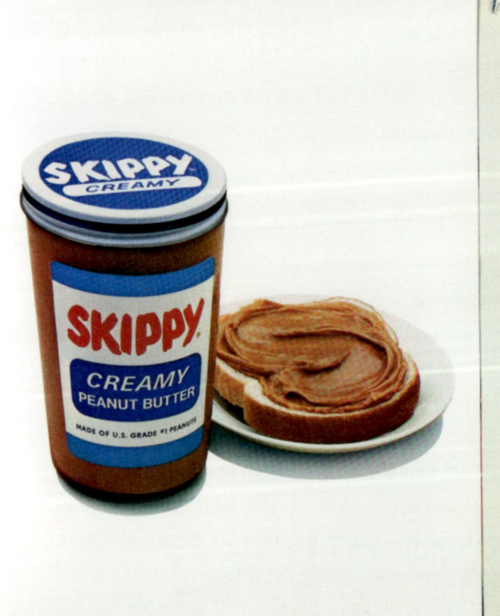

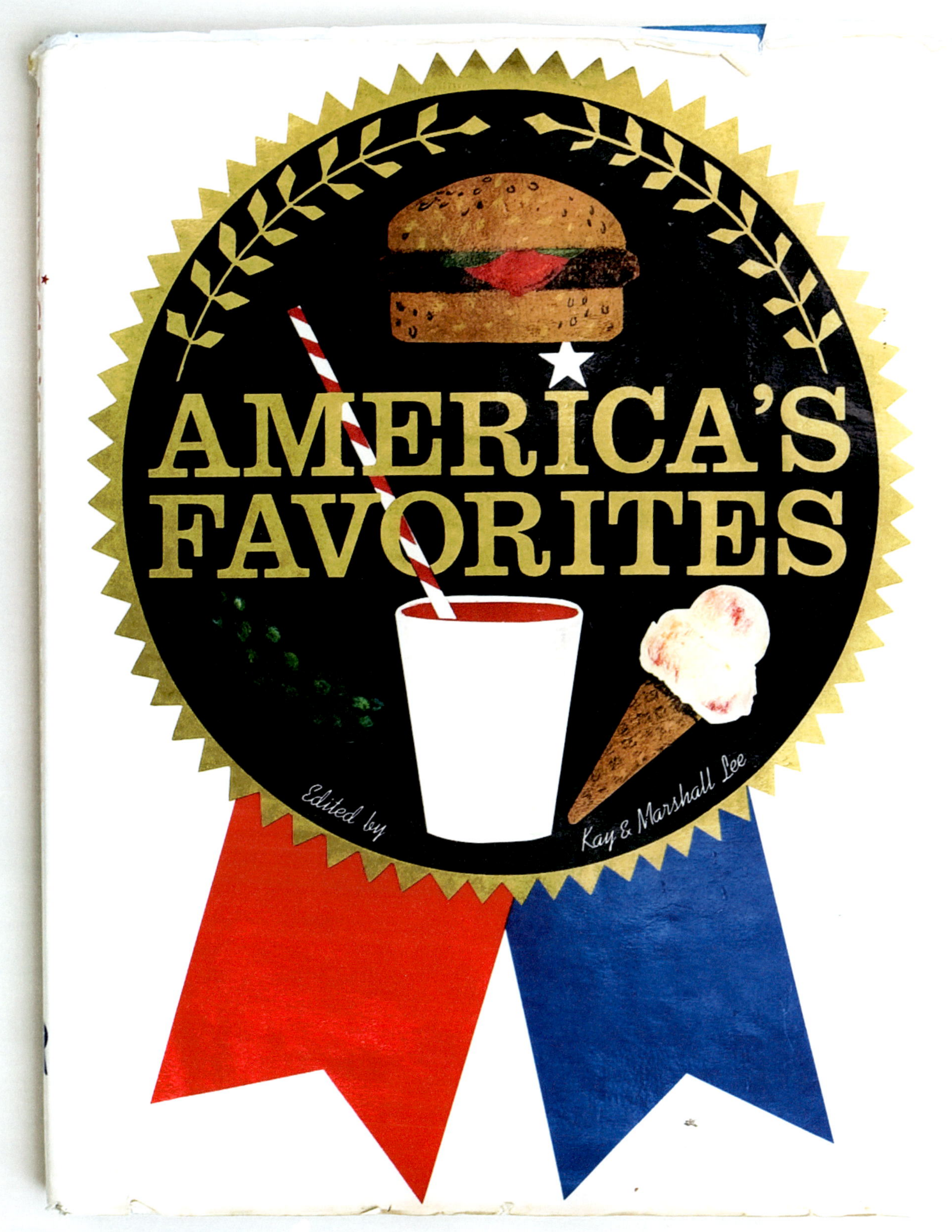
AMERICA'S
FAVORITES
Edited by
Kay & Marshall Lee

Three Shadows Photography Art Centre
Francesco Zanot in conversation with
RONGRONG

Three Shadows Photography Art Centre is the first contemporary art space dedicated exclusively to photography and video art in China. It was opened in 2007 in a building designed by renowned artist and architect Ai Weiwei. Situated in the Caochangdi district in Beijing, it is the place to visit for a look at the latest movements in Chinese photography. *Fantom* talked with RongRong, founder and director of Three Shadows Photography Art Centre together with his partner, Japanese artist Inri.

FRANCESCO ZANOT: *When and why did you decide to found Three Shadows Photography Art Centre?*

RONGRONG: We had the initial idea in 2005. The reason behind it is quite simple: photography is what originally brought Inri and I together. We had already been doing photography for several years but at that point I no longer wanted to focus on 'taking' photographs. It became more about releasing something that was within, putting something out there and giving something back. Initially, it was going to be a small library, with the aim of sharing our collection of photography books with the greater public. However, this basic idea gradually transformed into a larger project. I had looked for spaces eventually deciding to come to Caochangdi and then started speaking to Ai Weiwei about it. It's almost as if this little dream of ours slowly blossomed into something beyond our control.

Can you tell us something about your building?

Three Shadows has a very special architecture. When we began the design process I naturally thought of Ai Weiwei who has been a friend for many years. The design is based on the topography of the land so the architecture is triangular in form. We were aiming to create a space that is conducive to displaying and viewing photographic images; a space with the proper depth and scope to allow viewers to enter the works of photography while viewing them.

Do you think contemporary Chinese photography can be considered an organic body of works and poetics, or is it composed by different tendencies which don't permit a general approach?

Photography as an art form in China got off to a rather late start. Previously, it was purely used as a documentary tool, limited to photojournalism and propaganda. After the period of reform and opening at the end of the 1970s, the cultural scene opened up and those artists working in photography could be considered like an organic group. Later on, there was even more change and development within the field and eventually "official" Chinese photography societies and organizations were formed. On the whole, however, photography is a rather broad medium with a high degree of freedom and independence, so it's difficult to generalize. I suppose *New Photo Magazine*, which Liu Zhen and I founded in 1996, can be considered a group of sorts.

How do you plan your exhibitions? Do you alternate between Chinese photography and the presentation of international artists?

At the start we had an official in-house curator; subsequently we expanded to engage and cooperate with various international institutions. Our exhibition program has three major elements. The first is the annual Three Shadows Photography Award and subsequent exhibition, in which we aim to give exposure to new talent in contemporary Chinese photography. The second is to put on comprehensive solo exhibitions and retrospective shows of established artists. And finally, we hope to provide a platform for international artistic

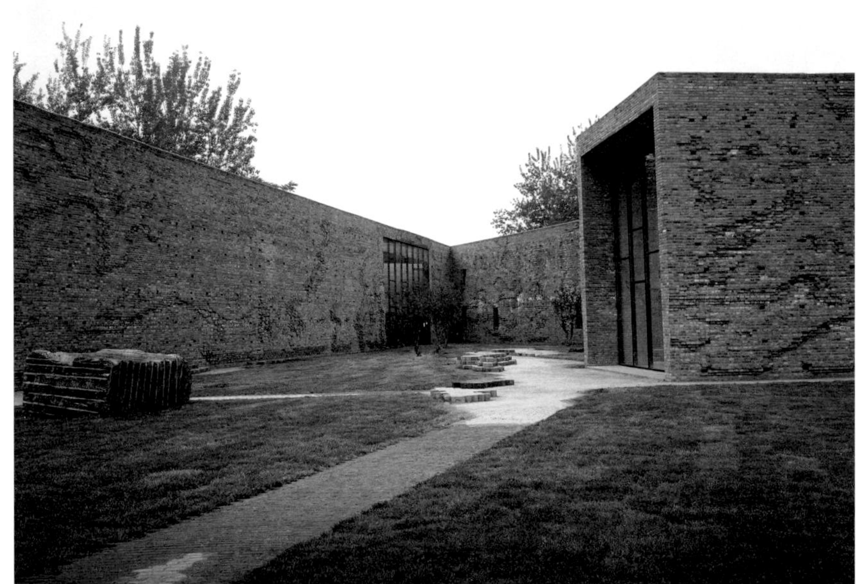
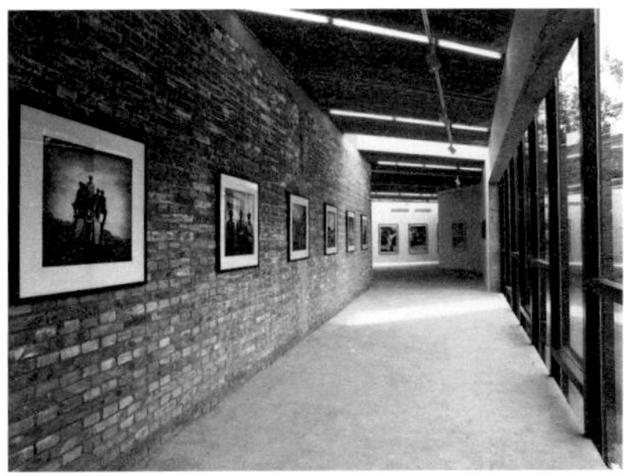
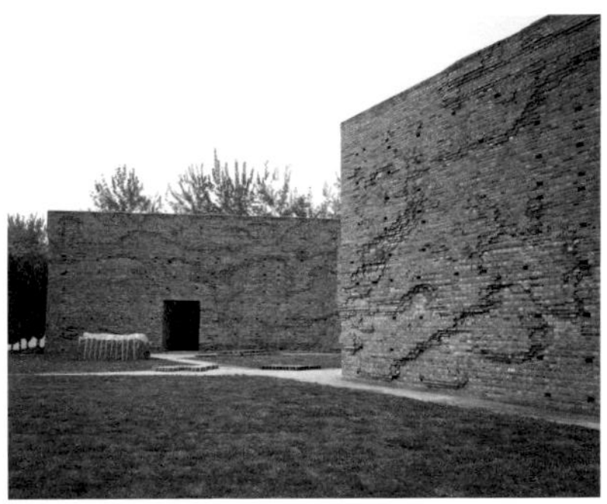

exchange. We have an Artist in Residence program, which hosts artists from China and abroad, who have the possibility to exhibit the works they created during their stay. Additionally, we have had shows that we curated go abroad. For example, we recently put on a show entitled *WATW (We Are The World)* featuring photography from China and the Netherlands, which will travel to the Dutch Cultural Centre during the Shanghai World Expo.

How many books does your library have? Any idea about the most requested ones?
When we started in 2007, it was just our personal collection, made up of under 1.000 books. Now, thanks to the generous donations of various organizations and individuals, there are over 3.000 volumes in the collection. In terms of what is most requested, it really depends on the type of reader.

Are you a publisher also?
Yes, Three Shadows is involved in a number of publishing projects. As far as photography publishing in China, it's basically a void, a blank slate. Previously there were some quality photography publishers, such as Zhejiang Photographic Press, but not anymore. There are fewer and fewer photography publishing houses; it's really quite a small field. There are great resources available here but publishing houses are not rising to the occasion. Publishing is a very important industry, but it has been relatively slow to react and adapt to the changes currently occurring in the field. And unfortunately, there still aren't that many magazines entirely specialized in photography.

What are your education programs at Three Shadows?
Our goal is to provide students with the opportunity to have close contact with the works of art and the photography creation process. We want to allow them to truly experience the photographic process, as well as the magic and mystery behind it. We also encourage our artists in residence to give lectures and interact with the community of local artists and viewers. With regard to specialized photography schools, what is most important is the actual program. How is the actual faculty? The environment? The equipment? Unfortunately, some are just about the big name and there's really nothing behind it. For example, we had a group of students from Tsinghua University and we invited them to explore our darkroom. They were thrilled to see film negatives because they had never seen them before. They even took out their cellphones and digital cameras to take pictures of the negatives! Things are developing too rapidly, I fear we are losing the historical process behind photography. The development is disrupted and discontinuous. Within China, photographic organizations and institutions are still quite weak. Even though there are photographers creating great works, we still need improvement in this area.

Where does the name Three Shadows come from (any references to Plato's allegory of the cave)?
This is actually quite interesting. There is no reference to Plato. More simply, it comes from the *Tao Te Ching* by Lao Tsu. The tao (the way) begets one, one begets two, two begets three, three begets ten thousand things. So we liked this idea of three. Also, with regard to photography, there are many elements relating to three: black, white and grey, RGB, etc. It is also tied to the western concept of the trinity, three forming one; representing myself, Inri, and Three Shadows. It was almost like our child. Three has limitless possibilities.

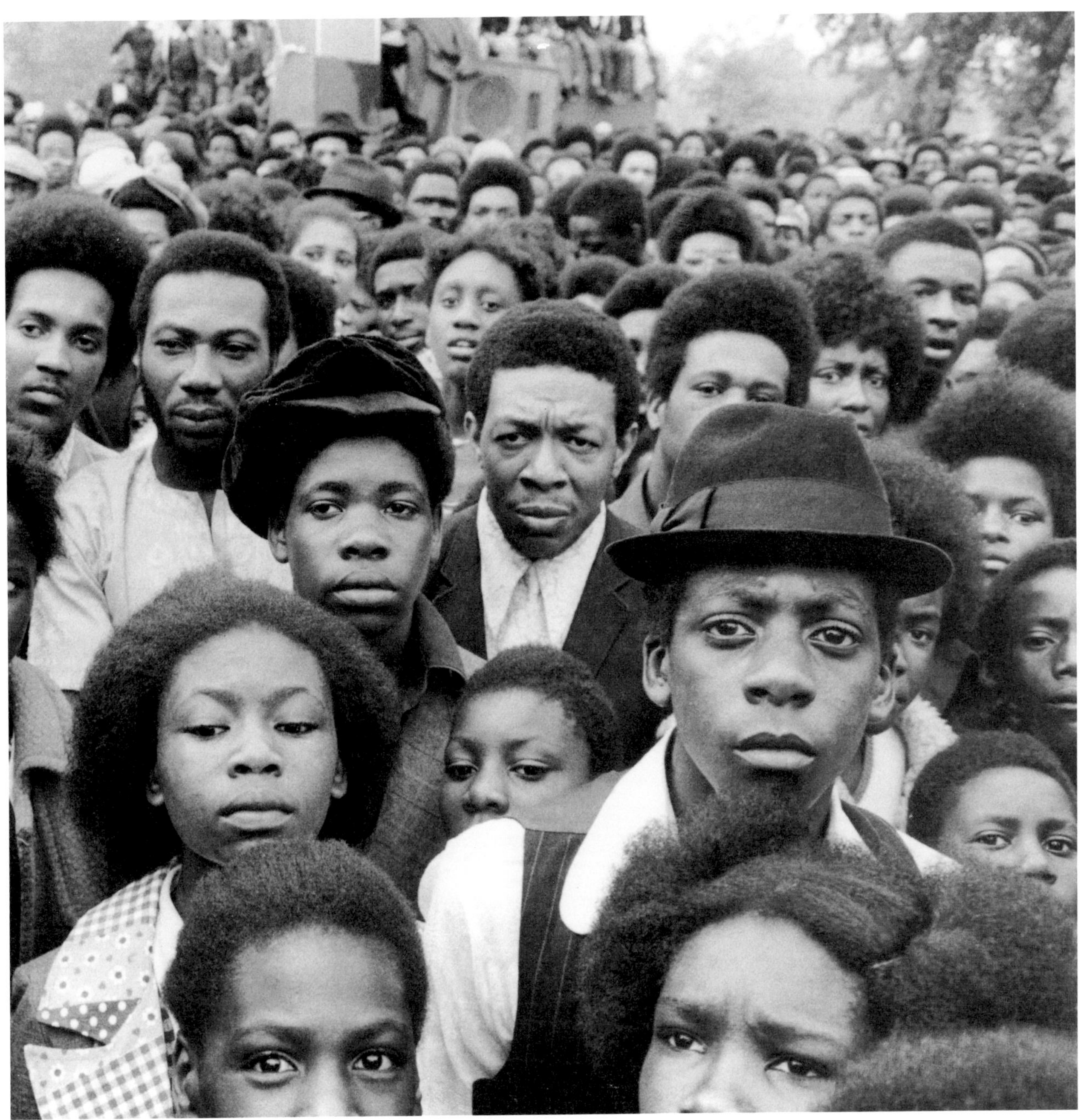

12.375 INCHES

Photography only record covers. No names, no claims. A selection of new (and not so new but awesome just the same) releases and reprints. An invitation to start collecting records again. And to collect photography in this wonderful form. The return of the vinyl is bringing back - with the resurgence of analogue sounds - the right breathing space for the art of the cover. Objects for lovers, a standard for all: 12.375 inches square. This is a farewell to the stingy cd jewel case, to boxes, binders and wallets. To the urge to give charm to an ugly product trying too hard with packaging and design. Let's start a collective museum. Send us your favorite photography only record covers at info@fantomeditions.com, we will publish them all on our/your website. Come on.

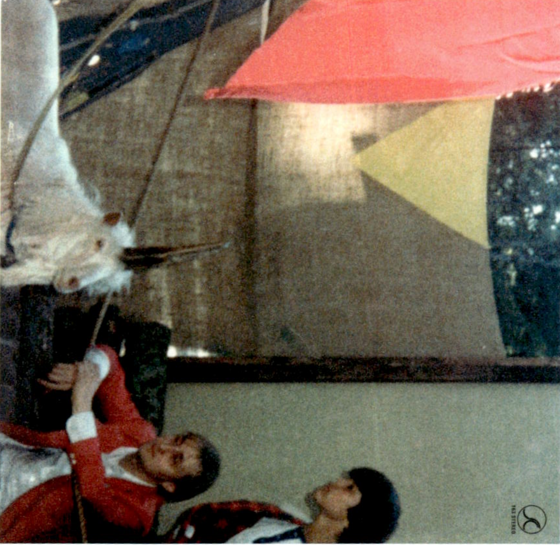
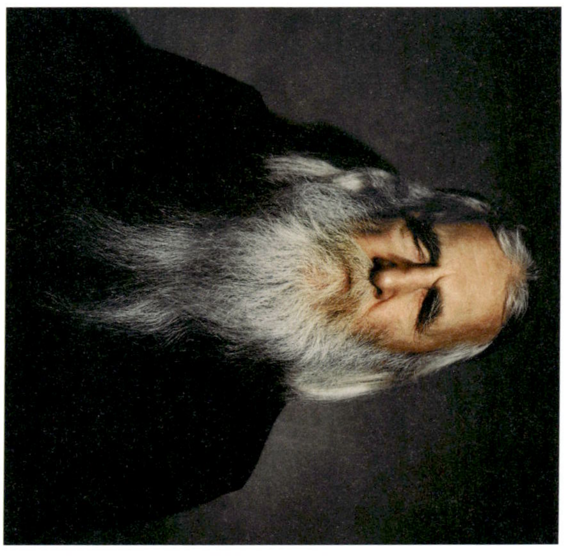
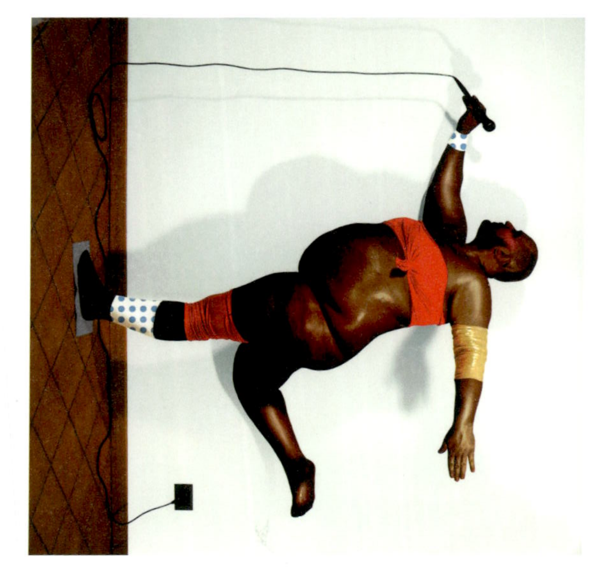
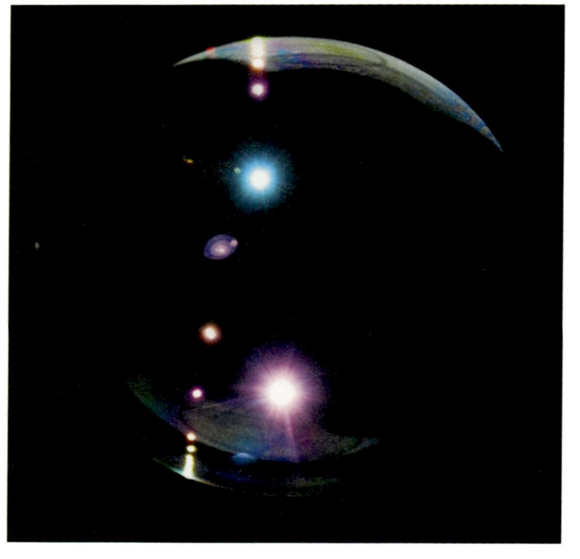
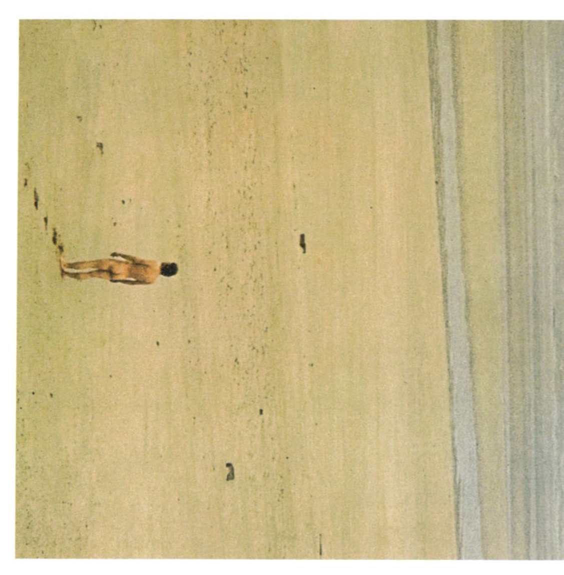
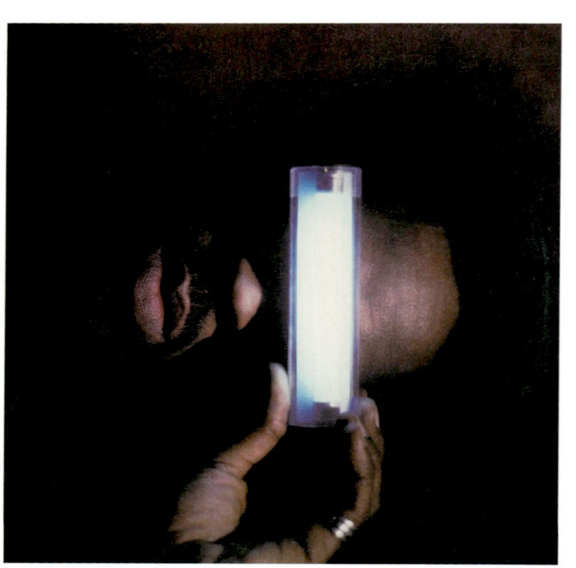

Previous page Various Artists, "Darker Than Blue: Soul from Jamdown", PK/Blood and Fire, original photograph: Chris Steele-Perkins, the crowd at a reggae festival in Blockwell Park, Brixton, 1974. *Here, from top left, clockwise* Hard Ton, "Selfish", International Deejay Gigolo. Randolph, "This Is... What It Is", Mahogany Music. "The Story of Moondog", Honest Jon's Records, photograph by Richard Dumas. Jean-Claude Vannier, "L'enfant Assassin Des Mouches", Finders Keepers, photograph: Tony Frank. Bobb Trimble, "Harvest Of Dreams", Secretly Canadian. Simian Mobile Disco, "Temporary Pleasure", Witchita Recordings, photograph: Jane Stockdale

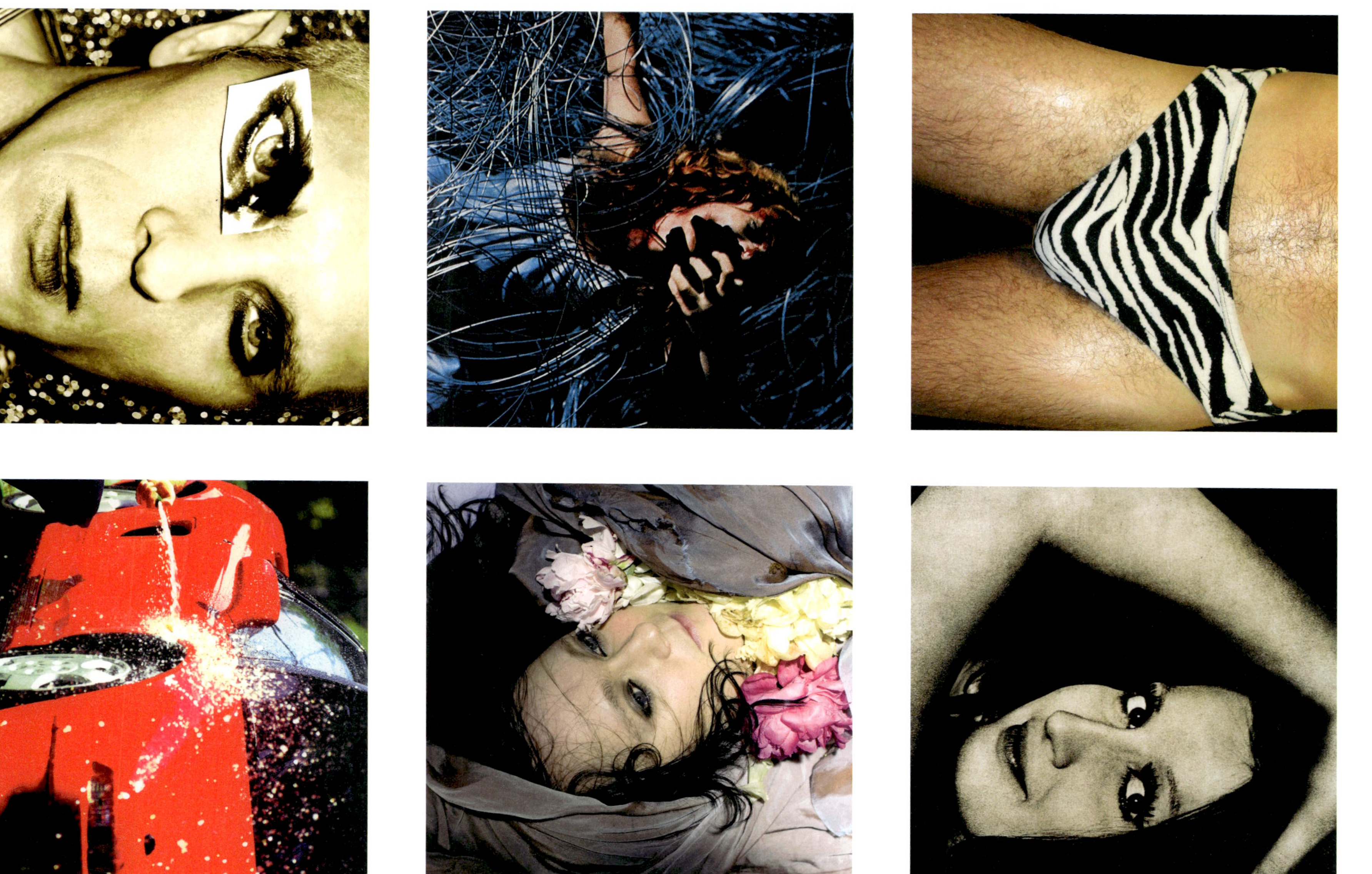

From top left, clockwise Hunx And His Punx, "Gay Singles", True Panther Sounds. Mina, "Mina", Ri-Fi Records, photograph: Pietro Pascuttini. Goblin, "Suspiria", OST, Abraxas. Antony And The Johnsons, "Aeon", Secretly Canadian, photograph: Michael Sharkey. Mr. C, "Lunar EP", Wagon Repair. Various Artists (Johannes Wohnseifer), "Honda Beats", Bonner Kunstverein/Tropen Verlag

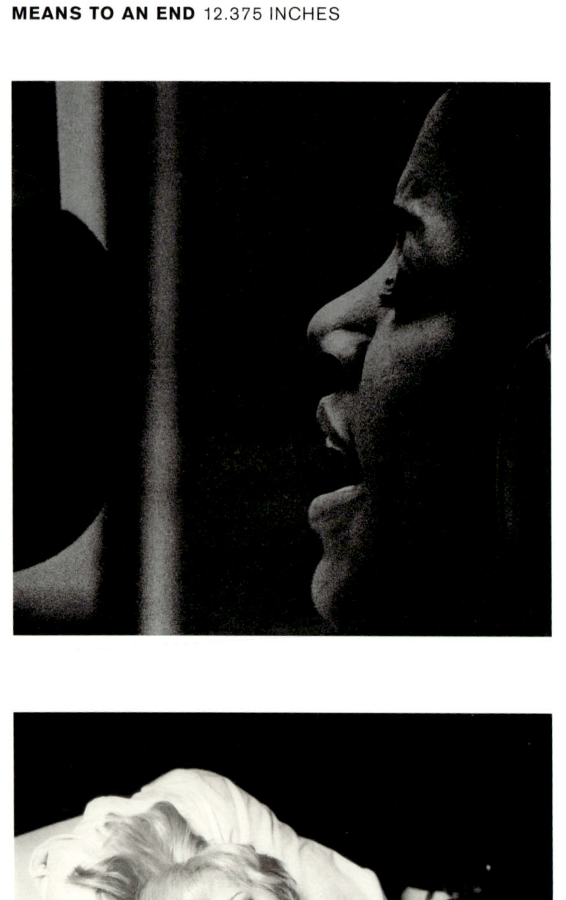
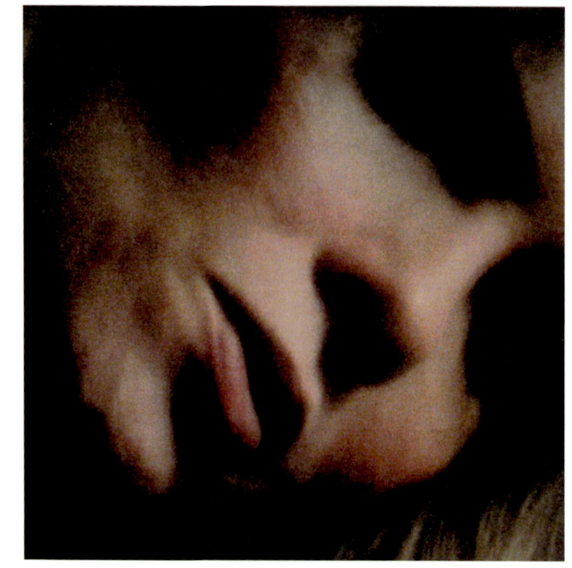
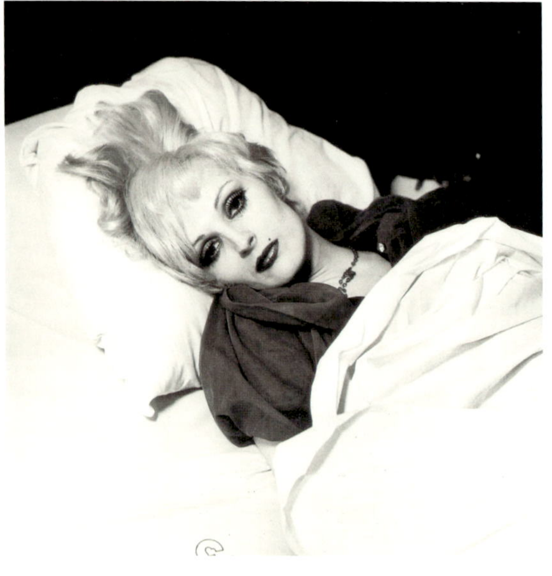
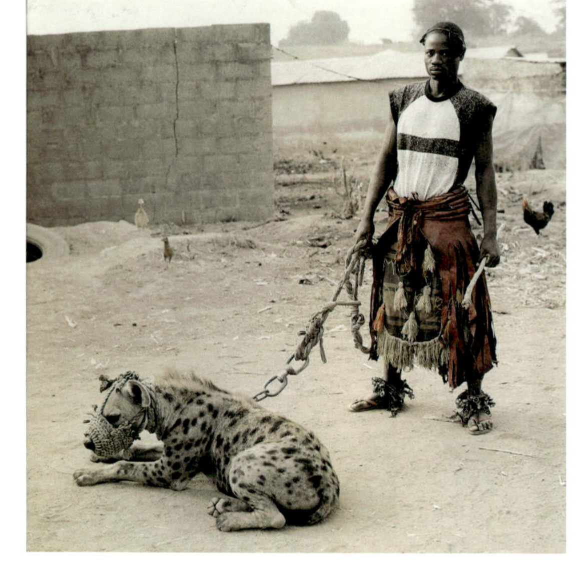
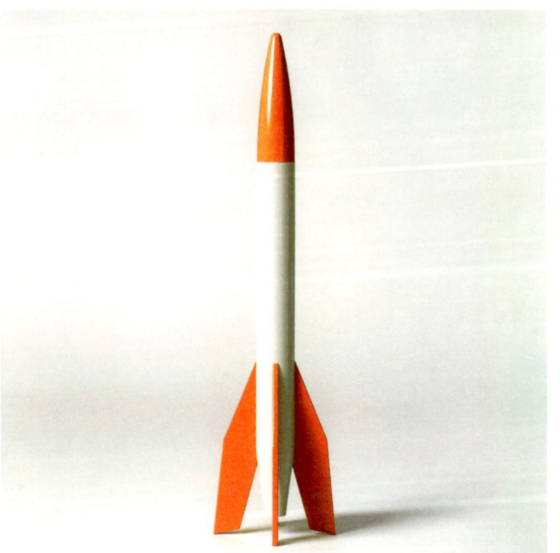
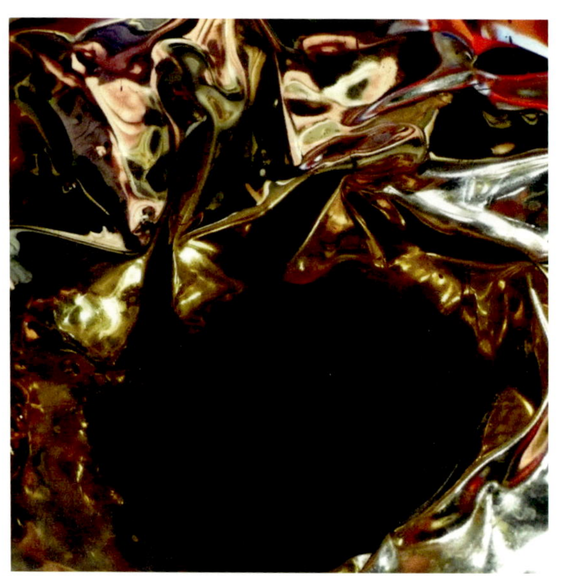

From top left, clockwise Bettye Swann, "Bettye Swann", Honest Jon's Records. Antony And The Johnsons, "Hope There's Someone", Secretly Canadian, photograph: Joey Gabriel by Glen Fogel. Antony And The Johnsons, "The Lake", Secretly Canadian, photograph: "Candy Darling on her Deathbed" by Peter Hujar, 1974. Various Artists, "Lagos Shake: A Tony Allen Chop Up", Honest Jon's Records, photograph: Pieter Hugo. Moritz Von Oswald Trio, "Vertical Ascent", Honest Jon's Records, photograph: Cosima von Bonin. Hypnotic Brass Ensemble, "Hypnotic Brass Ensemble", Honest Jon's Records. *Thank you Serendeepity Records, C.so di Porta Ticinese 100, Milano serendeepity.net*

TRUE CITY

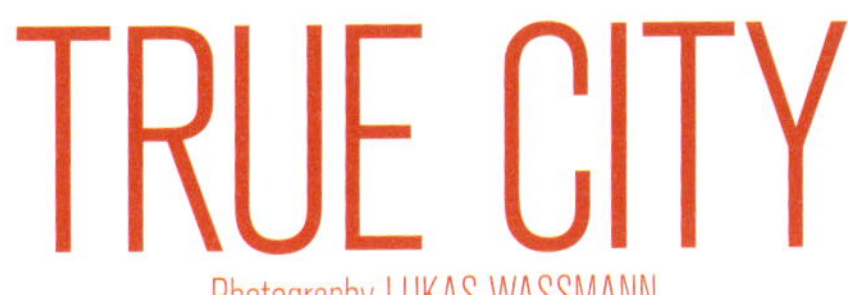

Photography LUKAS WASSMANN

To map is to invent. We wanted to take a portrait of Milan by looking at the new art scene, mapping the city through the eyes of the artists living in town. We get to know things, ourselves, the world through photography, art, writing, through their frictions, resonances, interactions. New connections, even temporary or inappropriate, create new worlds. *Fantom* is made here. And here is Stadium, the new Nike project space where they are pulling and pushing the city's active scenes: performative and creative. We spoke with them about the project, exchanged ideas, decided to go for it and asked a first group of artists, performers, curators, gallerists and designers working within and around the art world to choose a place - representative, evocative, pleasant - where they wanted their portraits to be set. Step 1: on location with Swiss photographer Lukas Wassmann, one of *Fantom's* companions. Next step: wait and see. *nikestadiums.com*

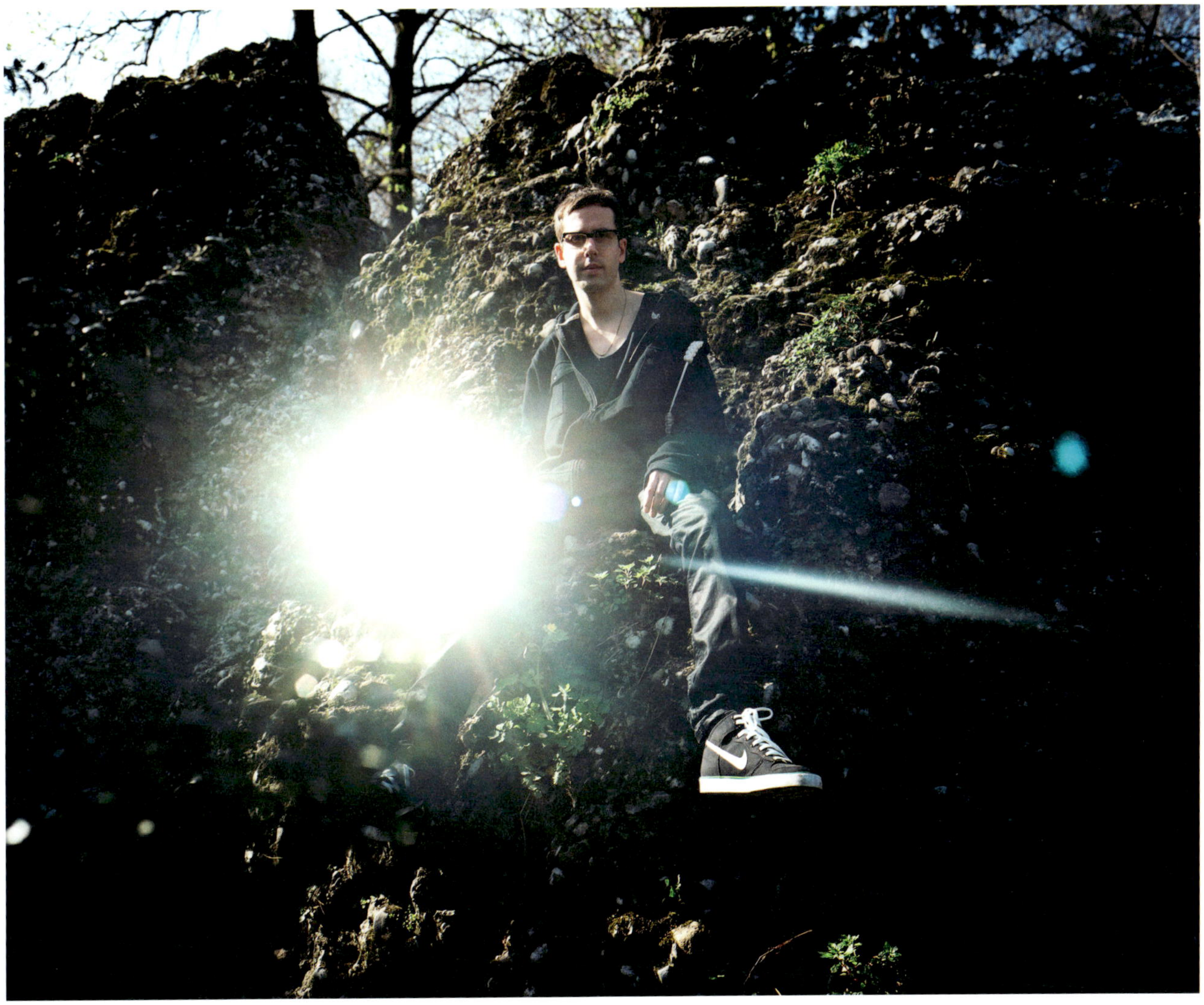

JACOPO MILIANI, ARTIST

Where are we? Indro Montanelli Public Gardens. A mix of young bourgeois families, cruisers, rock-climbers, joggers, teen-agers skipping classes; a charming non-place in the middle of the city.

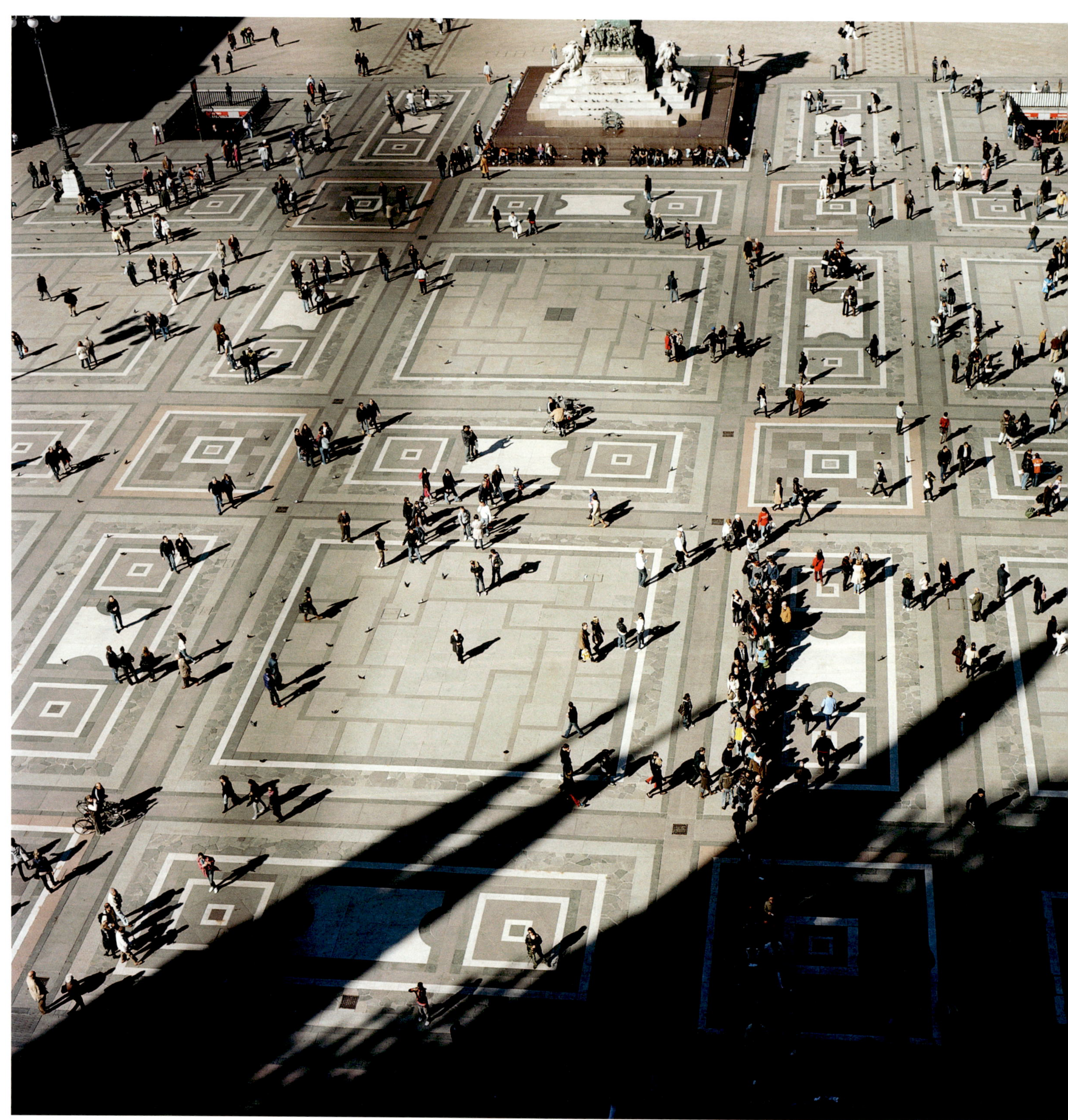

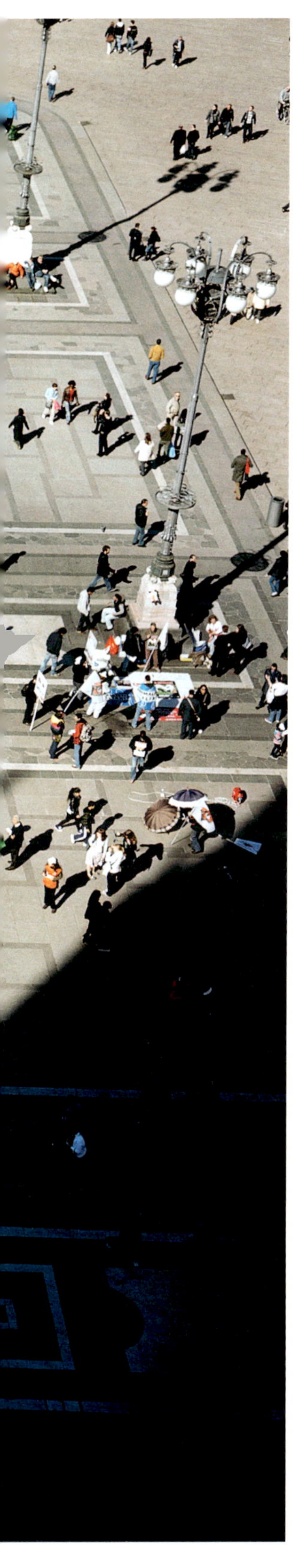

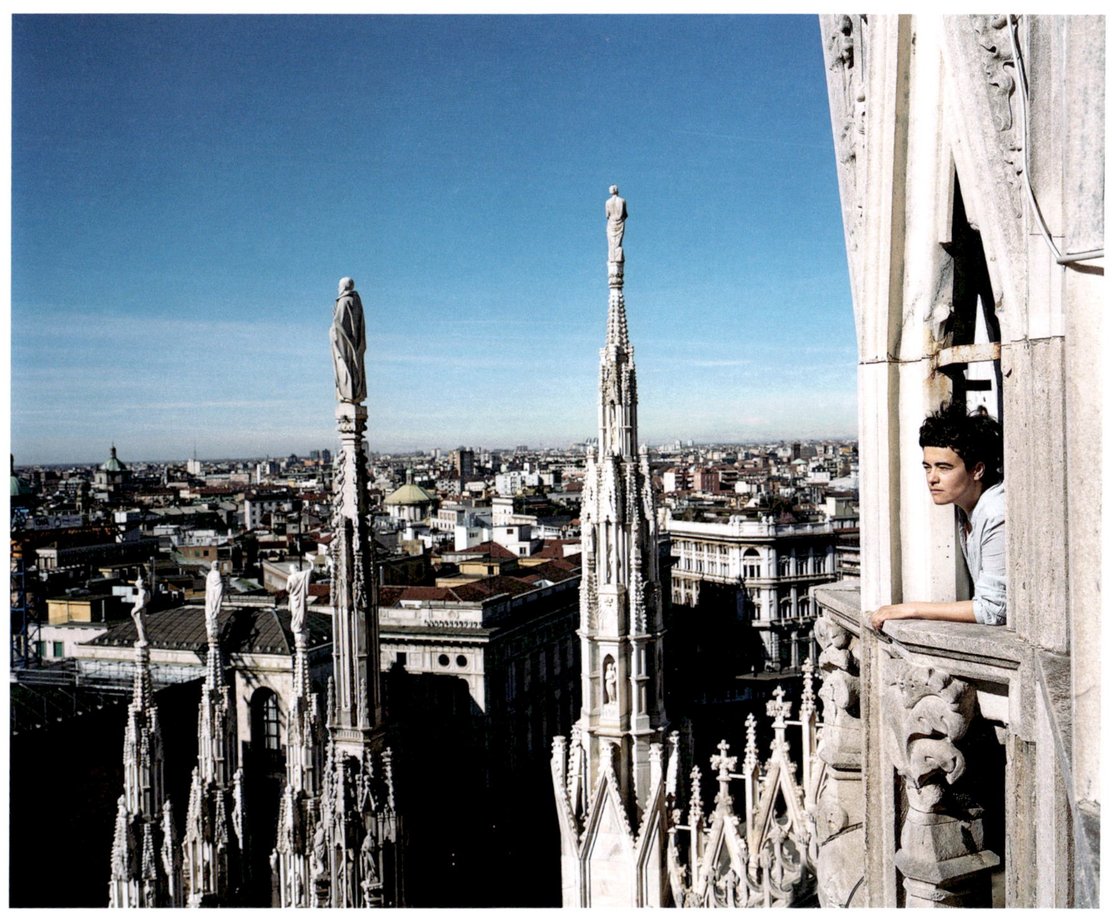

ALICE GUARESCHI, ARTIST

Where are we? On the top of the Duomo. Here the horizon is open and I like cities from above. *What do you think makes Milan special?* Some people who live here.

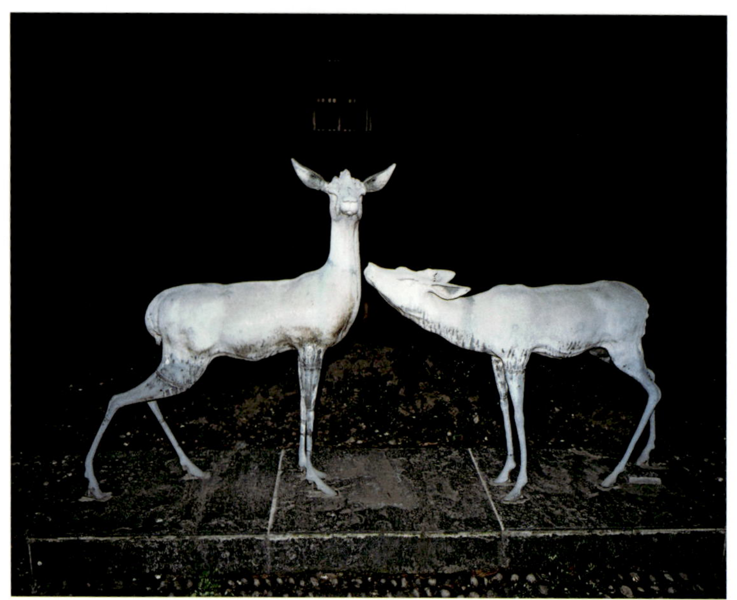

GIORGIO DI SALVO, GRAPHIC DESIGNER AND ILLUSTRATOR

We are in Lambrate, I was here last year for a party organized by some friends and the place really struck me. It's a surreal, post-apocalyptic urban landscape. *What do you think makes Milan special?* It's simply the place where I was born. I think that all cities are good or bad depending on how you live them. I like to think about Milan in the 80s when I was a kid, the fashion I did not understand, the furs, my mother's emerald green tailleur with shouder pads. *giorgiodisalvo.com*

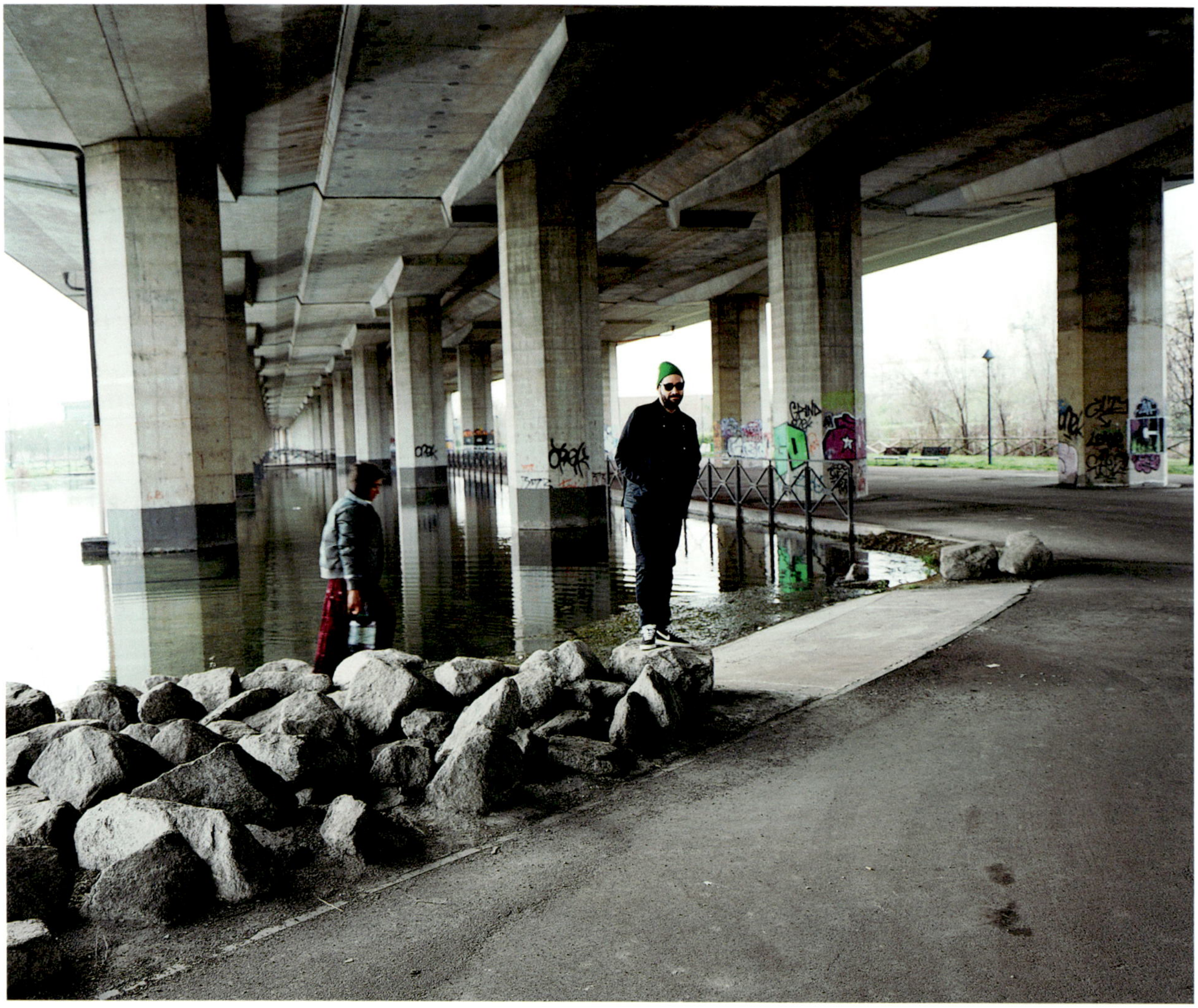

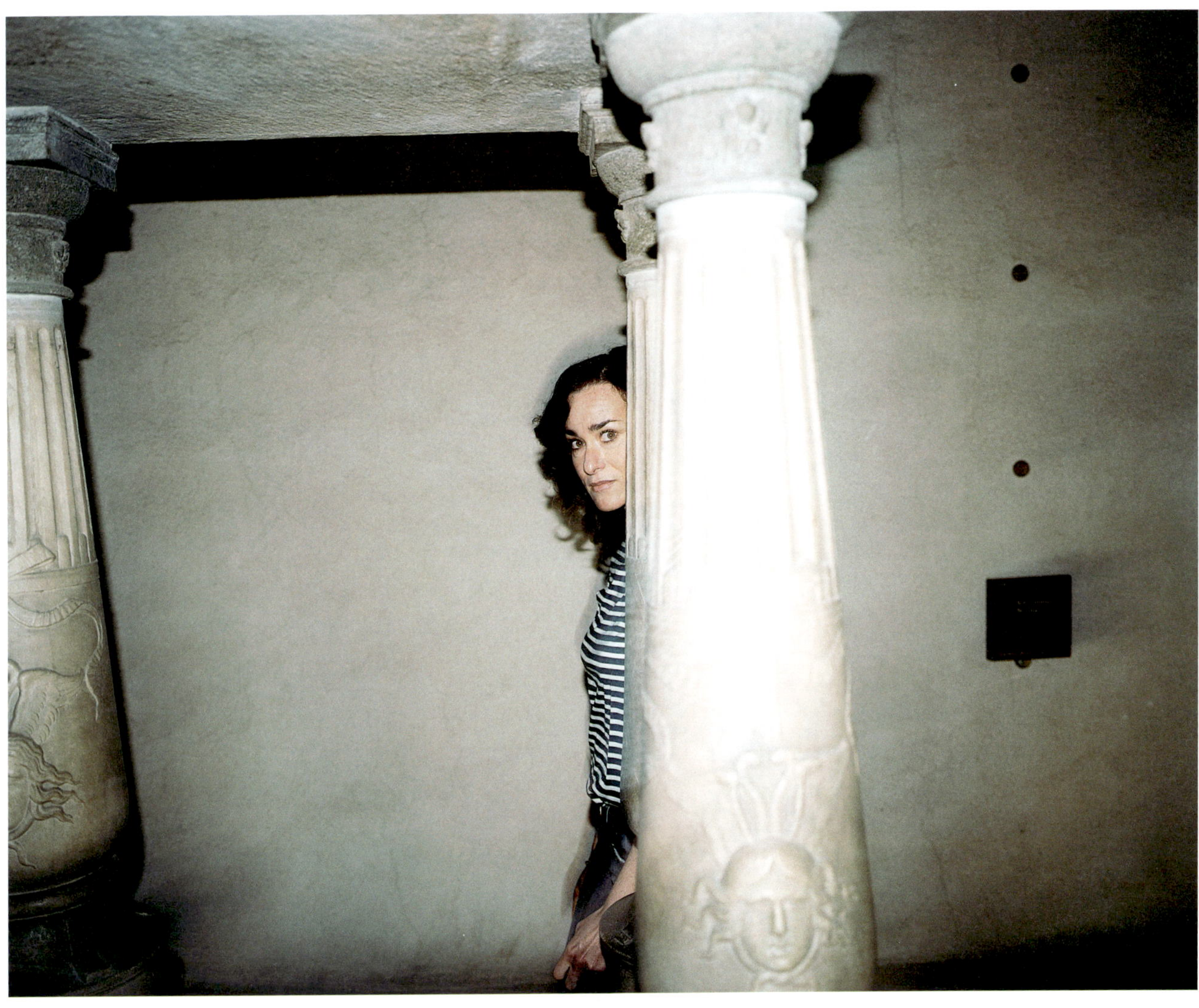

LINDA FREGNI NAGLER, ARTIST

We are in the Museum of Ancient Art, at Castello Sforzesco. I am really fond of it. It is extremely representative of the city. It was restored by the architects BBPR after the war and displays beautiful objects. I have been here many times, even just to walk through its rooms, and I participated in an exhibition within the Rocchetta, the section dedicated to decorative arts, where I spent time and could handle some objects. It's a place lit mostly by natural light, very romantic, right for a first date. *What do you think makes Milan special?* I love the old craftsmen and the fog. Milanese craftsmen are real workers, they know what they are talking about, know how to solve the problems of those who arrive with vague requests, are rough but become affectionate, and sometimes they still speak dialect, with their spectacles on the points of their noses. The fog makes Milan cinematographic. When there is fog, lamps have luminous edges, as if they were photograped with an open diaphragm, and the city turns into black and white.

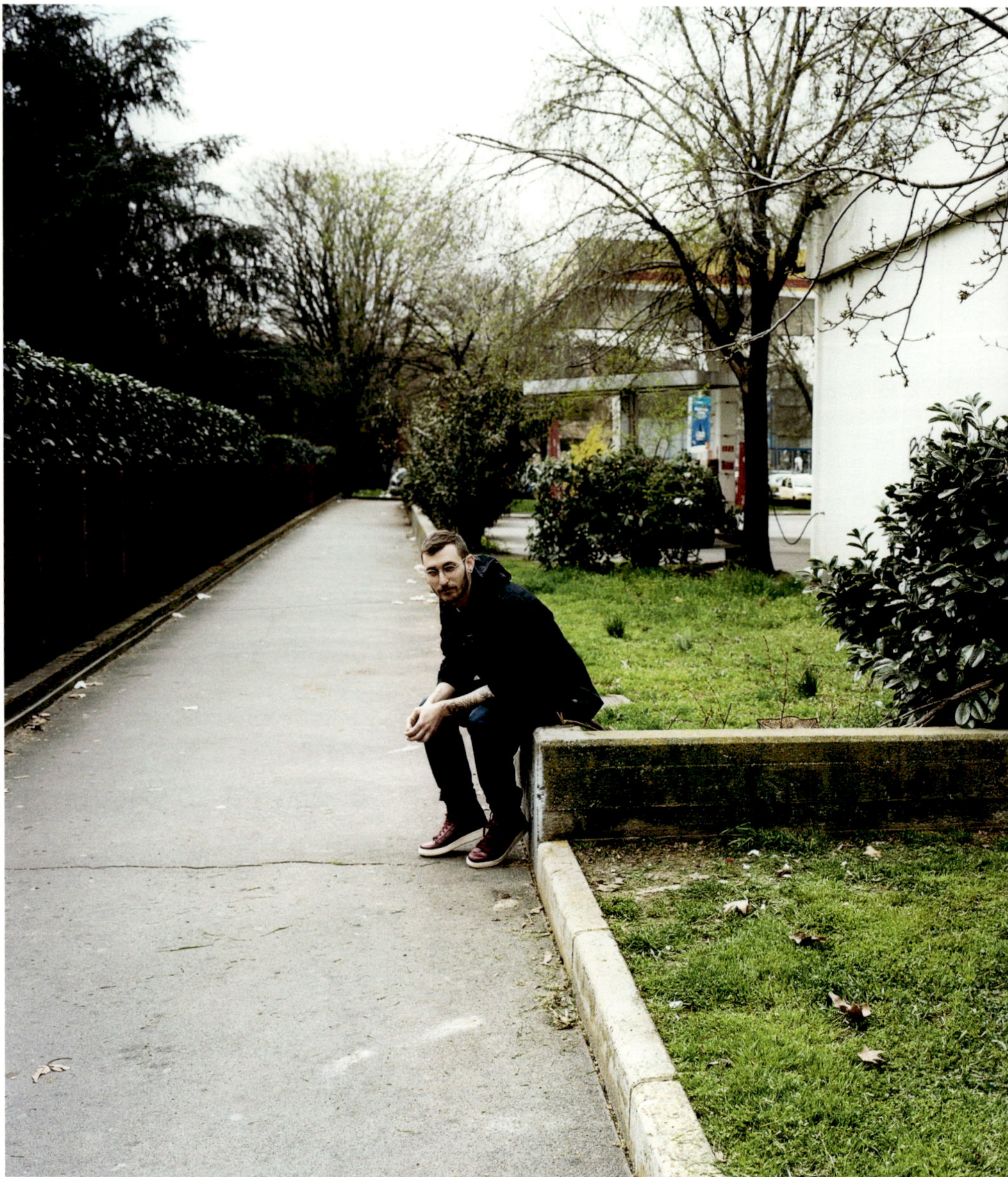

TOMMASO GARNER, GRAPHIC DESIGNER

This is Lambrate, on the outskirts of Milan.
The name "Lambrate" comes from the the river where
this village was founded, the Lambro, which means
"clear" and "teeming with fish". *Why did you choose
this place?* I have always been fascinated by the idea of
the back alley, the secluded lane, dimly lit, devoid of
any interest but full of activities that are better carried
out away from people. This in particular is a shortcut
to reach Via Ventura, the area of the city devoted to
contemporary art. *tommasogarner.com*

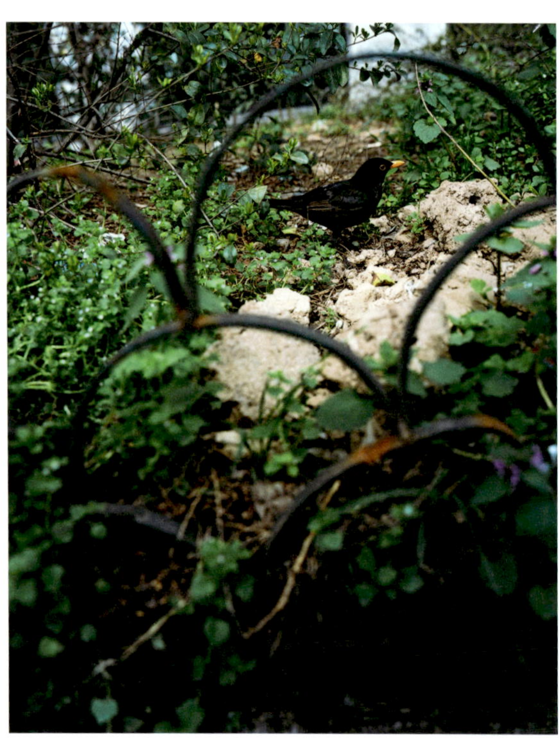

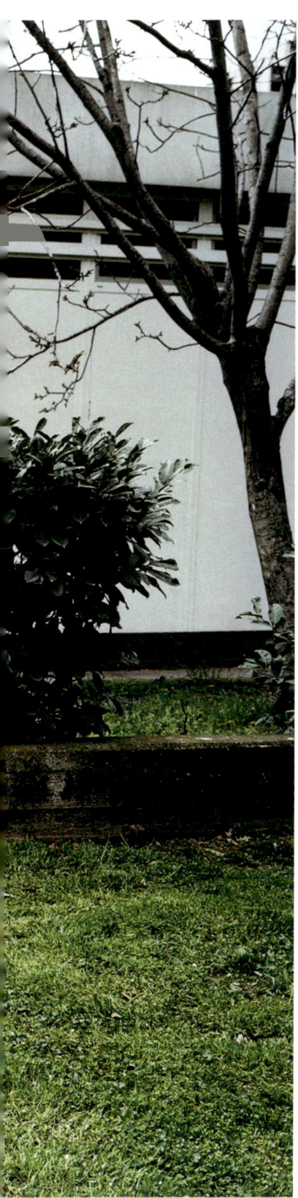

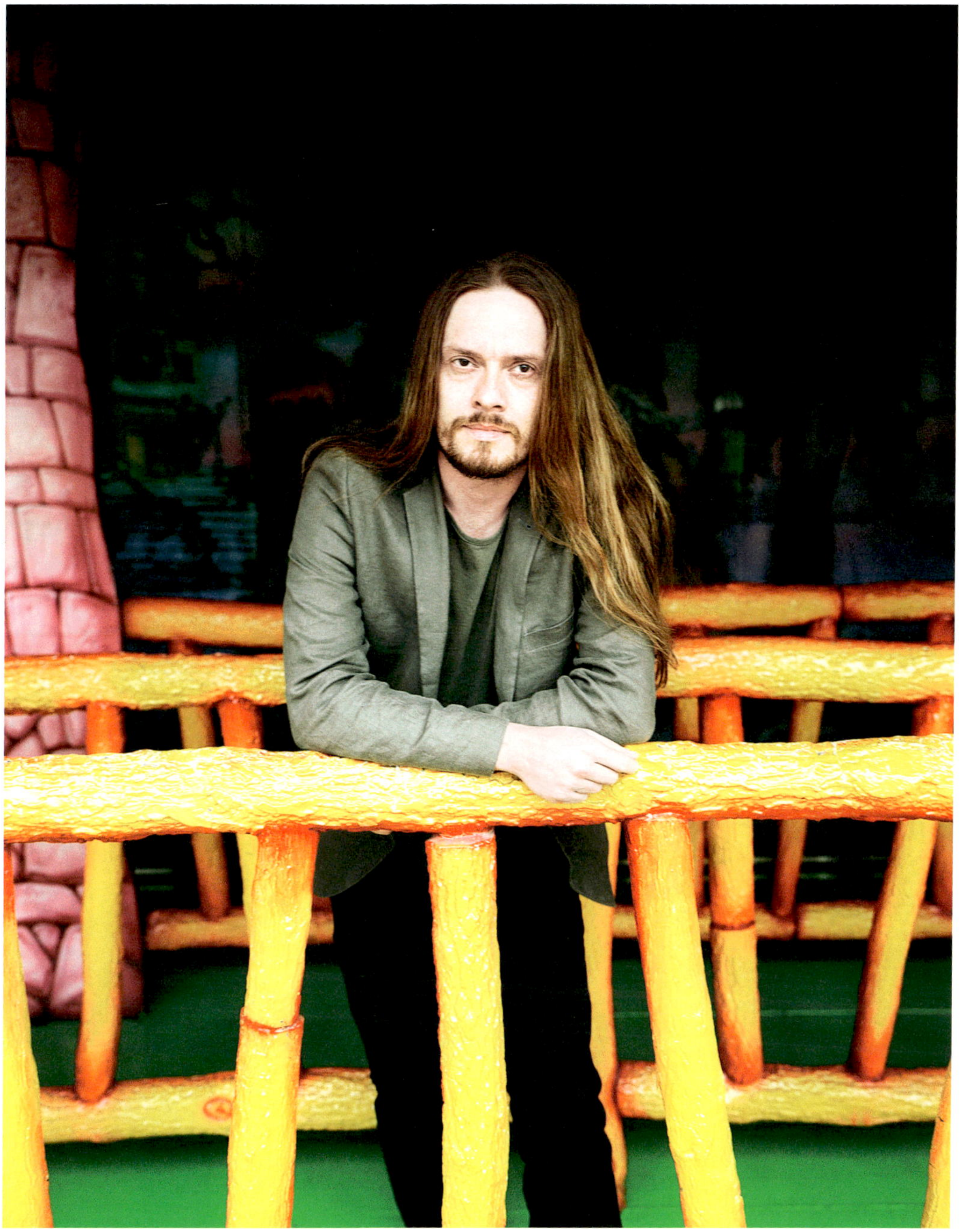

CHRISTIAN FROSI, ARTIST

We are in the area of the mining lakes. *Why did you choose this place?* Because it is the place where the city opens up and, elongating, produces constructions that mix with the countryside, with the periphery of small, rough football grounds, minigolf, disused amusement parks, and mysterious small buildings at the center of huge traffic circles. To live in Milan is a bit like living on Krypton, the force of gravity is triple in comparison to all other cities/planets.

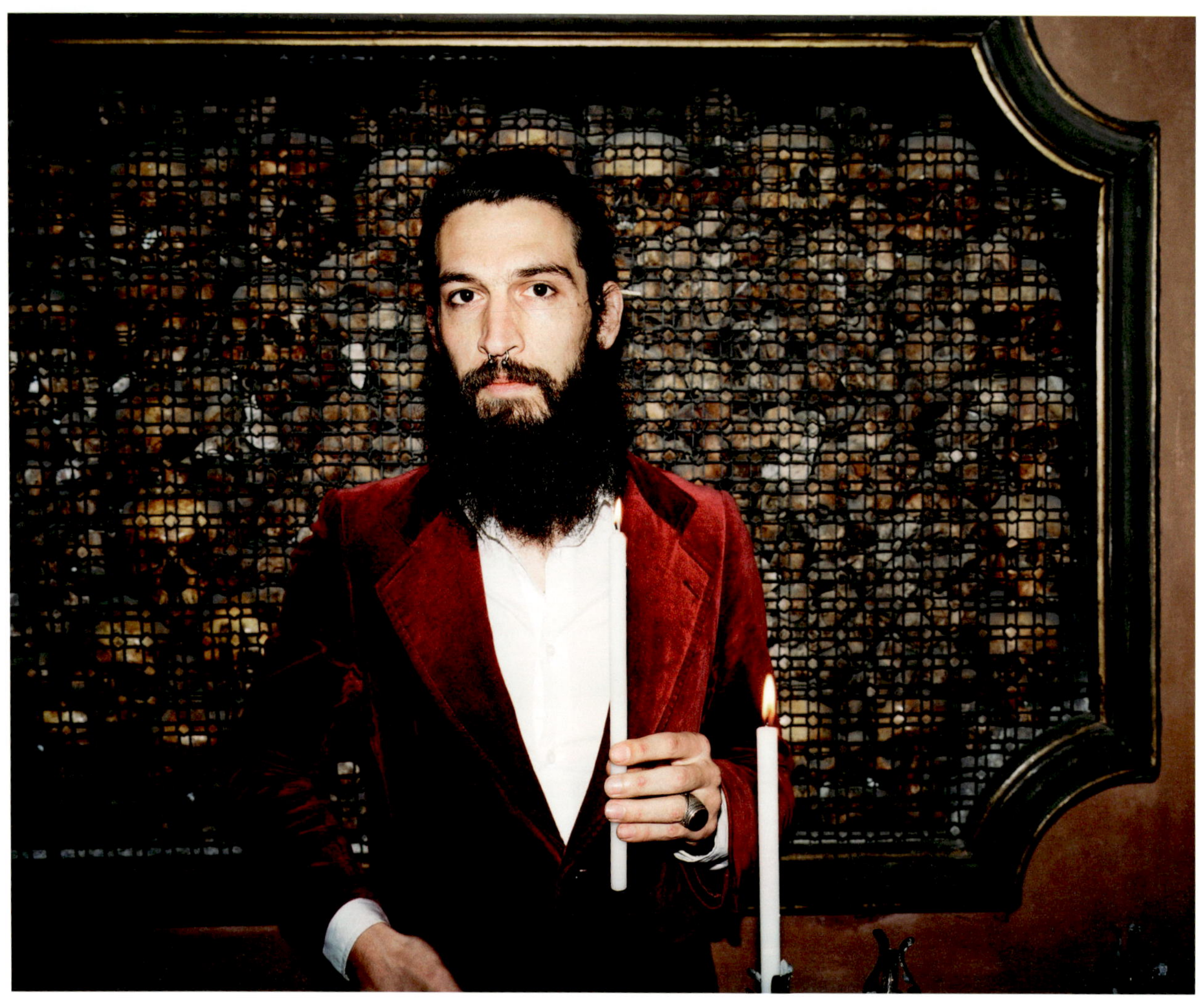

We are in the small crypt dedicated to Our Lady of
Sorrows in the Santuario Arcivescovile of
S. Bernardino alle Ossa, in via Verziere. Alessandro
Guerriero first brought me here. When I come here I
feel strangely at home; it reminds me of the Otranto
Cathedral where they keep the skulls of the martyrs
decapitated by Ottoman invaders in 1480. I can almost
hear the sound of the sea. *luigipresicce.it*

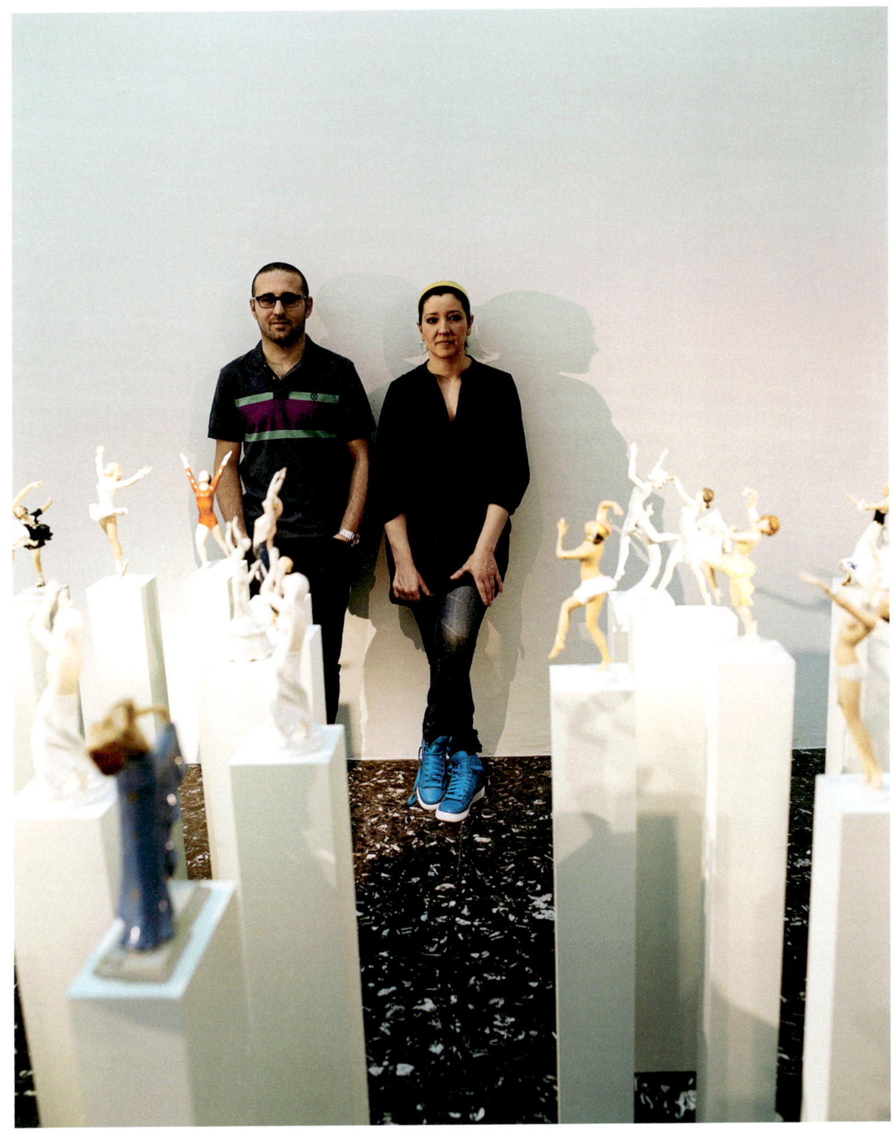

PEEP-HOLE PROJECT SPACE AND EDITIONS
(VINCENZO DE BELLIS AND BRUNA ROCCASALVA)

We are in the middle of Alicja Kwade's exhibition, *Broken Away from Common Standpoints*, at Peep-Hole, the space we opened in 2009. It would be our portrait even without us. *peep-hole.org*

FLUXIA GALLERY
(ANGELICA BAZZANA AND VALENTINA SUMA)

We are at Fluxia, the gallery we founded with our artist friend Luca Francesconi almost a year ago. It's our second home. *What do you think makes Milan special?* Orange streetcars and the angriest drivers in the world. *fluxiagallery.com*

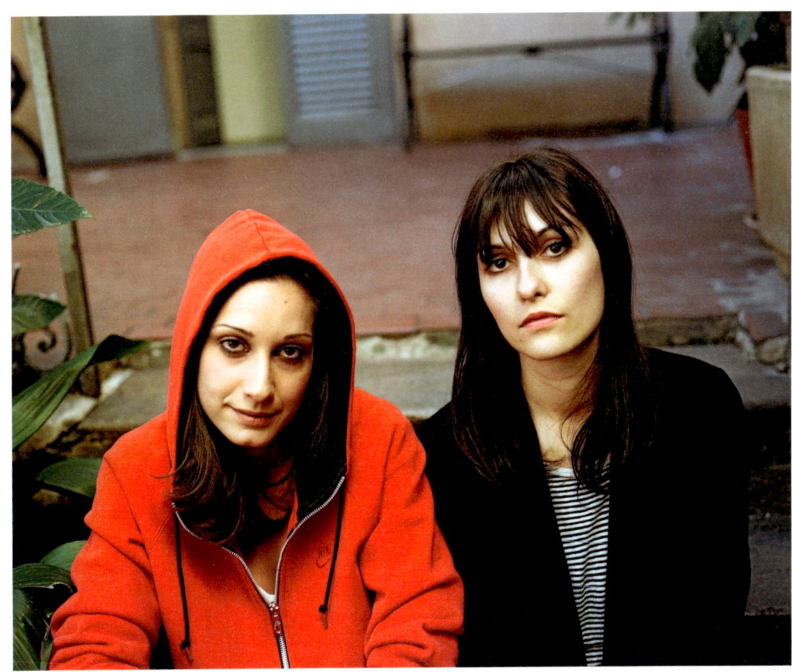

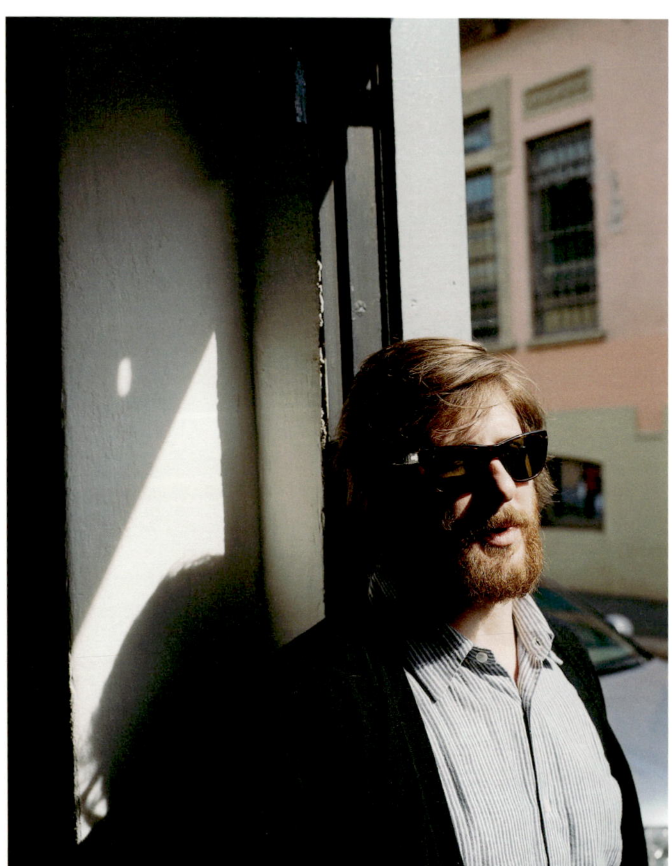

MARCO KLEFISCH, VISUAL DESIGNER AND ILLUSTRATOR

We are in my studio in Via Pestalozzi 1. It is where I develop most of my ideas and work. *marcoklefisch.com*

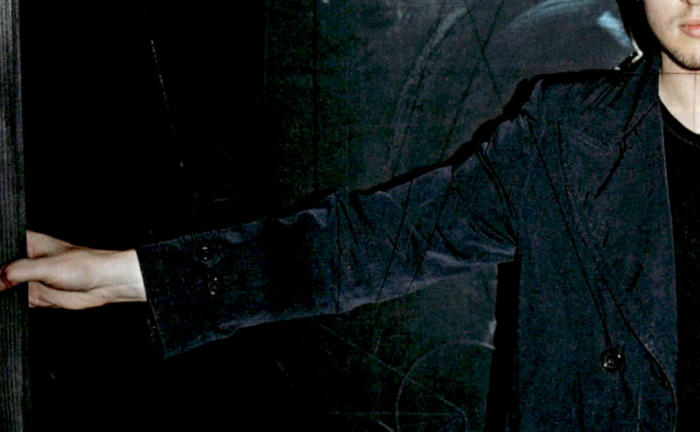

GIULIO FRIGO, ARTIST

Where are we? Within my installation *Impersonale* at DOCVA - Documentation Center for Visual Arts, my first solo show. It's like my mind habitat; I like the idea of being portrayed in a space that I have designed, an extension of my persona.

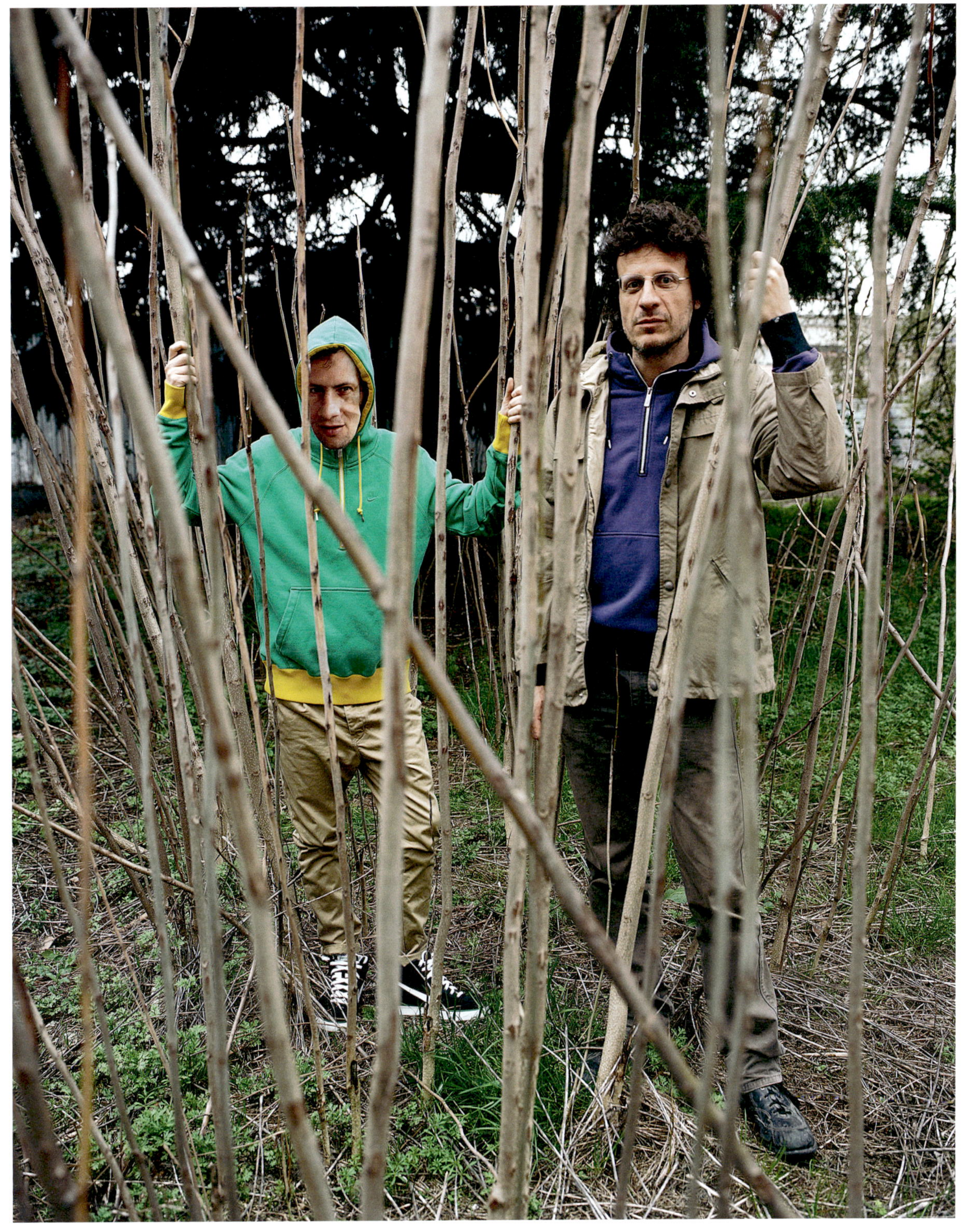

Where are we? Sebastiano: In an abandoned factory,
I suppose. *Why did you choose this place?* I didn't,
Colombo did and I like what he likes. *Colombo, why
did you choose this place then?* Colombo: I think I sought
shelter in the first uterus at hand; I love the gardens of
abandoned factories.

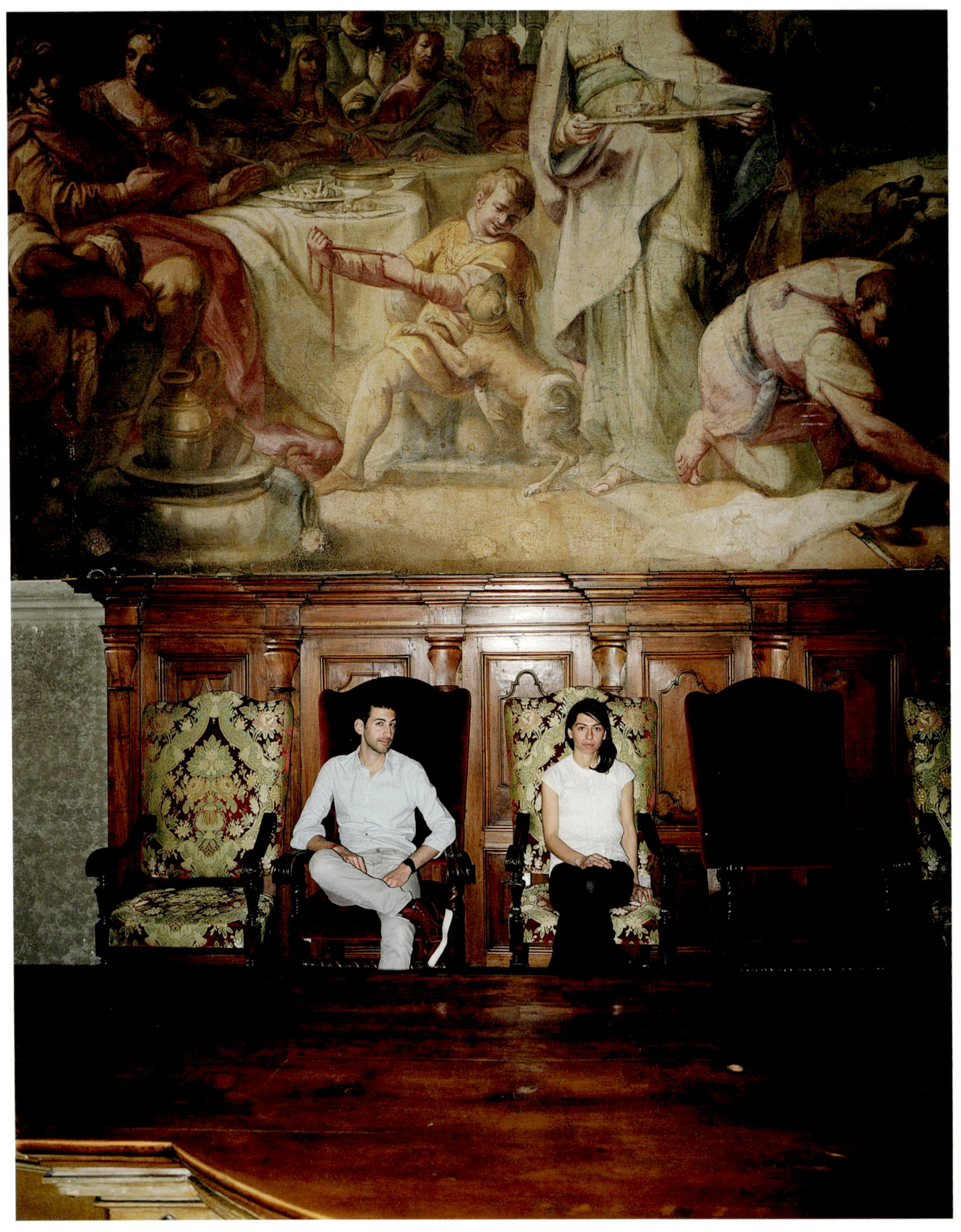

We are in the room dedicated to The Last Supper
in the Leonardo Da Vinci Museum of Science and
Technology. Our work combines art with strong craft
and mechanical elements. In our shows the technical
and the research of materials are in dialogue with the
movements of the body, so this museum is a place that
- starting with Leonardo - synthesizes these aspects
of our work. *What do you think makes Milan special?* It's
a city where a taste for classics is able to connect with
the ephemeral beauty expressed by performance and
fashion, it's a place where great traditions seem to be
able to compare with a creativity that is constantly
regenerating. *pathosformel.org*

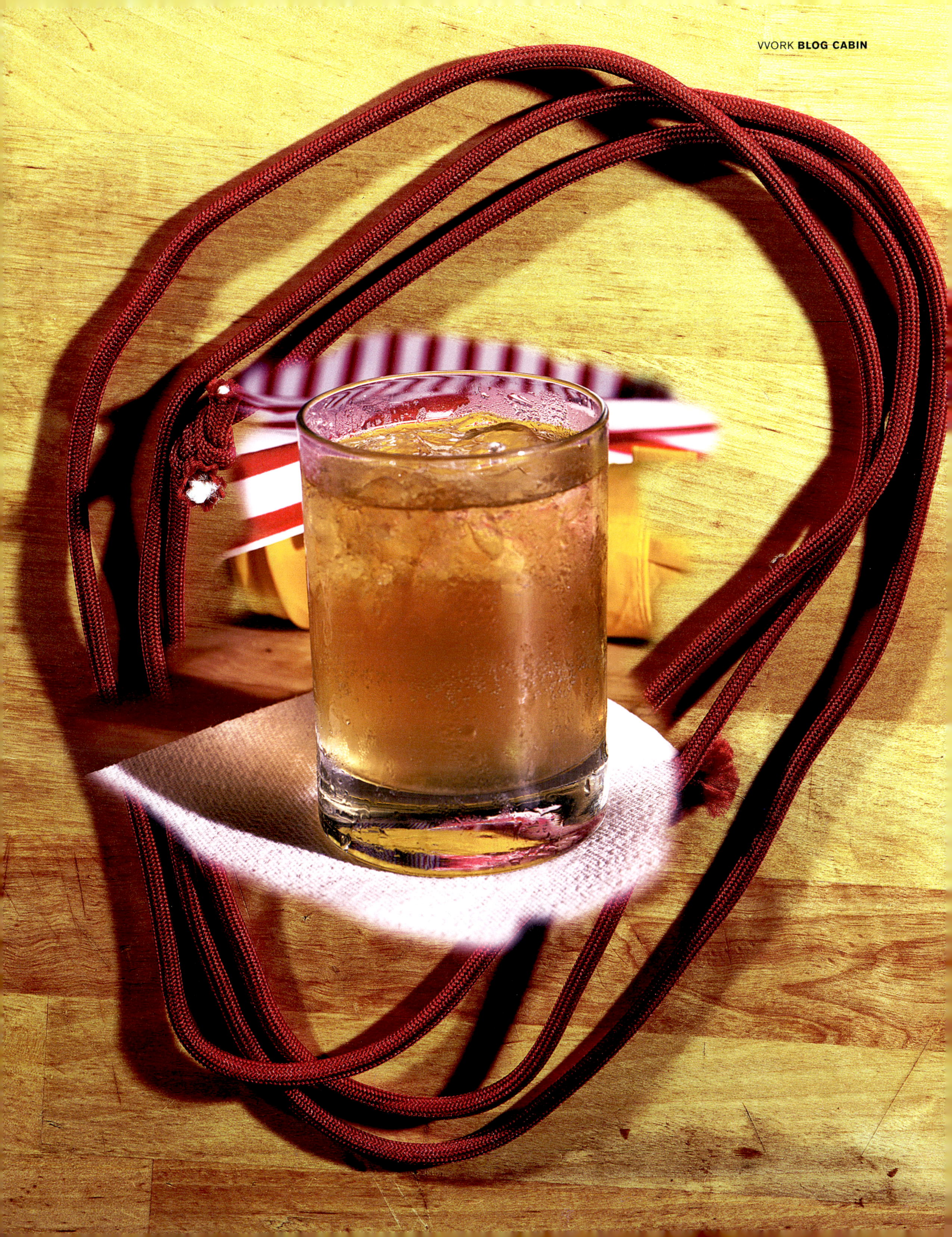

VVORK
by Alex Gartenfeld

The images published on the VVORK web site, edited by Vienna-based artists Aleksandra Domanovic, Oliver Laric, Georg Schnitzer, and Christoph Priglinger, run down the screen casually. The artists collect images of artworks from gallery and personal web sites, about three or four each day, and upload them with a title and the artist's name, hyperlinks and a tag that groups by city where the work has been installed. They don't bother with the cumbersome copyright information that bogs down publishing associated with institutions. The works are un-differentiated by contributing blogger. The sizing of the images is unremarkable, and not fit to any column width; the images are loosely connected - but not always - by the so-obvious-it-seems-arbitrary criteria of vague.

Today, March 7, there's John Transue's Running Scans, which look like scanning errors, followed by a diptych by Swiss artist Tobias Madison from his show at the Swiss Institute in New York; followed by a work by TWAIN (Santiago Taccetti and Natalia Ibáñez Lario) where a digitally smudged smiley face comes to look a little bit like a penis; and so on. The visual similarities are facile; they would be too matchy-matchy, even pedantic, in a group show. On a web site, they read instead as maybe a little too smart for their own good, lax, but mostly casual and affirmative - both towards the art and the rapid digestion of the blog format.

What the arbitrariness of the artist's most prominent selection criteria belies is the high level of taste, and the literacy and time spent wading through infinite web sites for the imagery. As someone who works on web sites related to art, I can say that it's difficult to chart what will be successful in terms of encouraging repeat traffic. A few things help: breaking original news; establishing regular franchises that create a site's personality. All of these are surprisingly contingent upon authenticity - either that of the news source or the credible familiarity of its author. I can't measure VVORK's level of success (I don't have access to their traffic statistics) but I can speak to an aura of singularity to the site, channeled through its louche sophistication. In any case, the site has advertising that indicates they've received institutional endorsement - and

there's another site, iwannabeonvvork.com, which presumably refers to this site. VVORK, unpronounceable but easily misread "WORK," brings out a niche in the new occupation known as blogging, and ties it into the making an of artwork. They call VVORK a "website" and a "curatorial project" - not a work of art. Furthermore, they use the format of a collective, a common trope for artists working in but without any defined vocabulary in the sphere of blogging. In its short history, one invisibly preserved in servers worldwide, and its unsteady value as a commodity with regulated exchange value, there are variables on all sides.

Recently, the VVORK blog has entered the real, as it were, by partaking in the first of Rhizome's *Silent Screening* series with a Variety Evening performance at the New Museum. The artists employed their peers and artists to re-enact eight works in sequence. These would then be digitized to their present video form, and stand as a script for further circulation and reenactment. A number of the works employed here made more or less specific reference to the work being done: *Exhibitions*, originally by Pierre Bismuth and Claire Fontaine and here activated by Amy Mackie, involves a woman using her long hair as a brush for the floor, where the impermanence of the public artistic gesture is compared with a domestic, gendered one. Critic Chris Wiley and the New Museum's own Laura Hoptman acted out two other instances from the *Exhibitions* series, doubling the confusion of roles implicit in the artists' of VVORK blogging practice.

To conclude, I'll focus on the reenactment of Kristin Lucas's Refresh, for which two audience members were invited to execute a cold-reading of a court case in which a protagonist looks to change her name to her own name. It's unclear from the beginning whether the person looking to "refresh" is a disembodied character or the artist Lucas (who often works at the intersection of web technologies) legislating her own new beginning. The role of documentation through technology-be it a diary, photography, video, or the performance script poses an interesting, age-old question about the work required to maintain memory in a landscape mediated by images and technology.

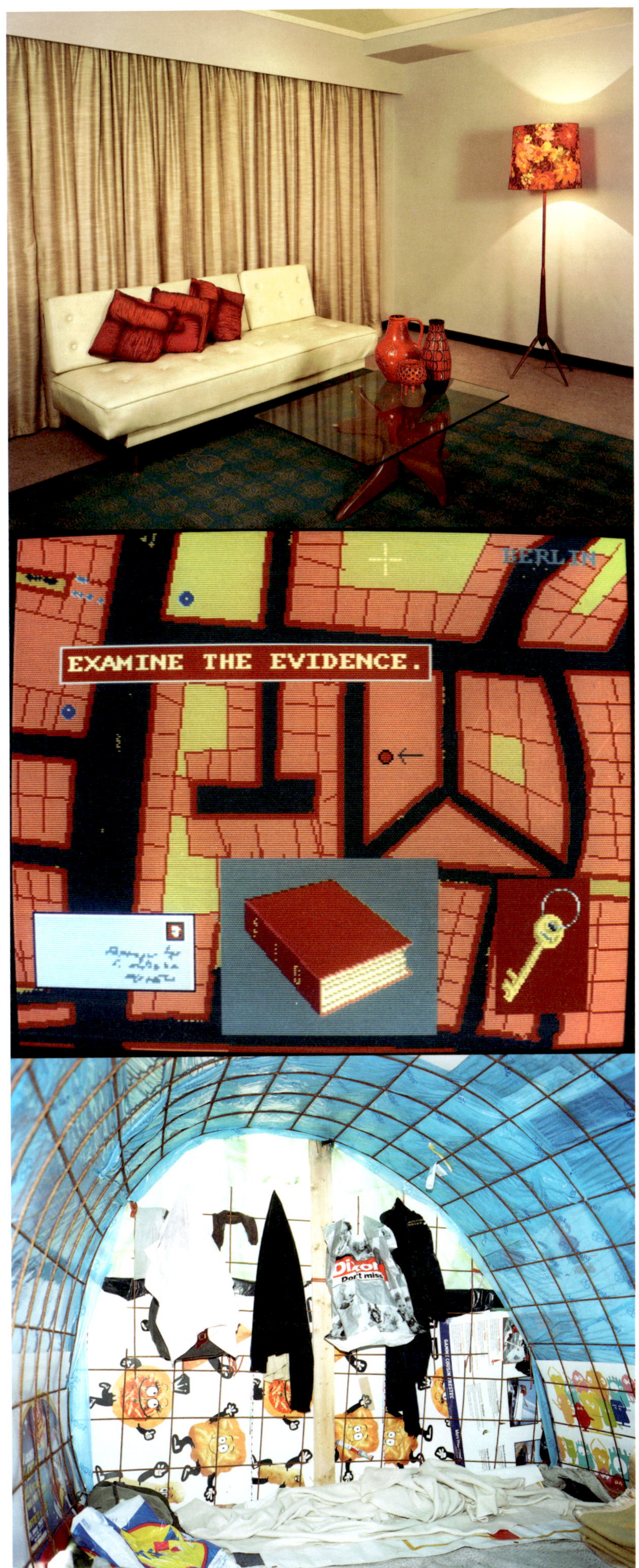

Here from top Ann Shelton "Modern Girl" 1999 © *the artist, courtesy the artist and McNamara Gallery, Wanganui, New Zealand.* Suzanne Treister "Examine the Evidence (fictional videogame still)" 1991, photograph (of the original work on the Amiga computer screen) mounted on aluminium. *Courtesy Annely Juda Fine Art, London and P.P.O.W. Gallery, New York.* Henk Wildschut "Calais, France, July 2009" 2009 © *the artist. Opening page* Lucas Blalock "Strange Loop" 2009 © *the artist. Page 66* Eric Tabuchi "French Countryside Skateparks" 2009 © *the artist, courtesy Florence Loewy, Paris*

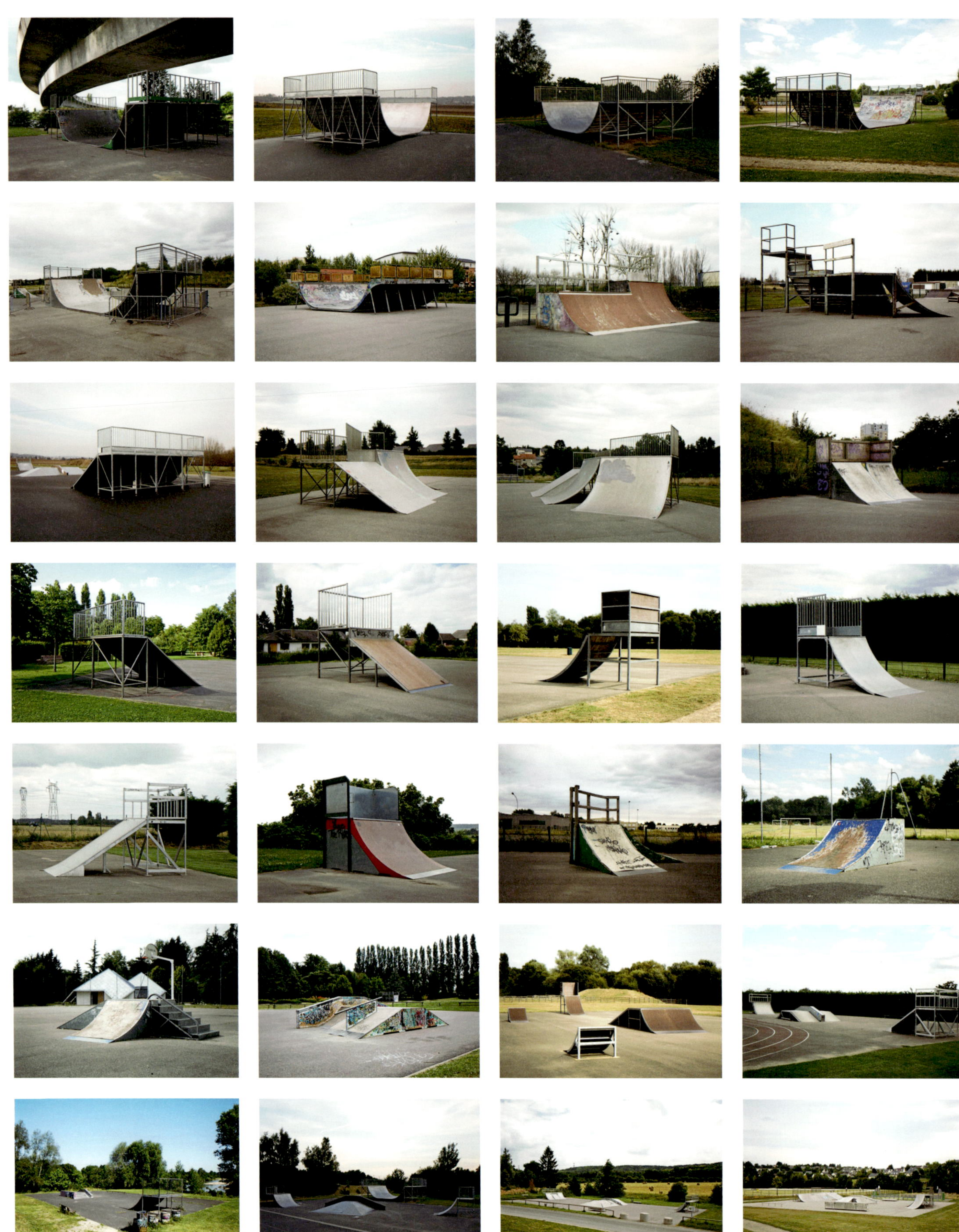

FRANCESCO ZANOT
VISITS THE COLLECTION OF
ADRIAN-SILVAN IONESCU

Adrian-Silvan Ionescu is an art historian and critic based in Bucharest, Romania. Now professor at the National University of Arts in Bucharest, he was formerly curator at the National Museum of Art and at the National Museum of History of the City of Bucharest. Along with stamps (which were his first love as a teenager), matchboxes, beer bottle corks and other trinkets, he collects almost everything that has artistic quality: contemporary paintings, tiny sculptures, graphic arts, fasion (military uniforms as well as civilian dress), African art, pipes. About his photography collection, which includes thousands of unique works from every one of the most important Romanian photographers of the 19th century and early 20th century, he says:

"Being an American Civil War buff I studied attentively many books and magazines connected with this subject. Most of them were fully illustrated and I learned a lot from them. I was able to recognize every important general. When I was a freshman and allowed to wear a beard, I used to make self portraits cladded as a Union or Confederate officer. That was in my twenties. In that period I acquired my first pieces of information about photography and photographers. Ever since then I have loved 19th century portraiture.

I began collecting in 1976. In that year I was writing a paper about Romanian Army uniforms during the Independence War of 1877-78. I came upon some old military men who agreed to give me parts of their old uniforms such as sashes, belts, kepis or other headgear, spurs, plumes, epaulettes or even a tunic or a greatcoat. Not all of them dated from the period I was interested in, but, unwilling to offend them, I accepted their offer with due gratitude. Some also threw in a few old pictures, showing them as young men receiving their first commission as lieutenant or their first medals.

Afterwards I became more interested in photography, especially 19th century c.d.v (carte-de-visite, small visiting card portraits) and cabinet pictures. My interest initially focused on military topics and children. Afterwards I diversified my collection. When my studies were related to 19th century fashion and artistic movements I acquired pictures which were relevant to such topics... Hairpieces, beards and moustaches were another motif in my collection. To say nothing of the backs of those pictures which occasionally yielded magnicent specimens of advertising and graphic arts".

1. IMITATION - FRANZ DUSCHEK Photography is a form of imitation. It may be an extremely close likeness of the original but the original is always something very different, distinct and separate. The same goes for the three noble women in this *carte-de-visite*, who, during the Russian-Turkish war of 1877-78, did all within their power to assist the wounded following the example of Elisabeth of Wied, wife of Charles I, the Ruling Princess (later Queen of Romania) and a poetess who used the pseudonym Carmen Sylva and who had an extraordinary influence on opinions, fashion and even the behaviour of her subjects. Vincent Van Gogh wrote to his brother Theo in a letter dated September 1889: "It's funny, just at the moment when I was making that copy of the Pietà by Delacroix I discovered where that canvas has gone. It belongs to a queen of Hungary or another country around there who has written poems under the name of Carmen Sylva. The article which talked of her and of the painting was by Pierre Loti, who made one feel that this Carmen Sylva was as a person yet more touching than what she writes…". *Caterina Cantacuzino, Maria Vacarescu and Smaranda Mavrogheni as volunteer nurses during the Oriental War of 1877-78, Bucharest, c.d.v.*

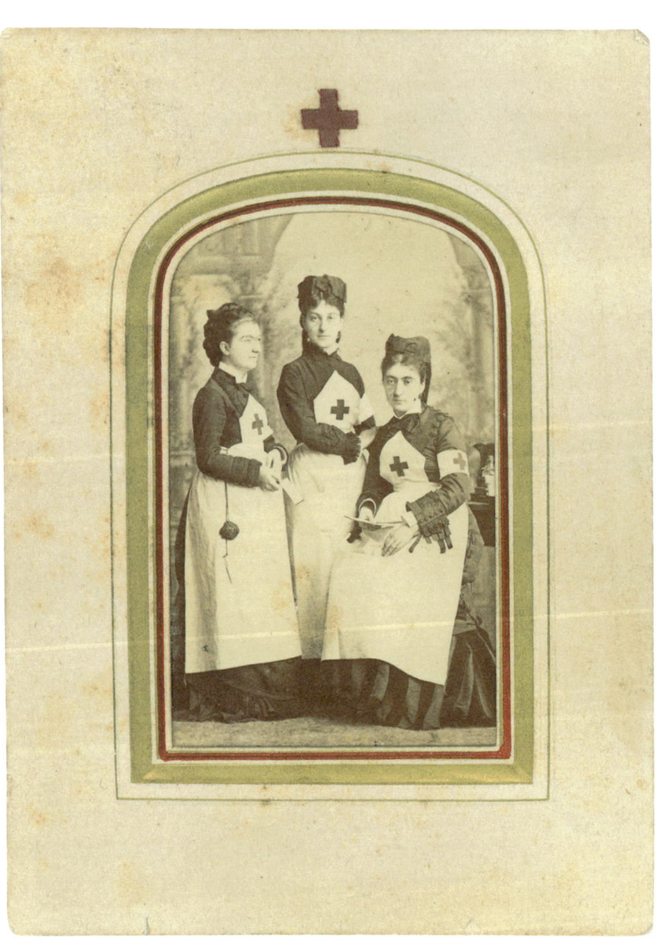

2. DEATH - IOSIF SZÖLLÖSY Photography entertains an ambiguous relationship with death. On one hand, it promises everyone the eternity of their likeness while, on the other, it freezes every body in a fixed pose. The point is made perfectly by this cabinet print, in which a child from a wealthy family is sitting astride the embalmed corpse of a colt made into a toy (one can glimpse the wheels under its hooves). Life and death find a balance in every photographic portrait. This fact, if the picture taken in Iosif Szöllösy's studio is observed for long enough, is quite frightening. *Girl riding a toy horse, Bucharest, cabinet, c. 1885*

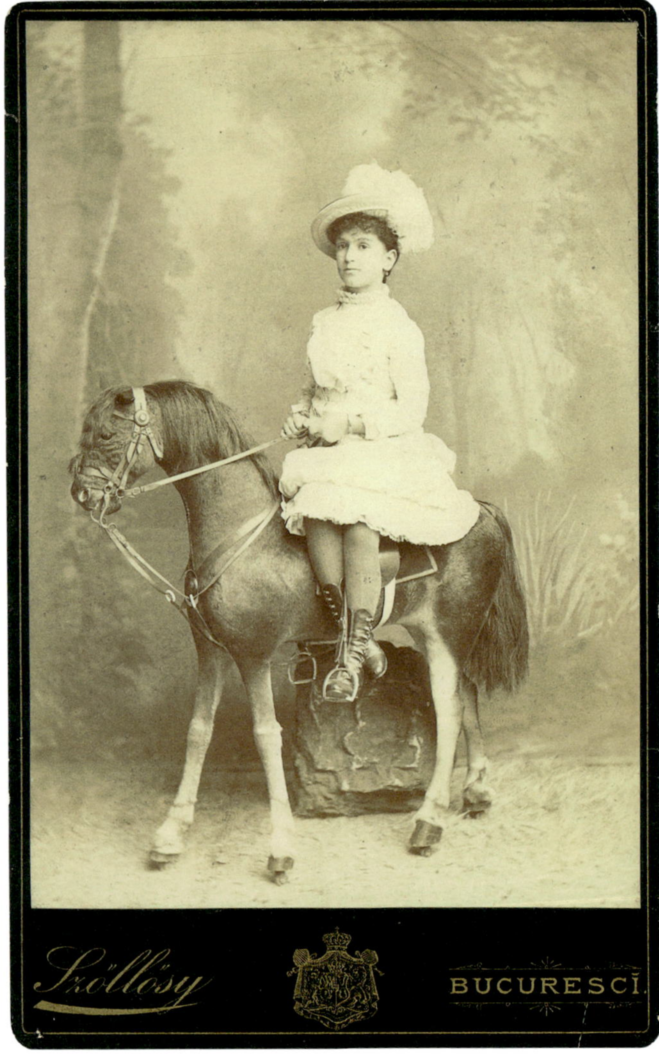

3. THE OMNIVORE CAMERA - FRANZ DUSCHEK The camera is an omnivorous instrument. It describes everything it finds in front of the lens and continues to do so with an equal amount of intensity. In order to make her daughter the only subject of this picture the mother turned her back to the camera and held her aloft. However, she had not considered the fact that in this way the photograph would show the details of her hat and the intricate geometrical appliqués on the back of her dress alongside the child's face. *Mother holding her little daughter, Bucharest, c.d.v., c. 1870*

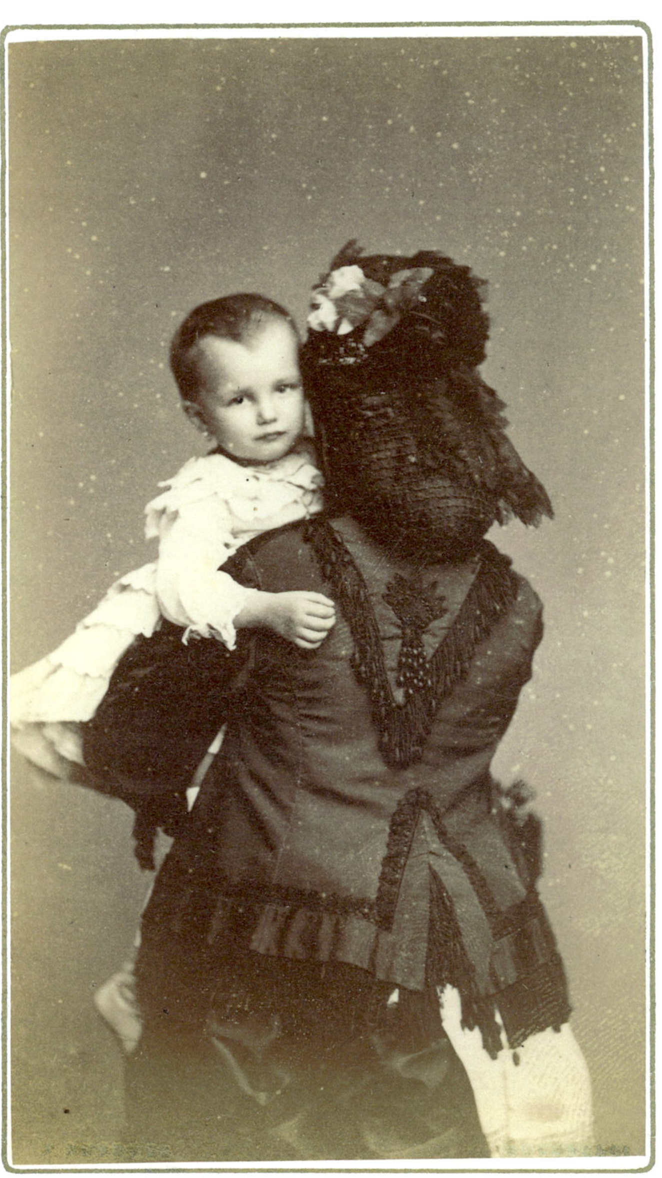

4. CLOTHING - ATELIER FANCHETTE In portraits clothing is a fundamental element in order to complete the description of the subject. This is especially true in the case of pictures taken in the 1800s, when having one's photograph taken was a sufficiently rare event to warrant special preparations. Without going into detail, clothing is the major means of codifying (and decoding) the class a person belongs to. It is a tool of social and political communication. However, this process of identification can be made difficult by the practice of dressing up. In front of a camera anyone can play a different role from his own. In this case a young aristocrat is dressed up in a typical peasant costume. Wearing a folk costume was a very fashionable thing for the Romanian elite to do at the turn of the century when invited to charity events, balls and even receptions at the Royal Court. *Lady wearing a peasant costume, Jassy, c.d.v., c. 1880*

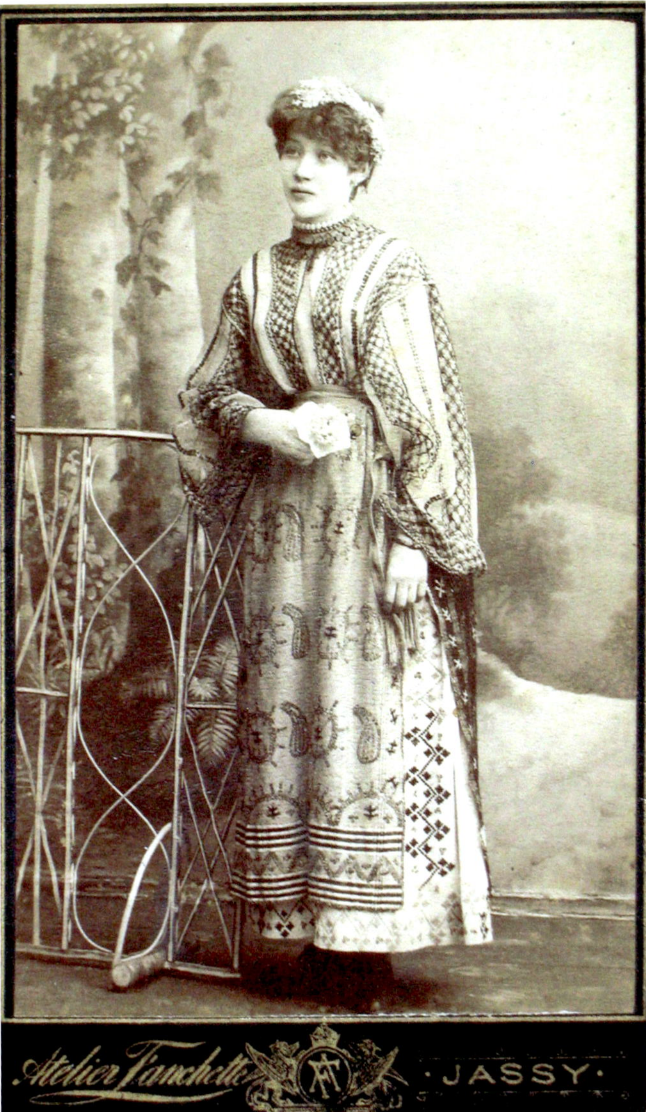

5. CIRCULARITY - D. HEITLER Portrait photography is a circular medium. This means that its popularity is limited in most cases to the family circle of the person portrayed. This is where it performs its principal social function. It roots the life of the observer in the past (giving it importance) and establishes a lineage. In photographs of one's ancestors one can recognize oneself. *Athena Zaharula Kindilide at age 5, the collector's maternal grandmother, Craiova, cabinet, 1895*

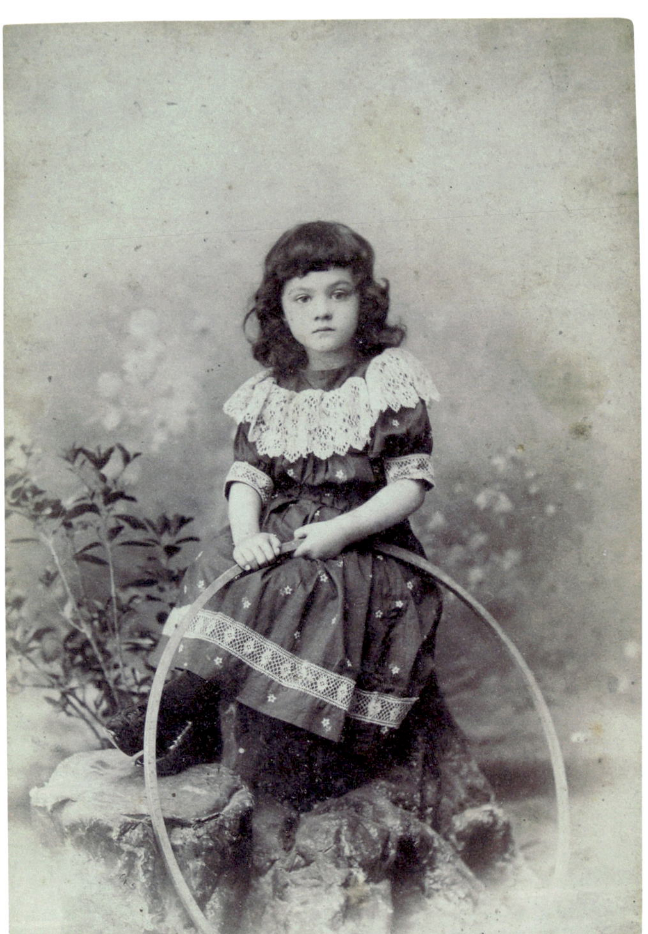

6. SCALE - IOAN SPIRESCU Photography is a scale reproduction of what is visible. Photography means you can keep an entire miniature universe in a drawer or, on the contrary, enlarge details that are imperceptible to the naked eye. There aren't any rules to say what the ratio between the size of a photograph and what it contains should be. Therefore, when the subject is framed, the photographer decides whether or not to introduce points of reference which enable one to determine the proportions of the subject (this is the aim of the human figures placed alongside monuments in the documentary photographs of the eighteen hundreds) or to prevent the viewer from measuring anything (how big is Edward Weston's well-known Pepper No. 30?) For instance, isolated from the context in which it appears, the cannon in the corner of this photograph might appear to be a highly dangerous piece of artillery. *Boy clad as a cuirassier posing beside a tricycle and a tiny cannon, Bucharest, cabinet, February 1899*

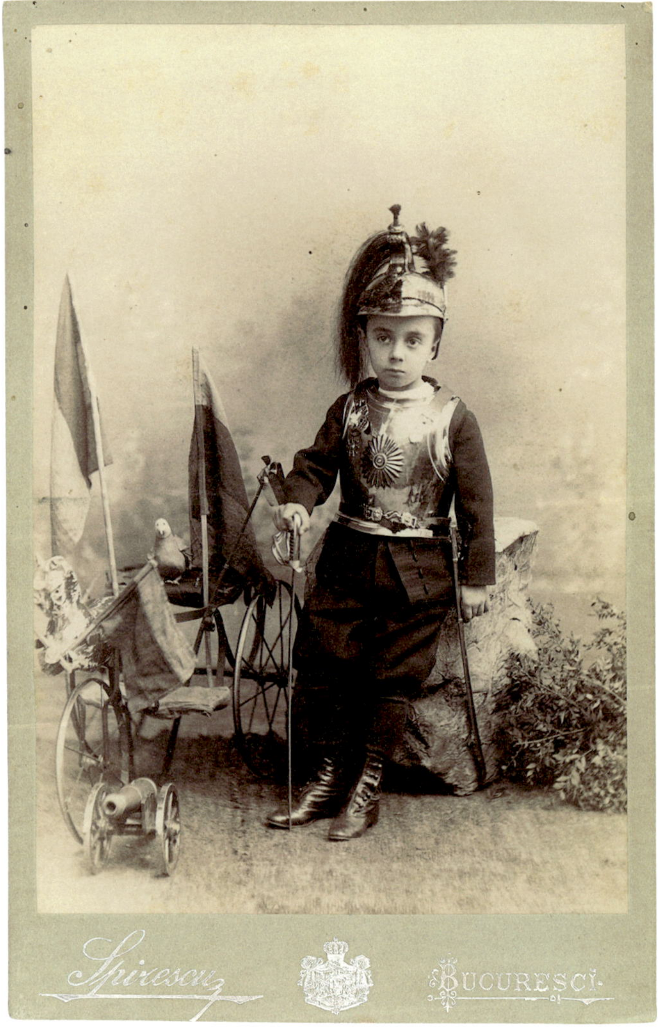

7. SHOOTING - W. WOLLENTEIT In its own way the camera might be thought of as a weapon. It is how it is used that permits this comparison. One takes aim and fires. Many people have spoken of this. Photographer Walker Evans said "It's akin to hunting too - photography is: and in that same way you're using the machine and you're actually shooting something, and shooting to kill actually. To get the picture you want - that's a kill, that's a bull's eye. Enormous satisfaction". Étienne-Jules Marey's photographic gun springs to mind. He invented this device in 1882 in order to aim at and capture moving subjects in sequence. He carried out some of his early experiments in Naples, earning the nickname "the crazy man of Posillipo" from the locals who observed him aiming at seagulls, pulling the trigger repeatedly without ever hitting the mark but nevertheless going away visibly satisfied. W. Wollenteit's photograph thus celebrates a double victory: that of its subject, the winner of a shooting competition, and that of the photographer who took the shot. *Target shooting contest winner, Bucharest, c.d.v., c. 1862*

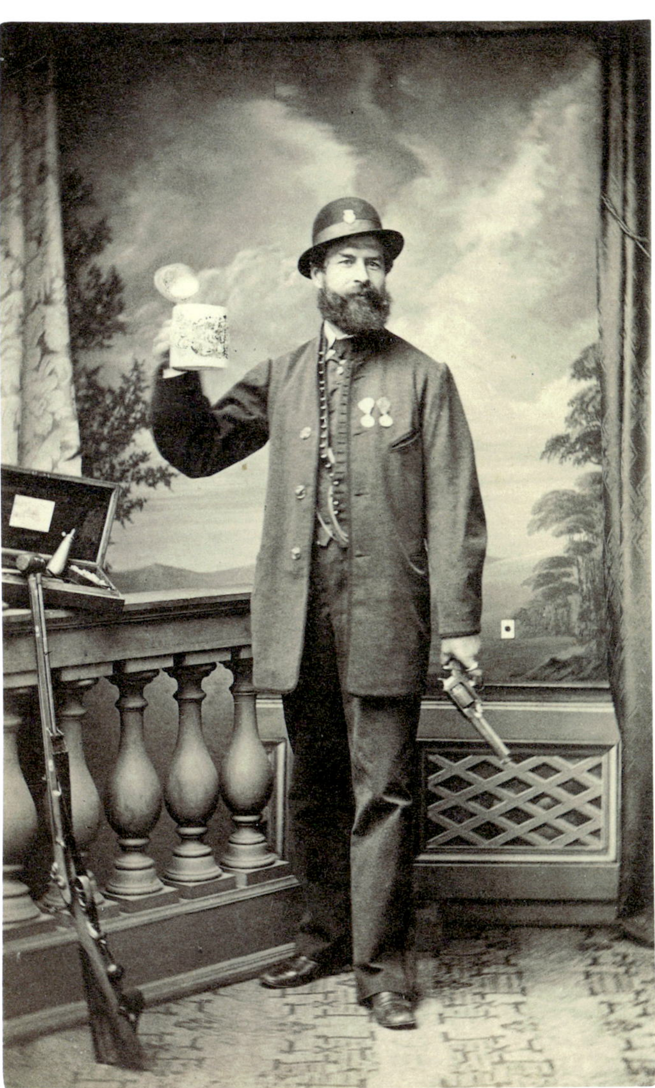

8. THE LEASH - CAROL SZATHMARI Photography is a predatory act. It means capturing a subject so that it will not vanish in time and space. It is a violent and selfish act. The camera is a leash which allows one to hold onto what might otherwise break loose and never come back. *Santry, Gypsy comedians with dancing bear, from a series of Romanian folk types and costumes, Bucharest, c.d.v., early 1860s*

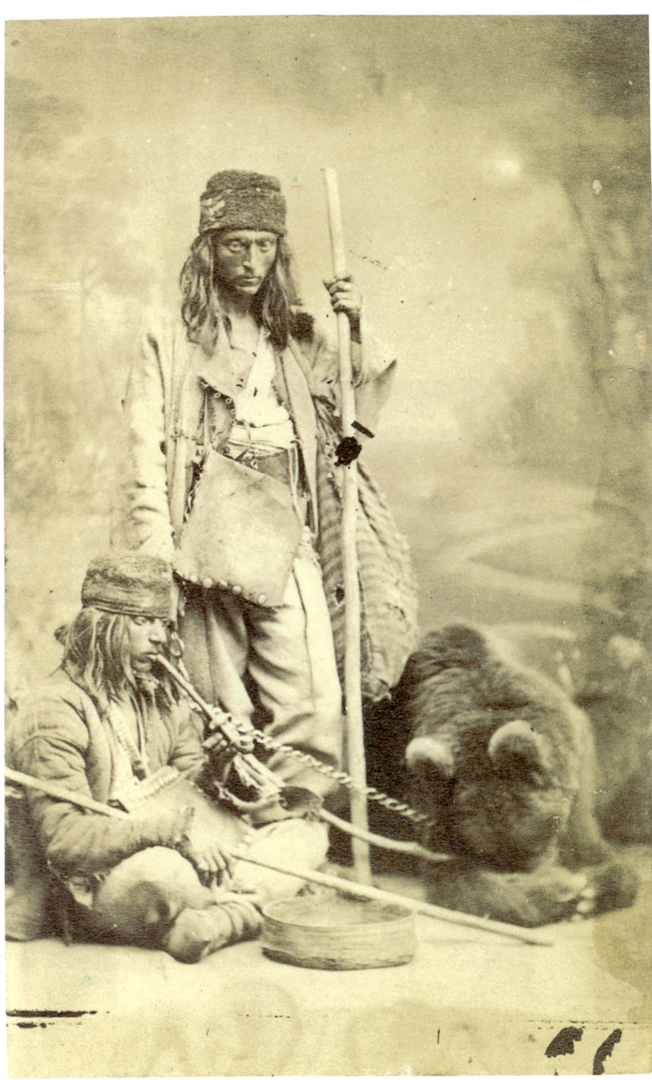

9. RETOUCHING - FRANZ MANDY The manual retouching of photography is a direct forerunner of Photoshop. It is merely one of the countless means photography uses to lie about its subject. It could be applied with astonishing results to any medium: from daguerreotype to salted paper, from ambrotype to tintype. It was used for the same reasons as modern digital manipulations: to repair any damage to the negative or the print, to eliminate or to add details, to modify colours. Now, as in the past, vanity is one of the major impulses behind this practice. Between the two pictures, both taken by Franz Mandy in the same year, 1894, of diplomat Apostol Manescu, what one clearly perceives to have changed is his clothing, from civilian dress to official uniform, and the amount of hair on his head, painted on in the second case by some skilled artist. *Apostol (Toly) Manescu in civilian garb/Apostol (Toly) Manescu wearing his full dress uniform of a Romanian plenipotentiary minister in Athens, Bucharest, 20.5 x 9.9 cm, c. 1894*

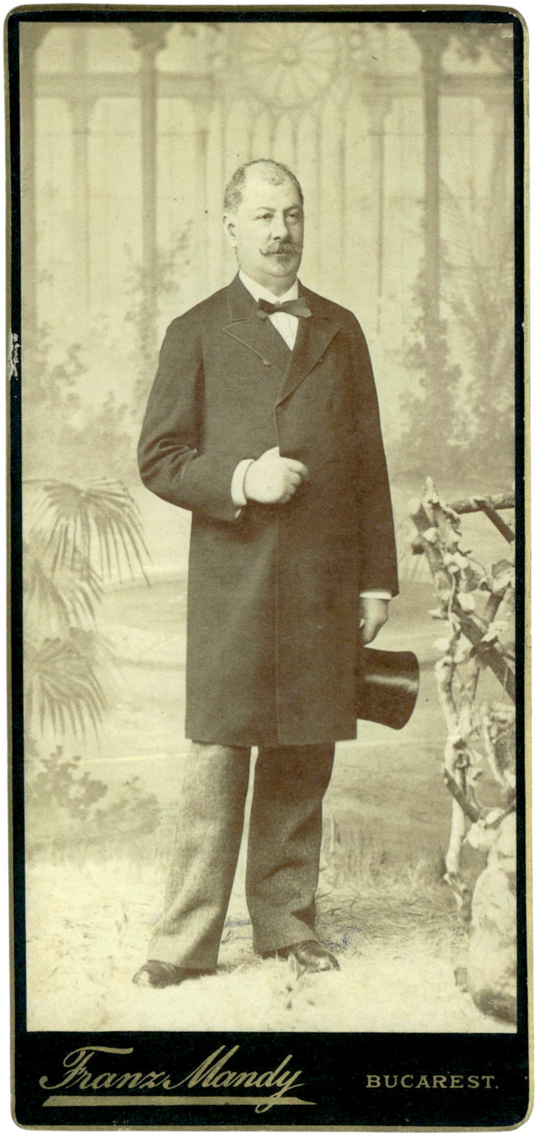

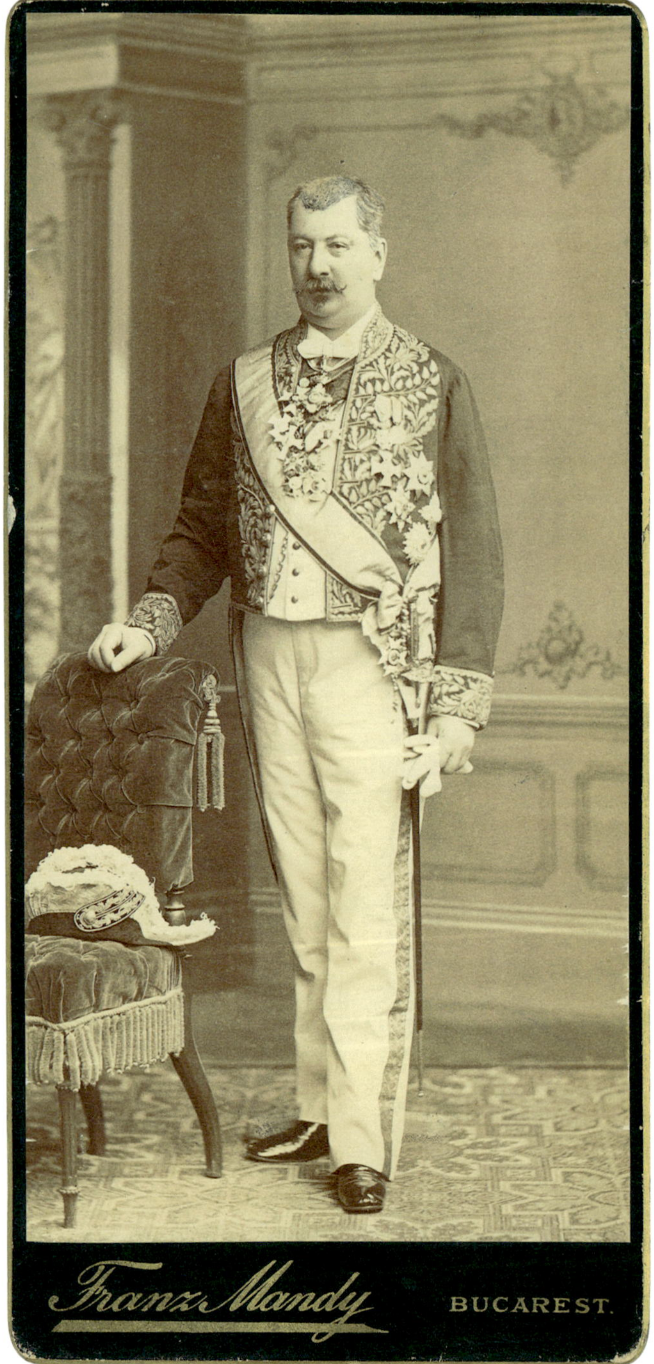

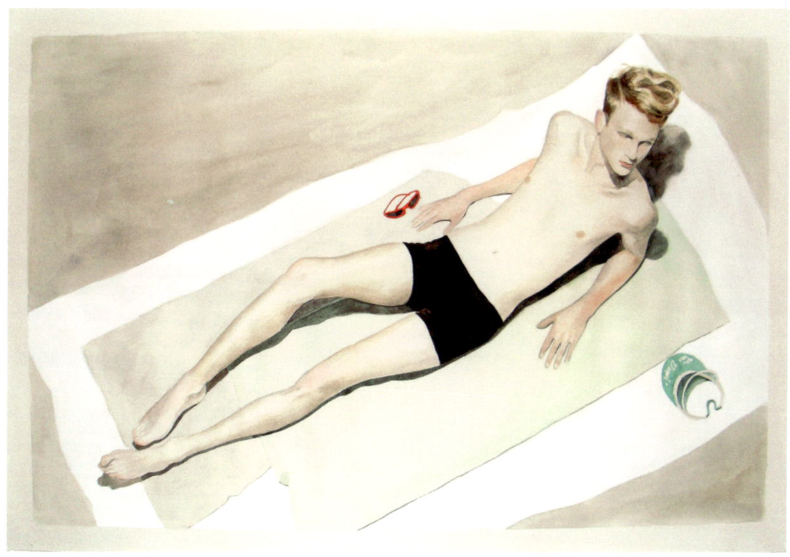

SLOW
MEGAN FRANCIS SULLIVAN
by Federico Sarica

"Slow down and dance with me, skip a beat and move with my body, come on and dance with me". In the chorus of Slow, one of those songs that you just can't get out of your head, released a few summers ago and whose video was held up by Megan Francis Sullivan as one of the major inspirations for this series of works, Kylie Minogue summed up, in approximately fifty words, the fundamental concepts upon which her global and timeless success are founded: dancing is like making love, moving in time with me is the sexiest thing in the world. Which is a little like what happens in the video of the song, in which a great many men and very few women in bathing costumes filmed from above surround Kylie, moving in time with her whilst lying on colourful beach towels.

Sex and movement. Could there be anything further from the sober effect created by the subjects Sullivan portrays in her *Slow* series? Perhaps just the sun tan oil on the biceps and buttocks of bubbly Kylie's dancers (nothing could be further from the soft and fantastic effects created by the watercolors used by the artist). And probably the undeniable and objective beauty of these images is due to their succeeding incredibly well in methodically cooling things, by means of a process which begins with an historical and anthropological study of the role of the male body in the history of art. Starting with a diligent casting and a photographic studio portrait taken from above, and culminating in the illustration - that which in nature and the collective imagination embodies warmth par excellence: the temptation of an almost perfect body, gleaming in the sun (and all this without relinquishing one iota of color, which is the biggest novelty compared to the American artist's previous works).

Sullivan's perspective is deliberately - by her own admission - a perspective which tends to investigate young males from a hidden and distant angle that never enters the sphere of desire. It is the opposite of the voracious and authentic Kylie Minogue, who at least touches young males. When she doesn't eat them.

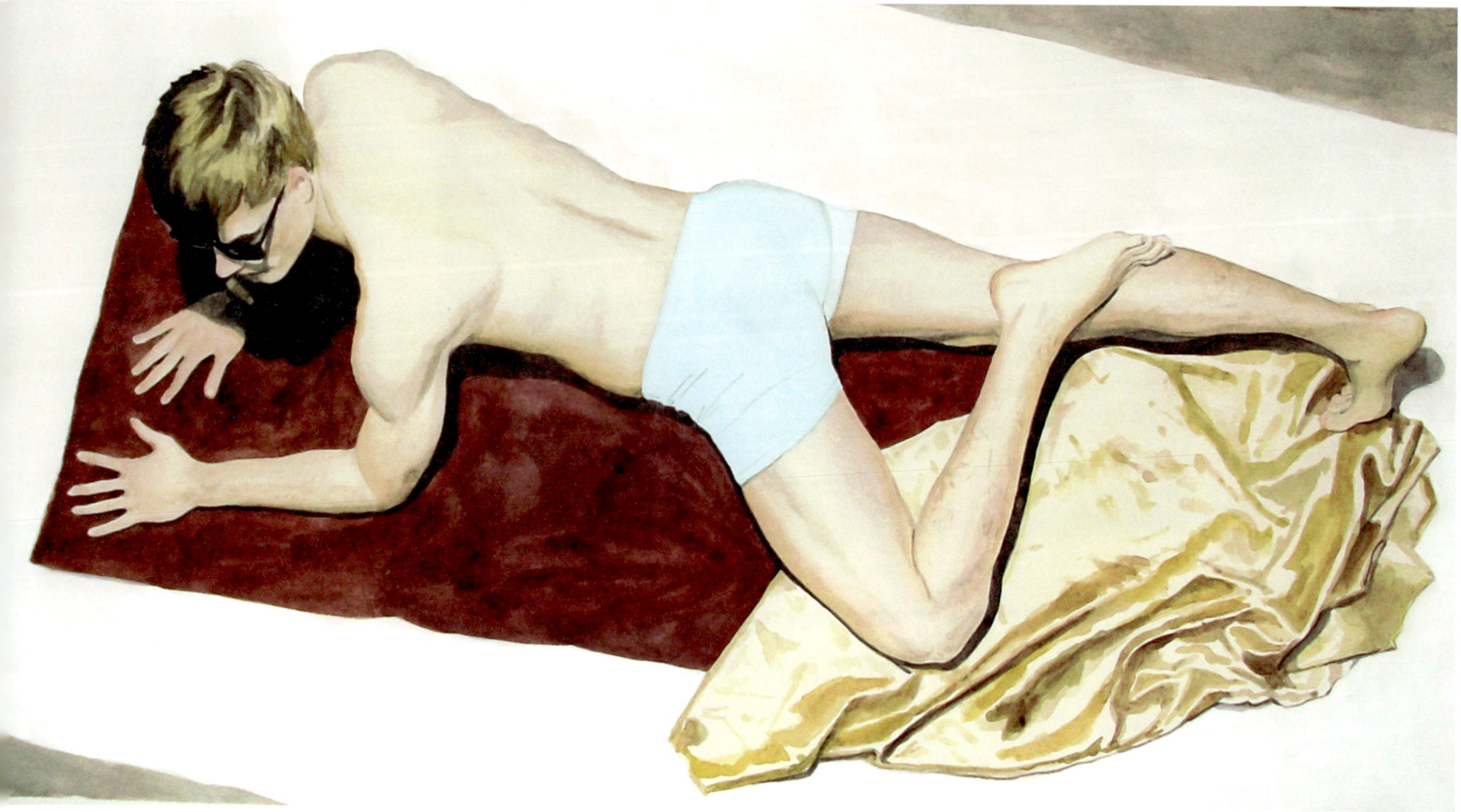

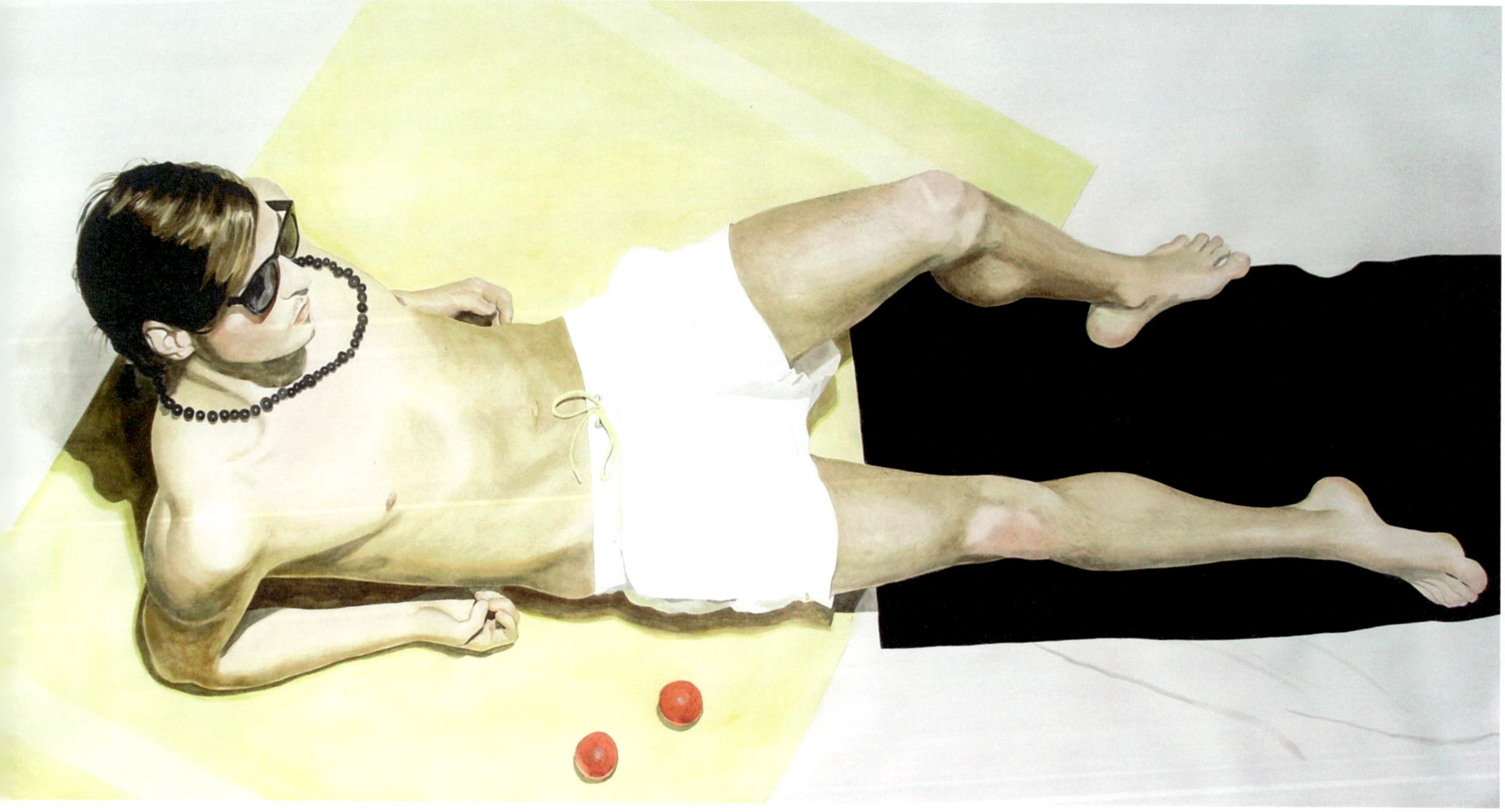

Top Slow (Marius) 2009, *gouache on paper cm. 57 x 31.5; bottom* Slow (Justus II) 2009, *watercolor and gouache on paper cm. 190 x 113. Previous page* Slow (Hannes) 2009, *gouache on paper cm. 57 x 35.7*

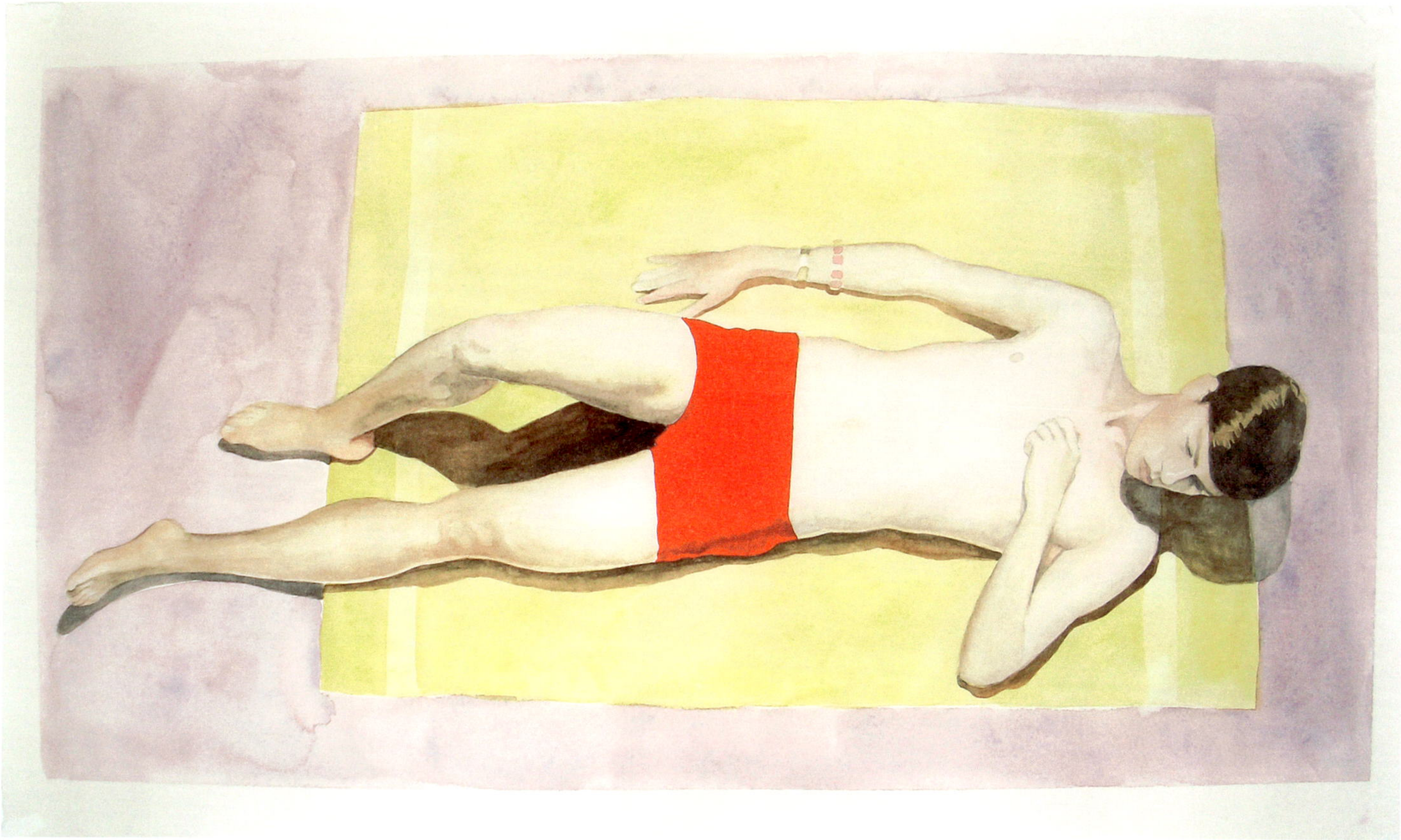

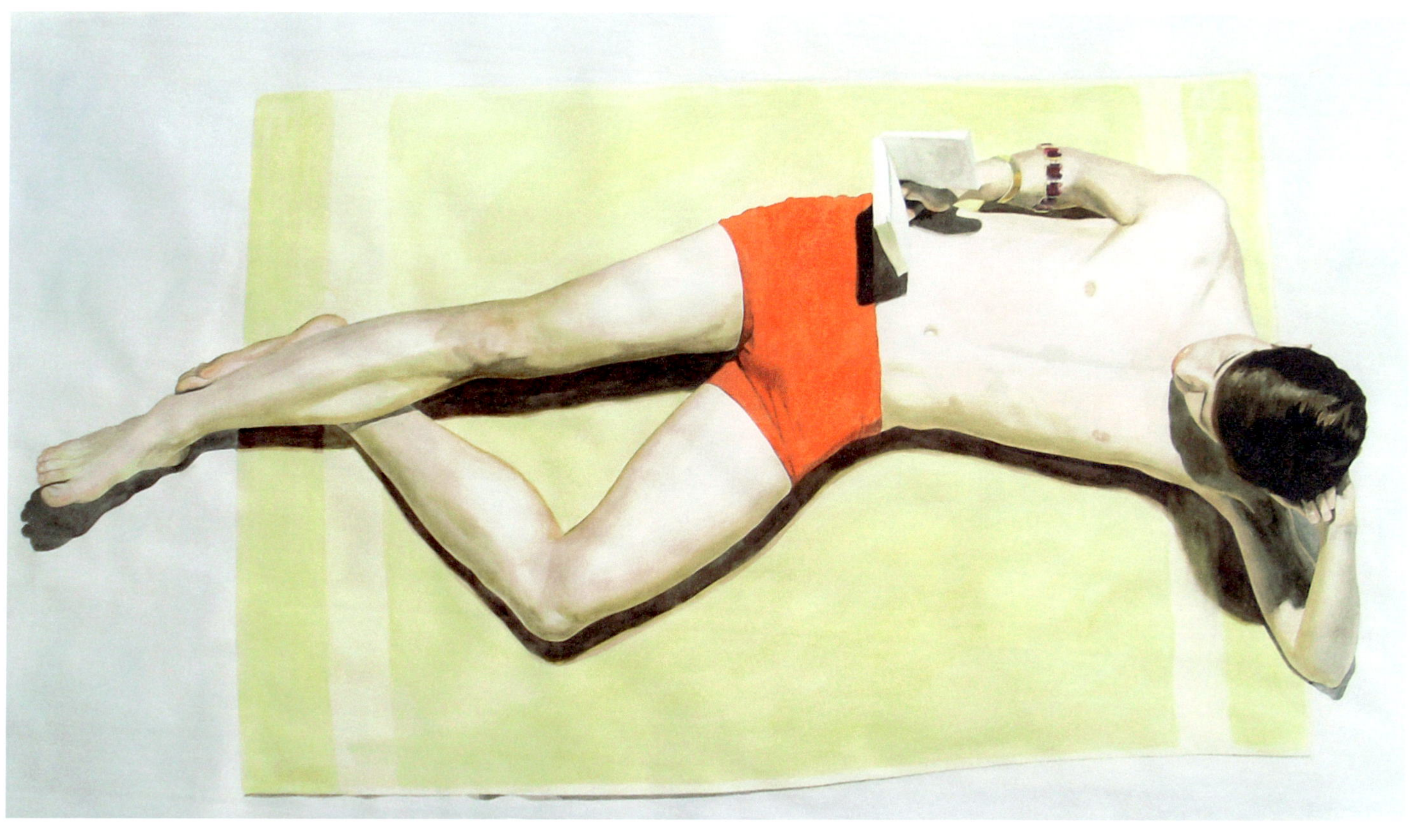

Top Slow (Oscar I) 2009, *gouache on paper cm. 57 x 33; bottom* Slow (Oscar II) 2009, *watercolor and gouache on paper cm. 190 x 113. All images © the artist, courtesy Freymond-Guth & Co. Fine Arts, Zurich*

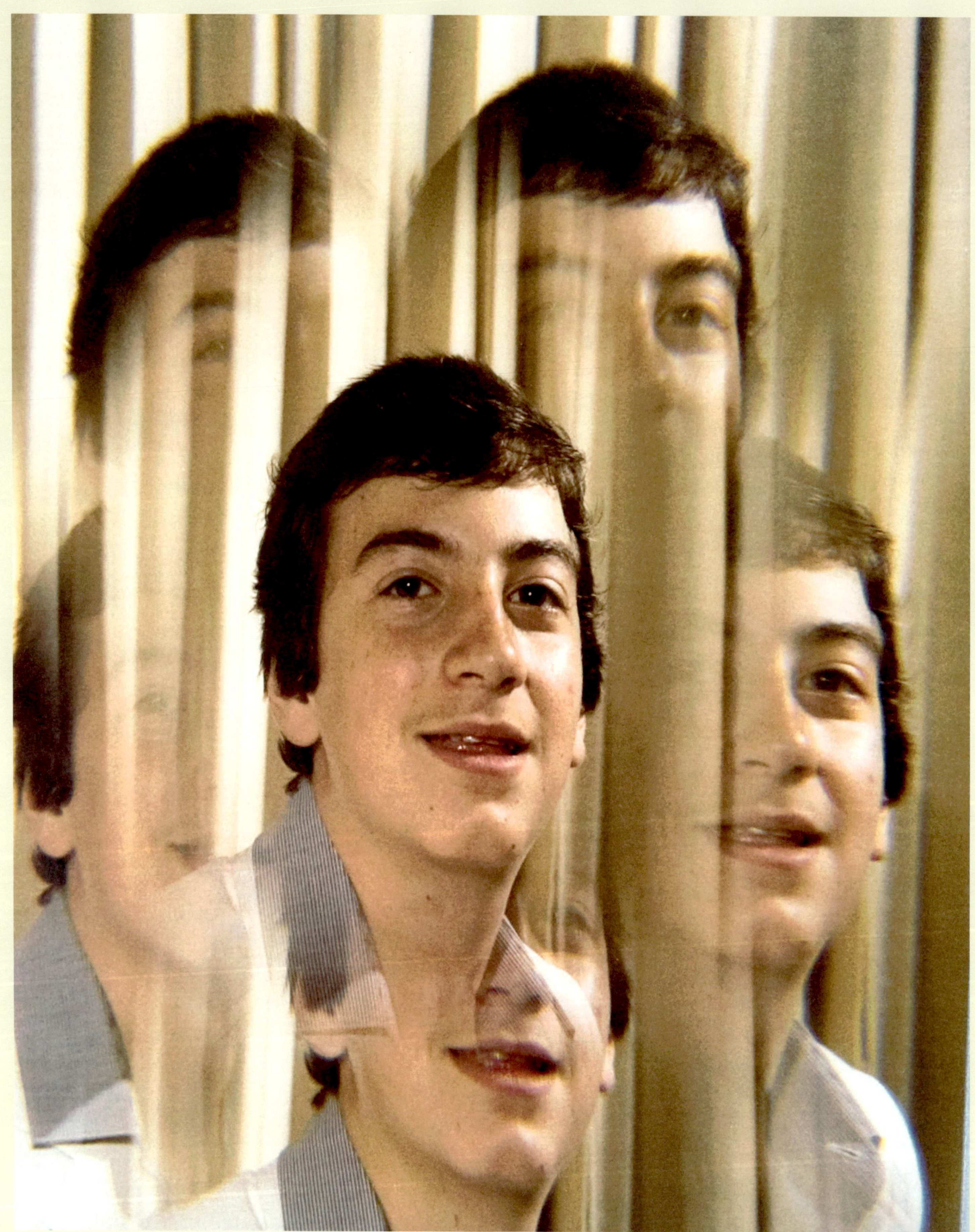

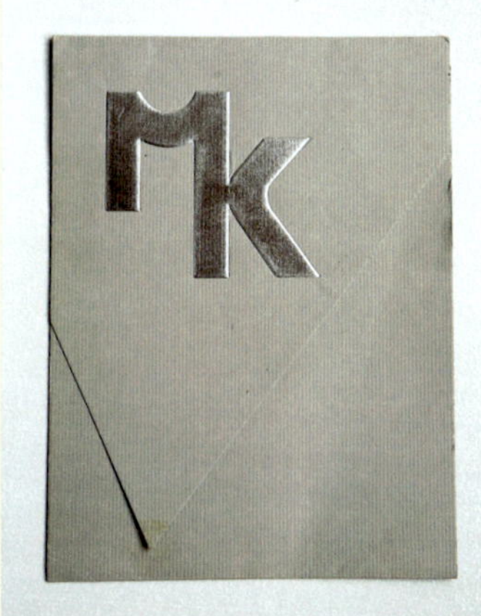 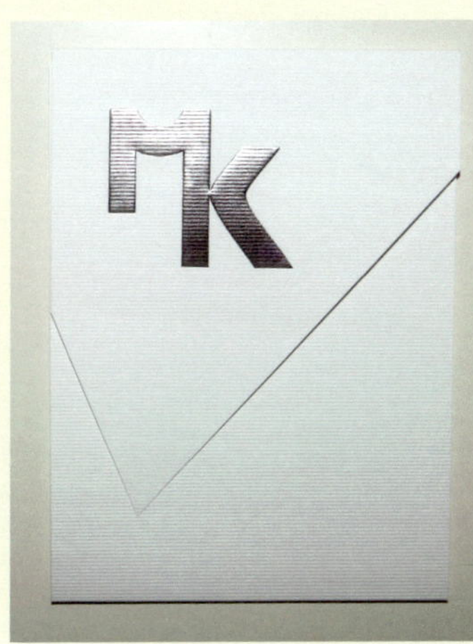

Marcelo Krasilcic
JUST LIKE THE FIRST TIME
told by Gilda Rachel Wajnsztejn

Just to understand the history: a Jewish boy celebrates his Bar Mitzvah upon reaching the age of 13 years (and a girl 12) making their Jewish adulthood - and thus their responsibilities - official for themselves, their families, and to the community. It is extremely important to all Jews from the orthodox to the more progressive.

The fact is that I had the delicious experience of reliving moments of a Bar Mitzvah that was long gone: as in a movie, I was led to experience the Bar Mitzvah of the Bar Mitzvah's Bar Mitzvah of my nephew Marcelo.

Let me explain: 26 years after his Bar Mitzvah, he decided to celebrate the second 13th anniversary of the date. I believe that the initiative was the result of a youthful mental creativity, despite his 39 years of age, coupled with the desire to reunite loved ones at his home in Sao Paulo - which has been for a few years his base every time he comes to Brazil, since moving to New York. And maybe even, dare I say, the reaffirmation of his maturity, since the event, the Bar Mitzvah of his Bar Mitzvah's Bar Mitzvah, replayed what happened in 1982.

And when I say replayed I mean just that. Guests were assembled, mostly those who had been at the official ceremony when he completed 13 years of age. And his guests, when informed of the meeting were surprised by invitations that were replicas of the original.

Although almost three decades later, those who remembered the party, as I did, were moved by what they found: the Bar Mitzvah man was contagious with his love, joy and satisfied smiles. And he welcomed us wearing an outfit similar to the one he wore as a boy. In one corner of the room, decorating the environment, a table stood out, covered by the same towels, flower arrangement, napkins and dishes used in the original party.

And as if that was not enough, in another corner, a movie and digital images from the first Bar Mitzvah played continuously - the host boy in his suit, the ballroom tables, family members and guests on the night of the feast of his 13 years - taking us back to the future.

Such care, commitment and emotional investment led us to make instant trips back and forth in time. Either we entered the memories of that time, or we congratulated one another for the reunion. And so, we toasted and danced to the Bar Mitzvah of Marcelo's Bar Mitzvah's Bar Mitzvah, as inebriated as he was.

I have many memories in my life that are happily unforgettable. But I can say I had the privilege of being among those people who had a wish come true that I believe is in the imagination of all of us: to relive a moment with as much emotion as the first time.

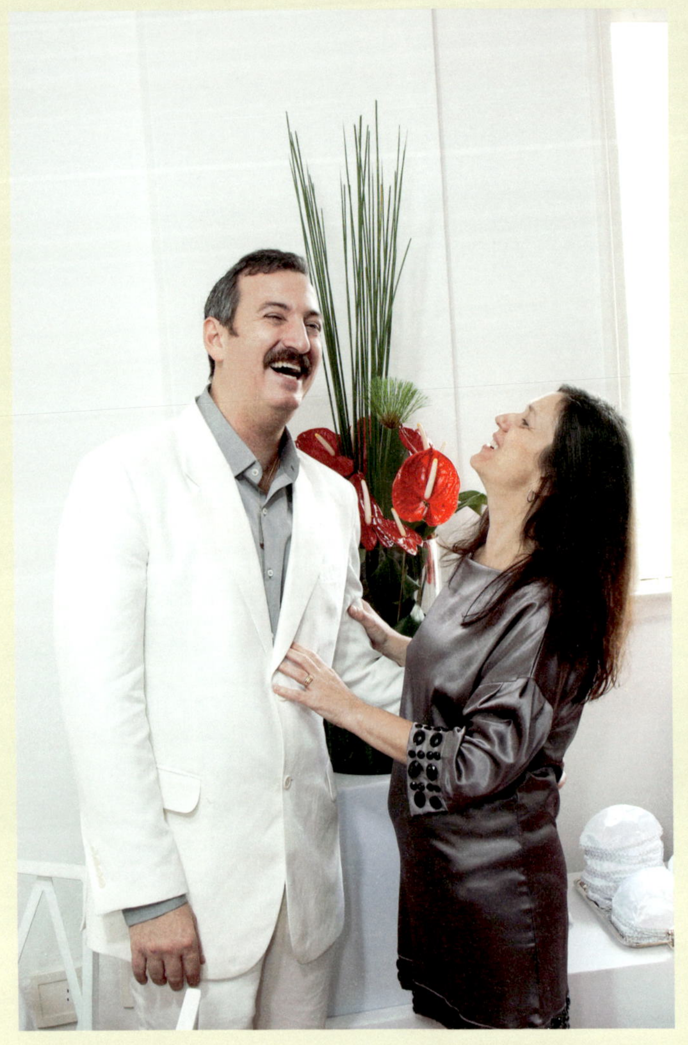

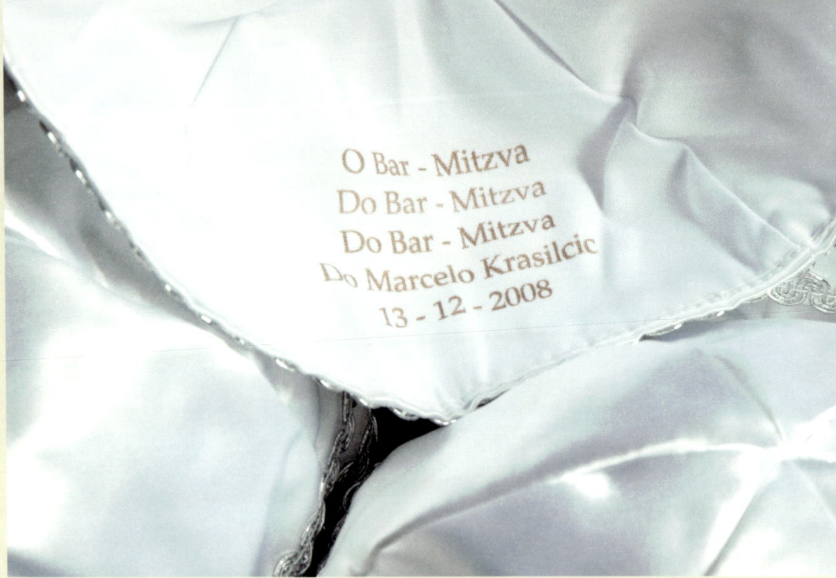

O Bar - Mitzva
Do Bar - Mitzva
Do Bar - Mitzva
Do Marcelo Krasilcic
13 - 12 - 2008

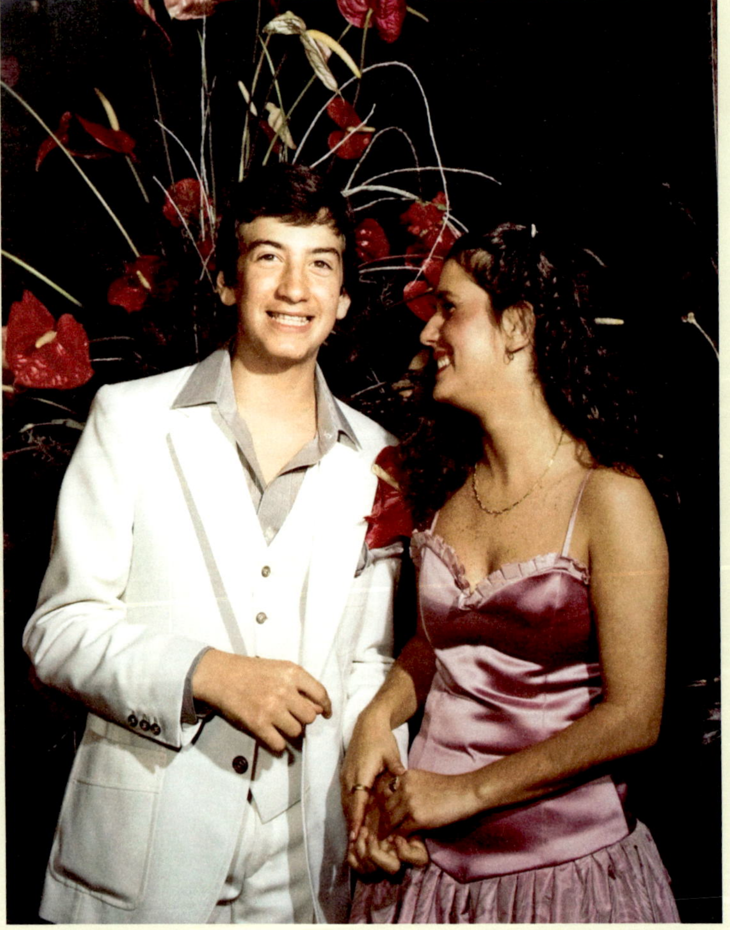

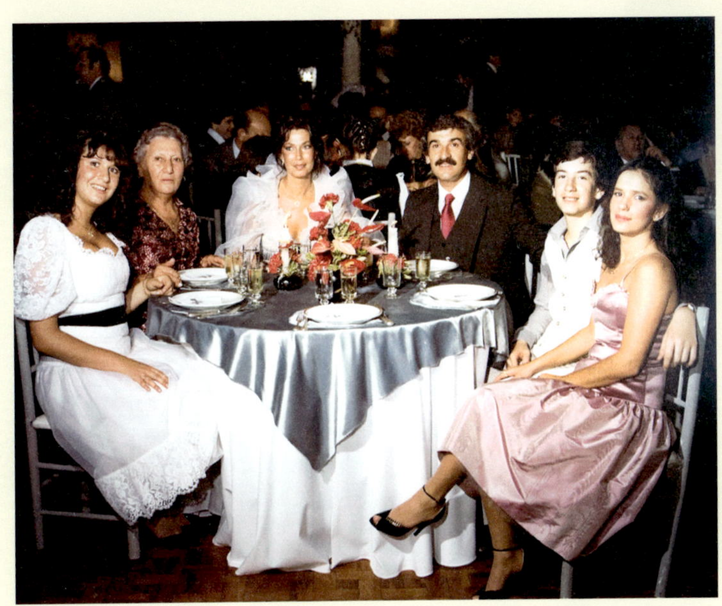

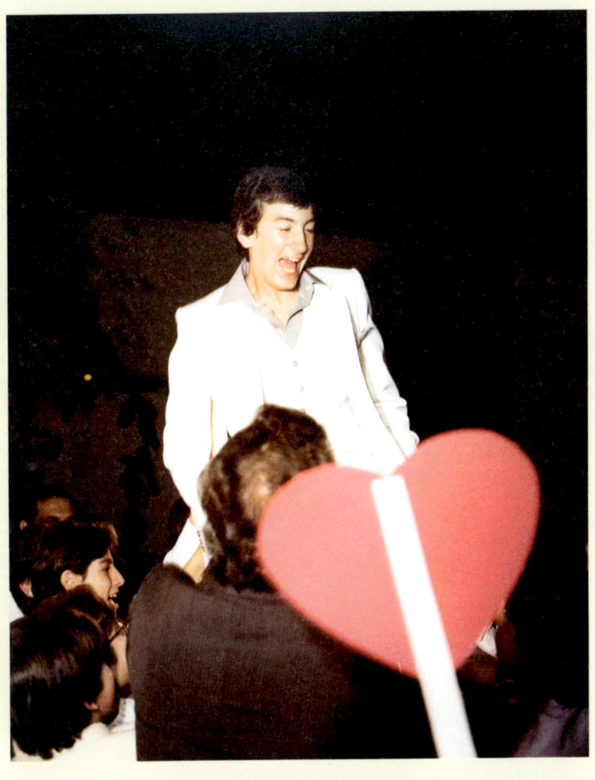

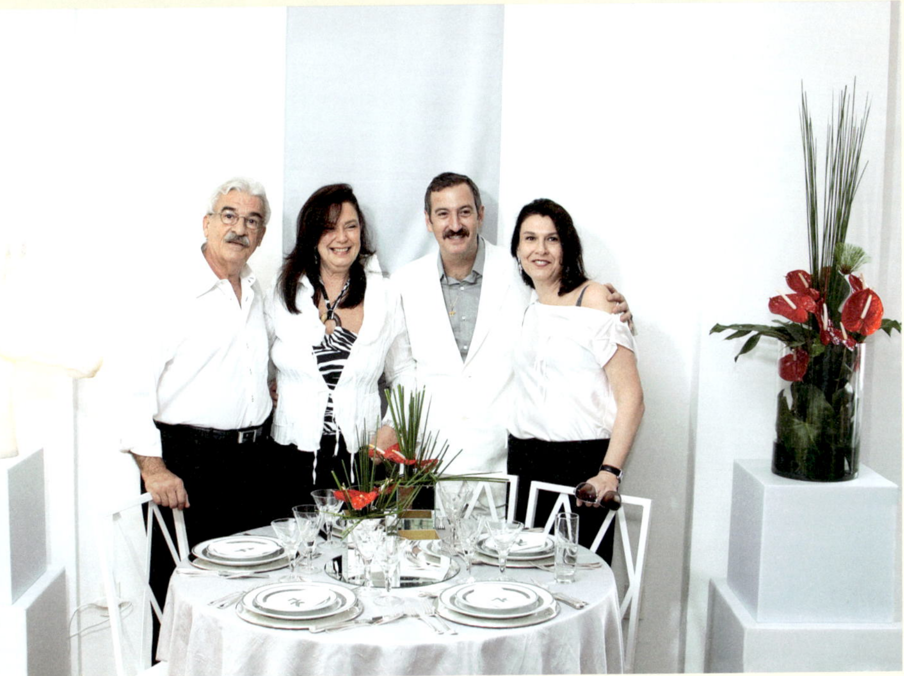

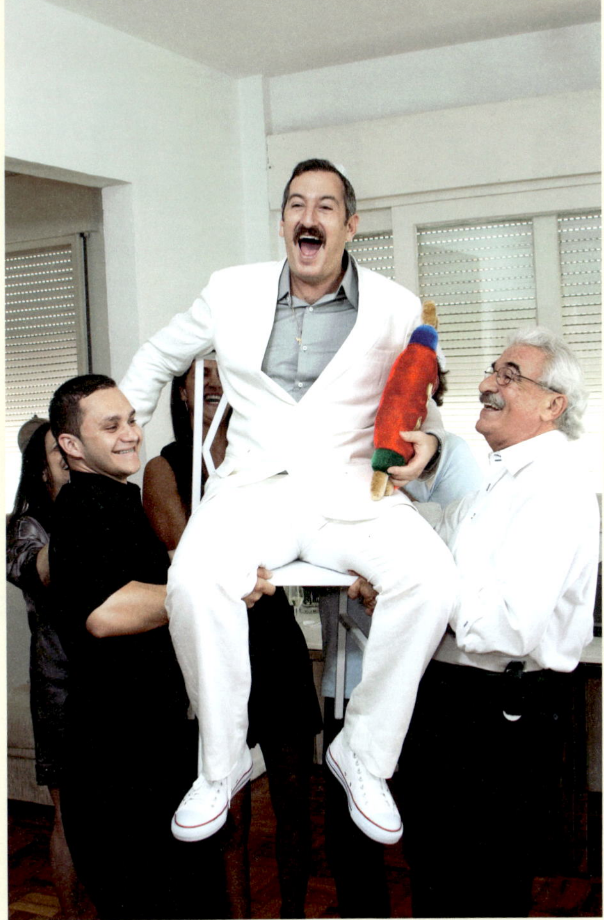

From left clockwise Family Table 1982; Chair Lift 1982; Chair Lift 2008; Family
Table 2008. *Previous page clockwise* Aunt Gilda 2008; Yamaka Inside Writing 2008;
Aunt Gilda 1982. *Page 76* Kaleidoscope 1982. *Page 77* Invite 1982 and 2008

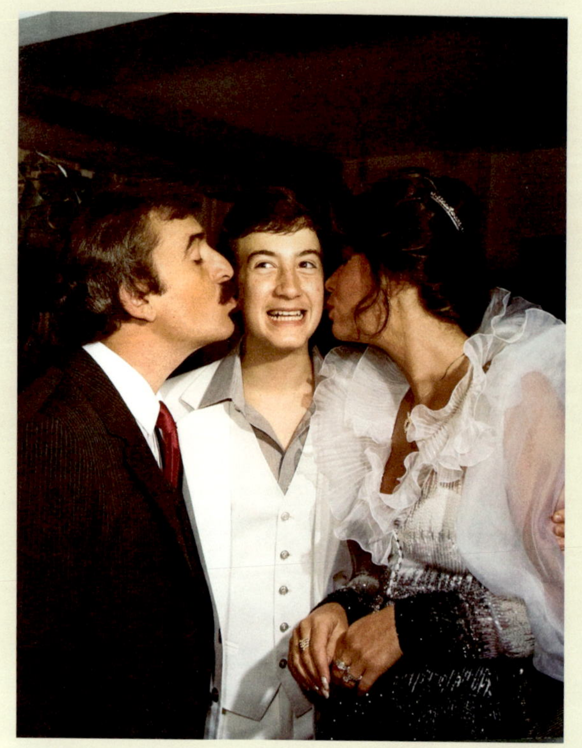
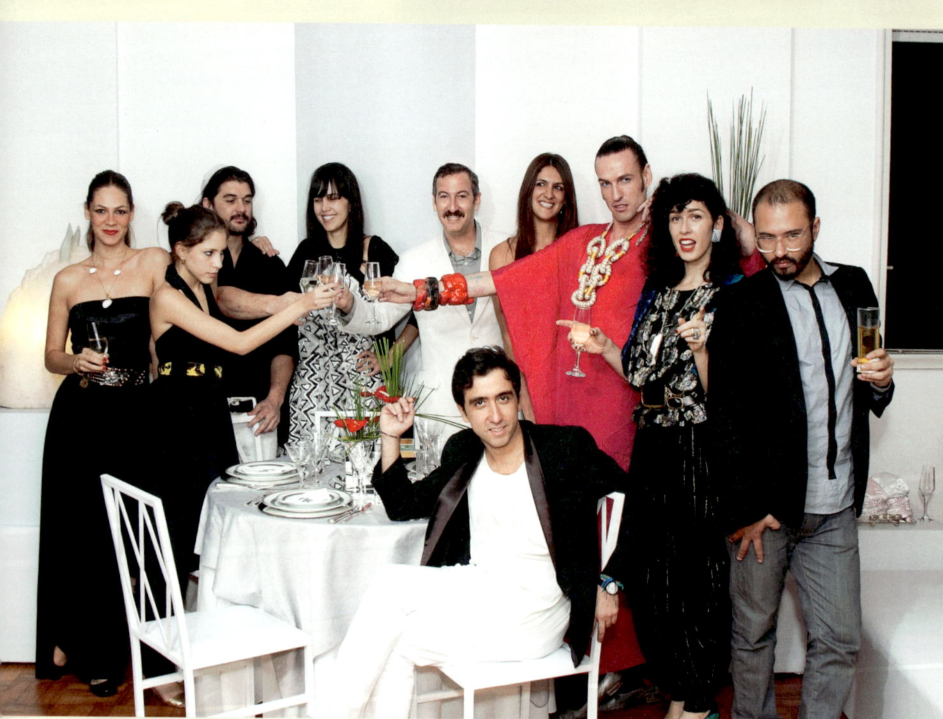
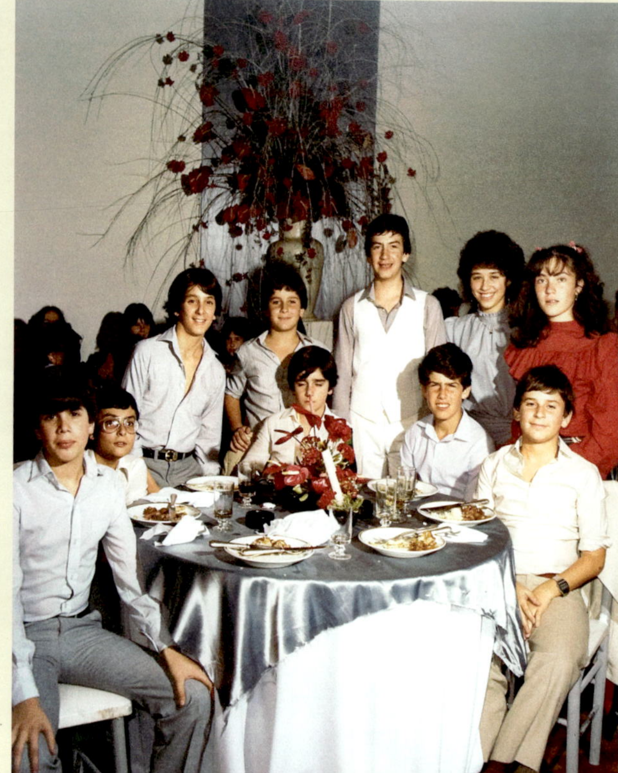
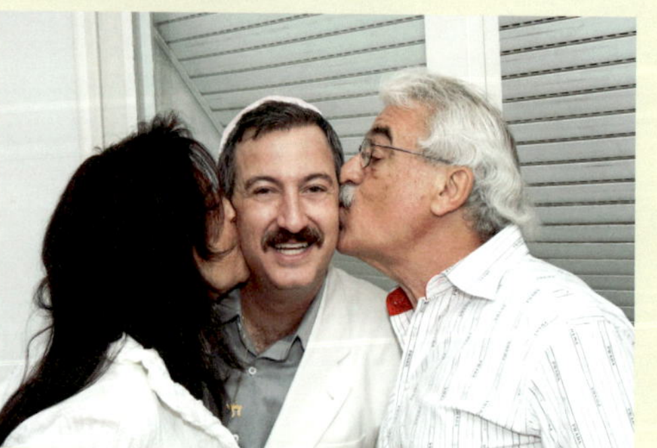

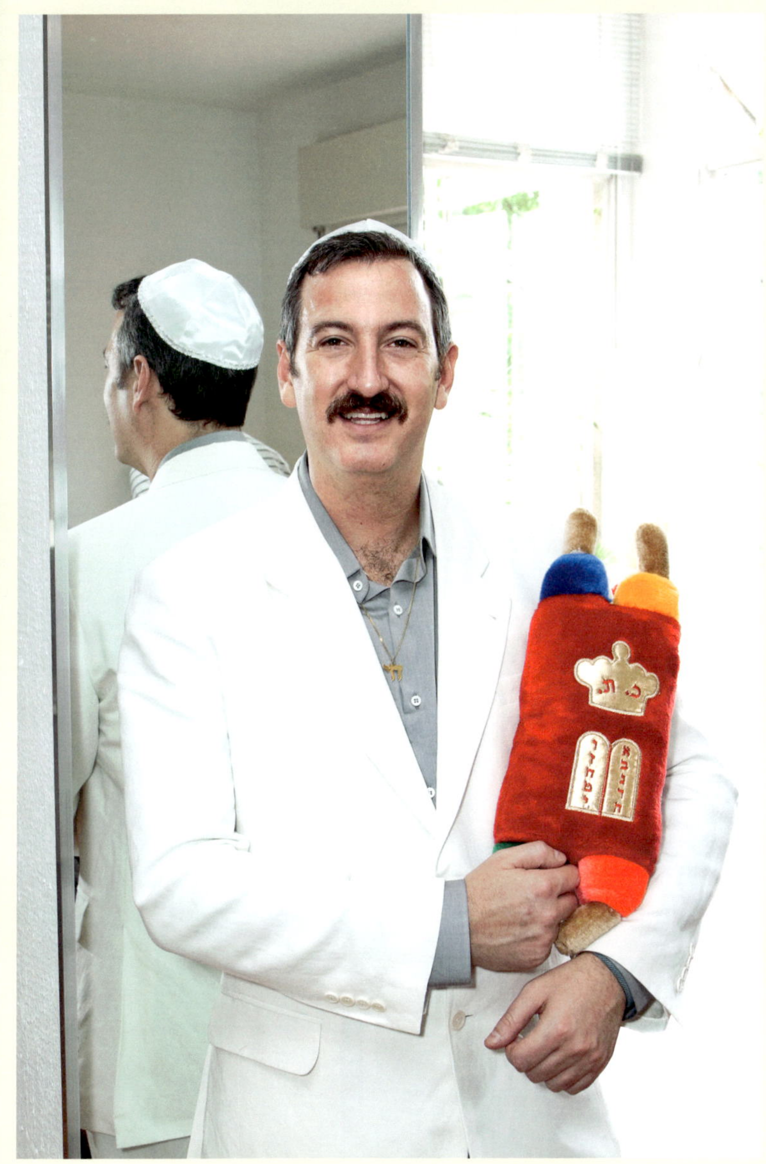

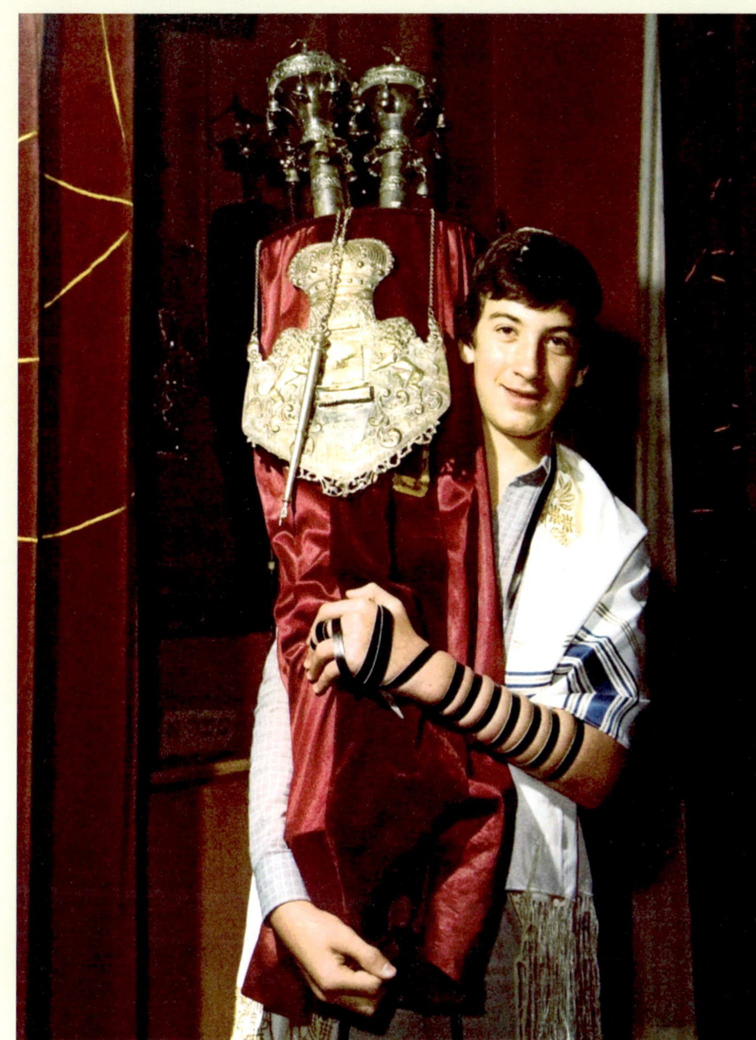

Left Pillow Torah 2008. *Right* Pillow Torah 1982. *Previous page from top left clockwise* Parents Kiss 1982; Friends 1982; Parents Kiss 2008; Friends I 2008. *All images © Marcelo Krasilcic*

Untitled (Rainbow Form 2) 2009

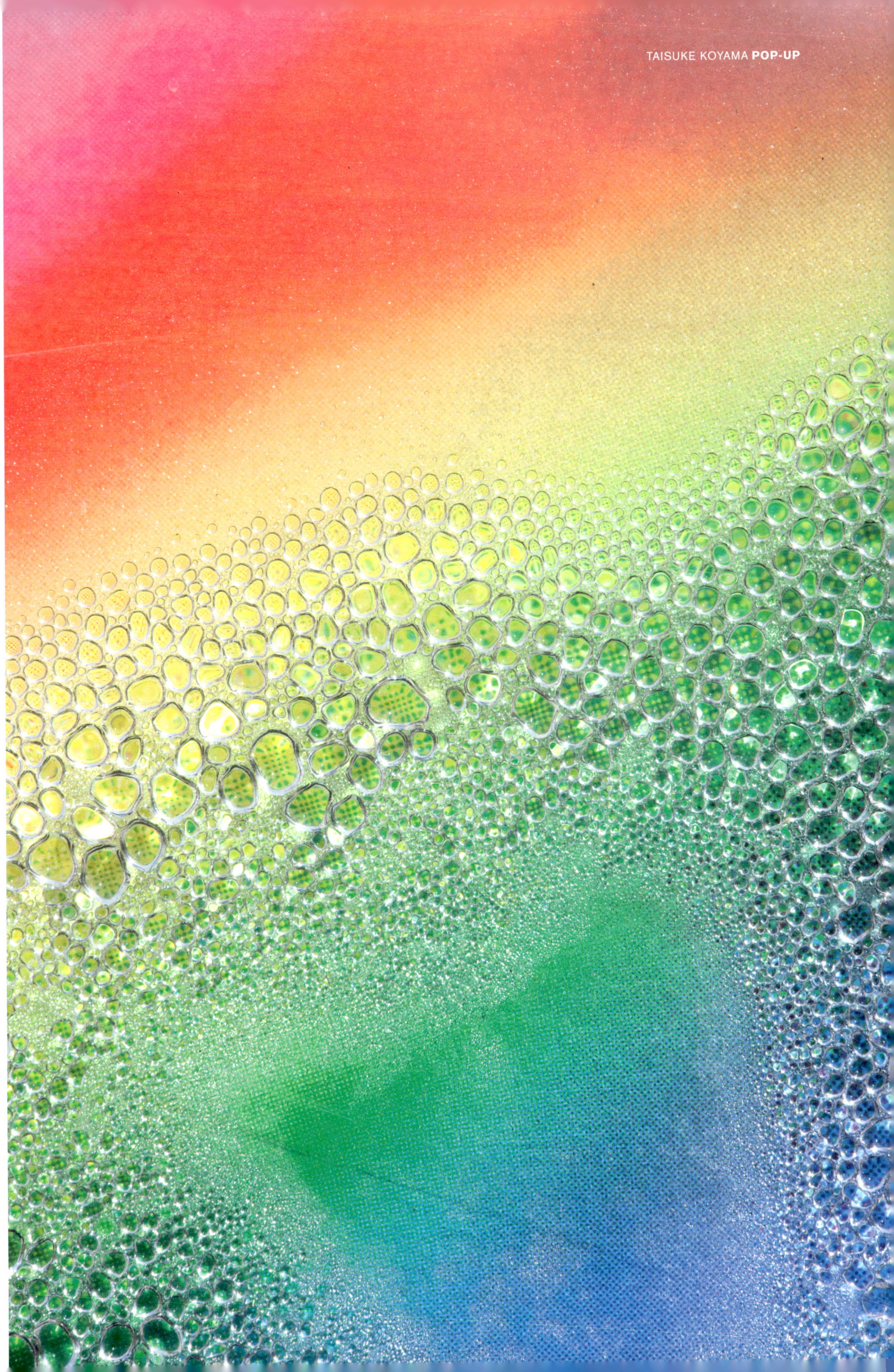

Untitled (Rainbow Form 11) 2009

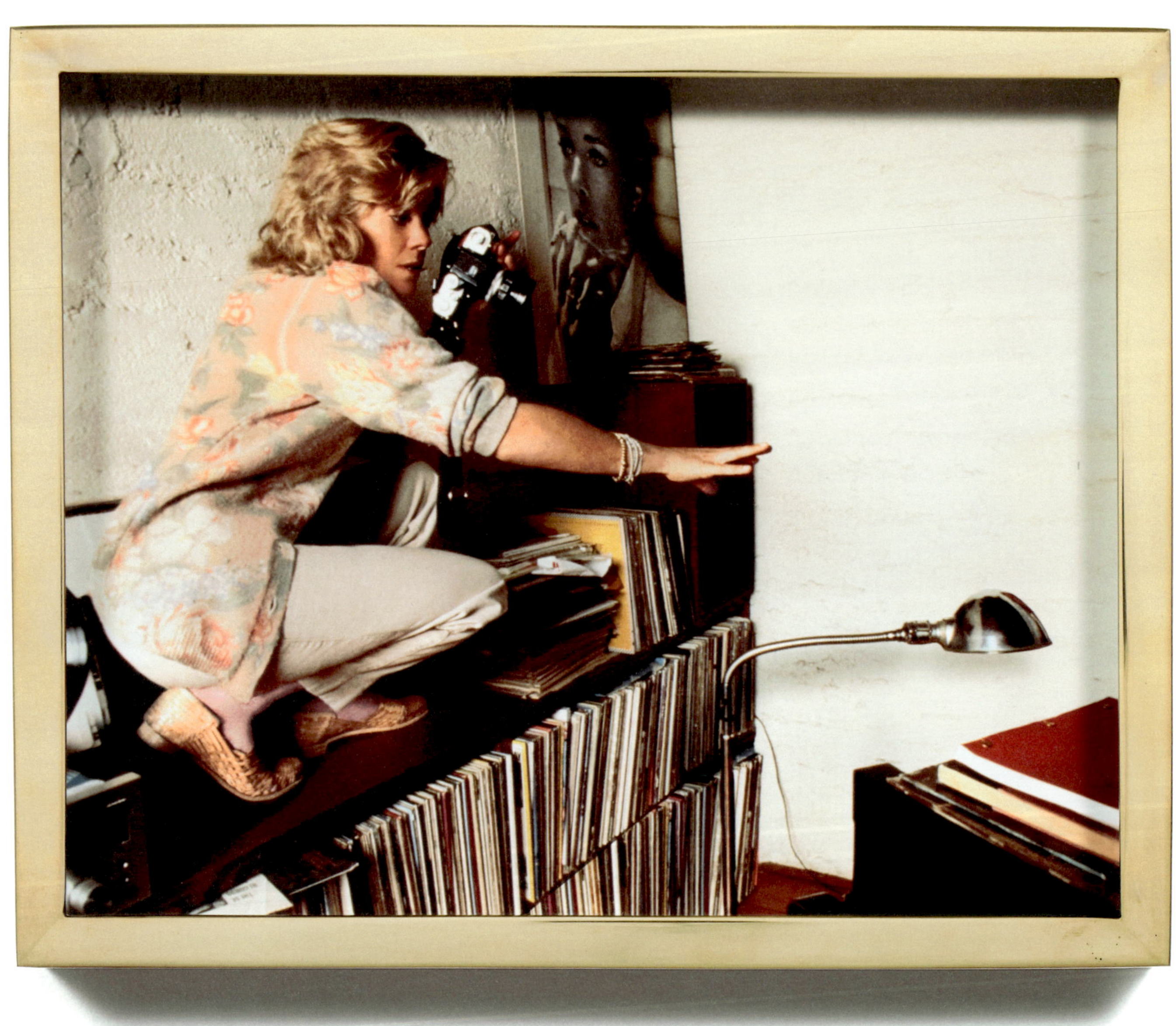
Woman (Camera), 2010, *C-print, framed, 20.3 x 25.4*

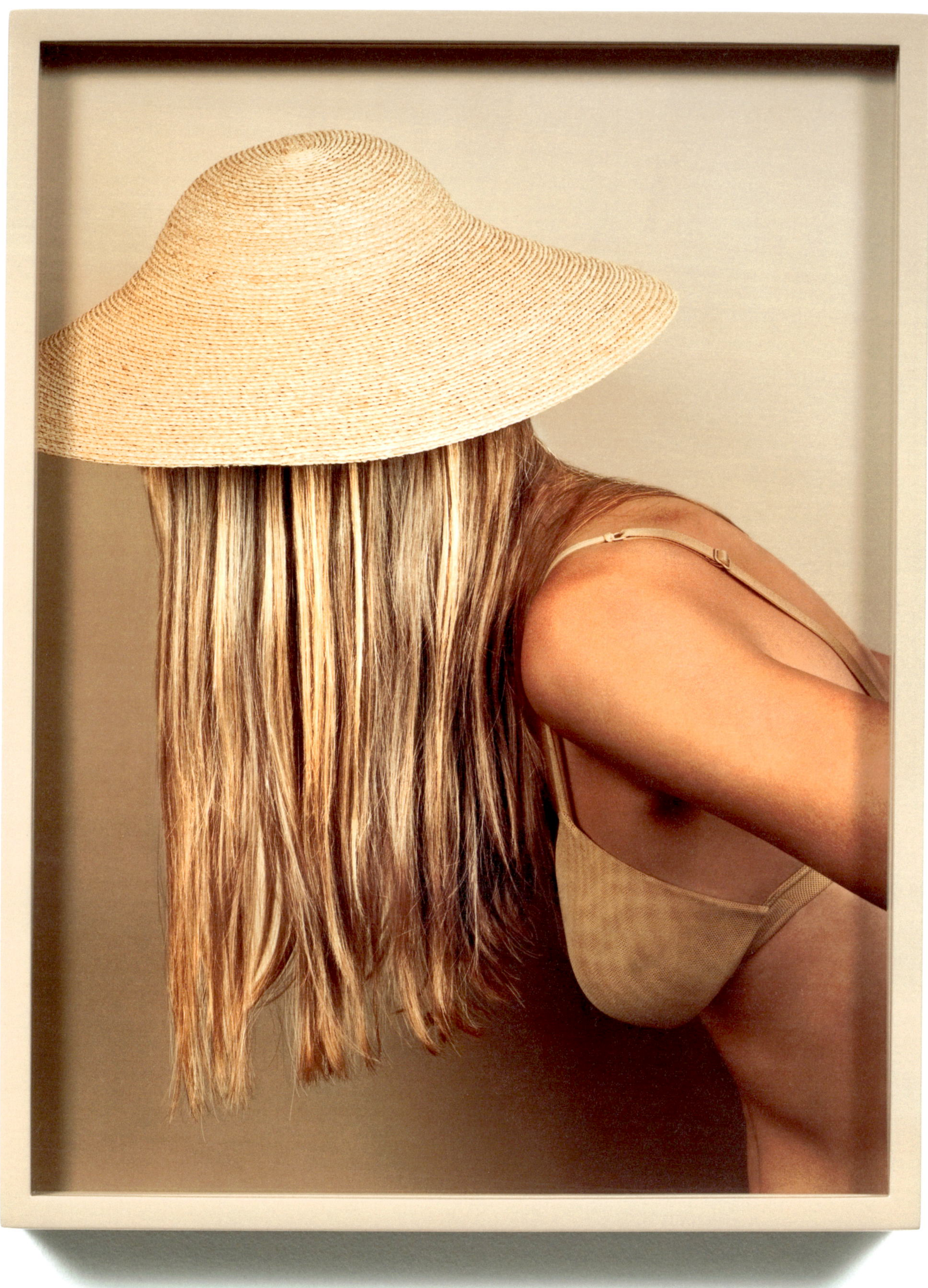

Blond Girl, 2010, *C-print, framed, 36.8 x 29.2*

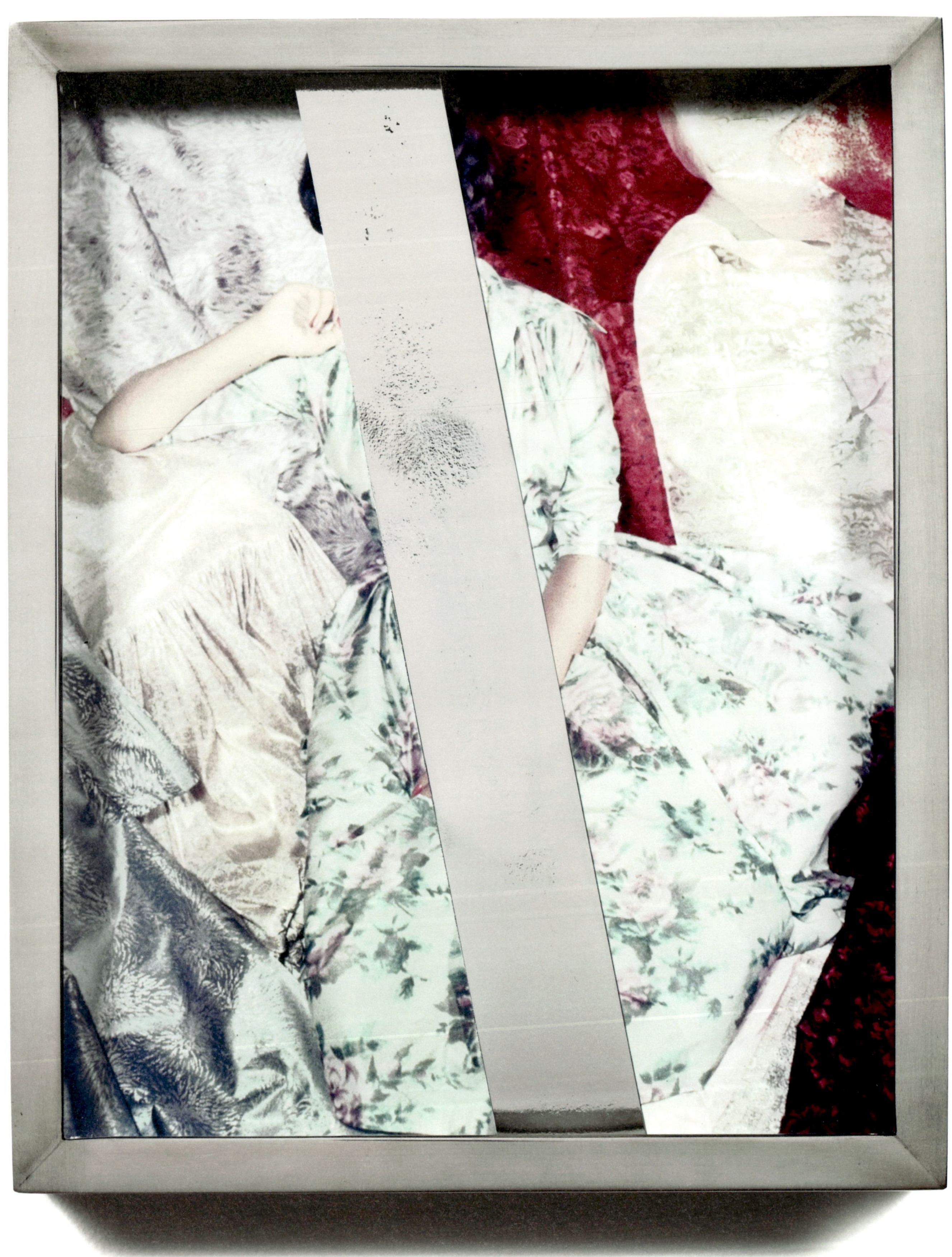

Untitled (Silver Diagonal), 2010, *foil on C-print, framed, 25.4 x 20.3*
All images © the artist, courtesy Galleria Massimo De Carlo, Milan

Hijacked in a Winter Garden Moment
Cay Sophie Rabinowitz with Erin Tao
in conversation with **ELAD LASSRY**

Elad Lassry, who was born in Tel Aviv, has exhibited in numerous group exhibition internationally. He has mounted solo shows at the Whitney Museum of American Art, the Art Institute of Chicago, and Kunsthalle Zurich. While his practice is indebted to canonical traditions such as conceptualism and structuralism, his method is incomparable and anomalous. Where a subject or image originates can be obscured just as the method of its production remains illusive. Lassry seems faithful to an analogue approach, but not merely in the way an image is completed, for his pictures at times involve digital processes. Similarly, the deeply personal significance that drives his engagement with a subject may never get exposed in the resulting imagery. The following conversation, that was conducted partly in Lassry's Los Angeles studio and partly on skype, reveals how his interests evolve in unexpected ways.

CAY SOPHIE RABINOWITZ: *As someone who works with various media, primarily photography and film, you seem to have an idea about challenging the authority of what media presents and achieves: for instance, the way a photograph defines and preserves the identity of a person, or how film professes to create narrative. Are these properties examples of an authority? Are they what you attempt to challenge in your work?*

ELAD LASSRY: Those properties certainly exist, but for me, tension starts the moment I make a photograph. My work speaks about what it means to photograph a subject where it is entirely evaporated, evacuated - a portrait emptied out serves as a stand-in for something else. The fact that it is an image is of secondary interest to me; there is an idea of detachment, as if it has been produced in a different context, with a different life - a certain separation from the modernist notion of the photograph. Something psychological, something historical about life and death, moves into a fetishized object. That is my relationship with film: I challenge places and settings,

questions of beginning and end, an institutional mortality. There's something regressive about the idea of film being no more than a sequence of photographs, especially in this time of technology; and there is something potentially analog about the things I've used and researched. I have an idea of a lumiere effect: can I have this moment again? Can I make this photograph move? Something about the film becoming a cinematic institution, with the folklore and ritual of watching - buying a ticket, sitting down, having a fixed proximity from the screen for a particular amount of time - fascinates me. Film helps me activate photographs to a place, like vectors that bolster each other; film and photography challenge each other in terms of the set of questions they ask.

Your interests in the realm of film and photography seem to have been inspired, at least in part, by autobiographical events which translate to structural functions. In each of your examples, you've mentioned something about the ways people conventionally approach images; you discuss the ideas of shared experiences and expected performance within a space. There is some sort of sociological translation in your work, if you will.

Much of my works, particularly the films, follow a structuralist strategy. For example I have made work which are exact segments of one-minute rolls of film shot with a fixed camera. Yet, I would not call them structuralist films. Nonetheless, this kind of engagement would not be possible without an awareness of structural approaches to the medium because that is what establishes the limitations or conditions as something embedded. Similarly, with photography, I'm not interested in mapping the world with pictures, but my work comments on the practice. It acknowledges that photography contains the potential to depict a world, like conventional photo essays do - but this is not where my interest lies. I'm more interested in using photography's history and studying the tension that surrounds it. Recently, while in the process of making the images for my upcoming show, I noticed how much more nuanced and different my investigation has been than in the past - I am starting to put the images up and I've found that there is a drastic departure from these initial questions. For instance, there is something about my images that are very engaged with space, which is very strange to me because they end up being flat works. To me, space is something more vitrine-like, as opposed to being a window to the world, that turns into a condensed object. But a lot of images start with objects that get rearranged. Often times I encounter a photograph on a particular object, and return to the object itself in order to re-photograph it. My photos are not utilitarian; they have not been taken for the sake of cataloguing or even showing work. They are meant to be interacted with even though photographs flatten the objects out.

This, in effect, would be very different from the work of some of your influences - for instance, Christopher Williams.
I've never consciously thought about how my work is different from people whose work I like. I don't photograph as a process of analysis; I'm not using photography to explain anything. There are photographic questions that are evident in the work, but there's something more complicated that viewers - and sometimes, even I - struggle to articulate.
I believe there is a substantial distinction between the depiction of an object and analysis of it. Many of my photos, rather than posing the question of 'Where is that photographed from?' ask instead, 'What am I looking at?' What a viewer sees in the most pictoral or figurative sense - for instance, a portrait - is actually as abstract as it is figurative. As an artist, a lot of things get activated through this tension.

Isn't every depiction also, in some way, also an analysis?
Traditionally photographic conceptualists have employed analytic strategies that I feel very removed from - for instance, seriality, which is really difficult for me to use; I'm always working against it. I prefer to consolidate items into a single image. Permitting, or even suggesting, variations on an object is a privilege that I infrequently afford. I have a

very hard time with that. Another example is acknowledging the source of an object. I try to move away from practices that rely upon the history of an object that has been photographed. I like the notion of divorcing things from their pasts. When I find an object that I want to photograph - even if some sort of history exists, I know the work cannot be about that. True, history adds questions and complicates things. But it is not where the tension lies for me.

A term you don't use is "reception", but at the same time, you repeatedly refer to things that have conditioned the way one sees. For instance, if you had an image with woman wearing a chef's hat, many viewers would associate her with a cook. When you ask, "What are we seeing?" you seem to suggest that there are viewing habits to be broken. Is reception codified?
I think perception is more dominant - I hope there is a perceptual exercise that happens within the work. I do try to employ different technical strategies to that effect. Like when I place the cut out of a man to be looking out from cut out concentric circles, which is a very analogue "trick" similar to a old, bad, theater set made to create special illusion. Or like in the arrangement in space of a puzzle made in the shape of a woman. I shoot in a very high F-stop to get the backdrop in as much focus as the subject, which leads to a very confusing visual experience. For example, if the background is a floral textile, the subject can't help but become involved in the pattern, and the image flattens out. So, perceptually, there is a debate: what exactly is the subject of the photograph, and how do we treat it?

Using media to explore these questions involves a substitution of language to explore your construction - as much as language helps, it runs the risk of shutting it down.
So much contemporary work is full of moments where things fall apart. It would be naïve to think that there is a way to have a singular thesis that summates a foolproof way of viewing. But, I still think something like a cook can be abstracted - I can see the hat becoming another head. I think

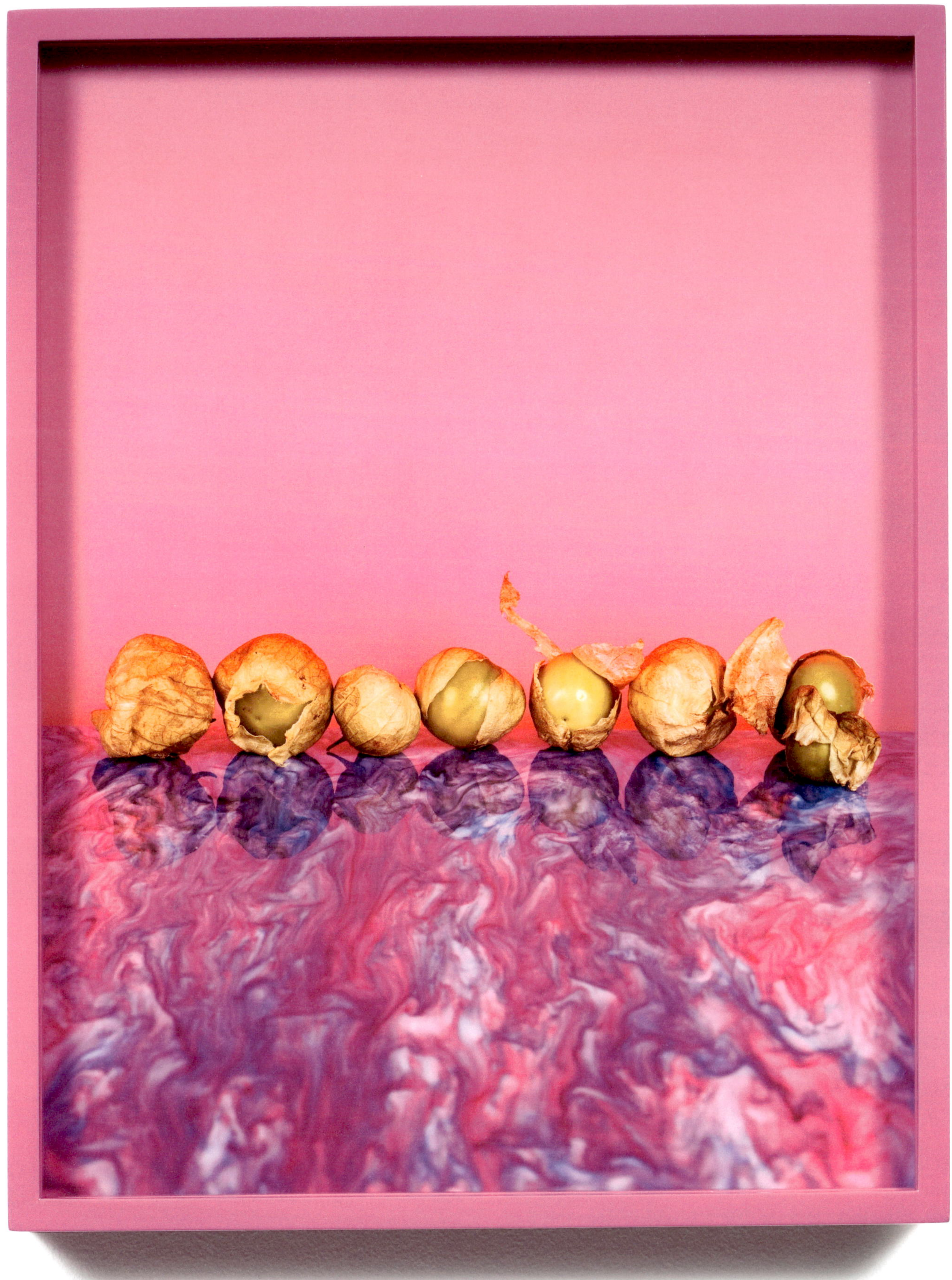

Tomatillos, 2010, *C-print, framed, 36.8 x 29.2*

maybe that's the nature of a picture. We had to write a thesis for graduate school, and most of mine was about the paradox of how much I didn't believe in photographs. Yet, there was an entire chapter devoted to 1950's pictures of Anthony Perkins, which led me to question that belief (or rather that lack of belief). I fell in love with and through these utilitarian photographs that had mostly been produced by the film studios. I made an archive and I learned to believe in it. But I had to acknowledge that there would be exceptions. I became hijacked in a Winter Garden moment. What is in a photograph you find (or keep) is something more than what was in it before. Pictures have that sort of duality - they can become an investment. When I appropriate an image, I'm not giving it baggage to make a statement. I'm just using an image that works, that has to be utilized again. I acknowledge appropriation, but I'm not interested in what that means, or taking on the question of authorship and originality. I definitely think that what we know about appropriation allows young artists to think in a particular manner - like Levine or Prince - but from that point on I need appropriated images to do more - to move to the next questions. The work, Woman Photographer, is also from the Perkins archive but the character actor himself has been removed from the image of Barry Bronson, Perkins' then future wife on location for *Interview Magazine.*

But there are times when you emphasize the re-presentation of an image from a particular source, as if to be an act of distancing from its original source. Your works that mirror magazine covers from the 70's are one such example.
When I use magazine images, I want to be able to sneak them in with a constellation of other images - I want them fit them into a category where they otherwise wouldn't belong. I want people to look at them and say, "Oh, of course you belong with other covers of 70's magazines!" I say this with a wink of sorts, because everyone is going to notice some degree of discrepancy - but the moment you potentially allow them to be categorized with another group is when the work happens. It is a challenge for me. When what used to be an advertisement passes as a portrait, then a photograph is successful. Its indexicality is not necessarily gone, even if I omit particular details like bar codes and dates from a page - it's more about allowing the space to interact with the work, permitting the picture to join another constellation of images, and by that, gain another life as something new.

So there are spatial ways that your found images are present. What about the addition of material? What about collage… and the surface?
Found images are where I experiment with silk screen, foil, metal, among others - they are where I address questions of materiality. Something about trying to print on photographs or magazine paper, or dealing with the physicality of how photographs register on another surface (while, in the process, erasing something that was preexisting) marks the transition from collage to film. There is an interference of surface. In relation to the other works, that interference becomes important to me. Some substances don't register - for instance, I'll heat a photograph with sandpaper, and then with foil. Something about this analog activity, something about butchering a negative on Photoshop and proceeding to edit out the things I don't like, remains completely valid. The end result for me is to escape photographic space.

While still using photography.
Yes, yes. I've mentioned the use of ghost photography. As a child, I believed in it; as I grew older, I learned more serious photo theories that allowed me to apply folklore to my work. I love the concept of an image being haunted by its own history. A photograph can have ghosts - even if they're not present, their histories still echo and interfere.

So there is still some autobiographical history embedded in your artistic practice.
Appears to be…

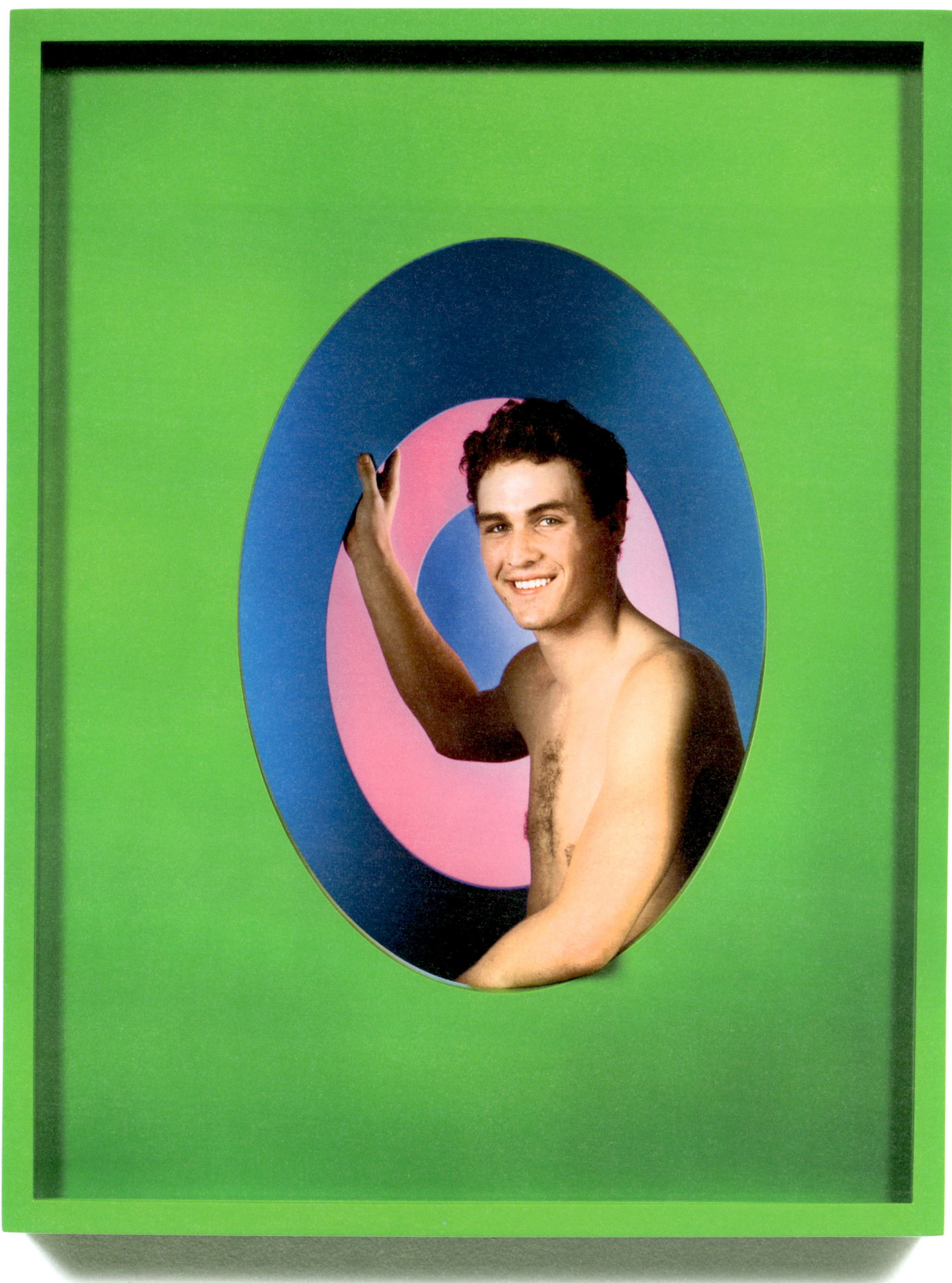

Dustin Christenson, 2010, *C-print, framed, 36.8 x 29.2*

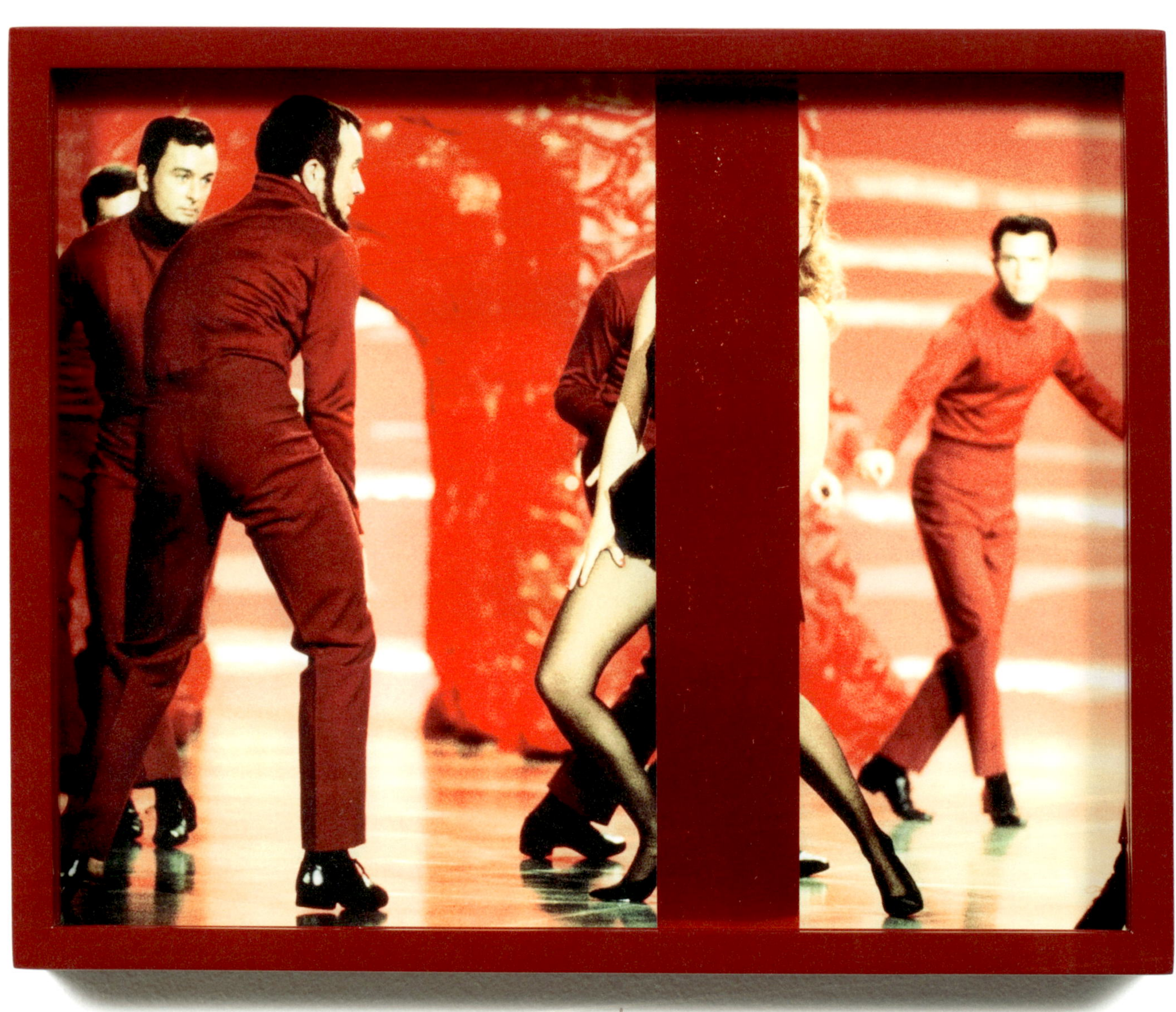

Untitled (Red Bar), 2010, *foil on C-print, 20.3 x 25.4*

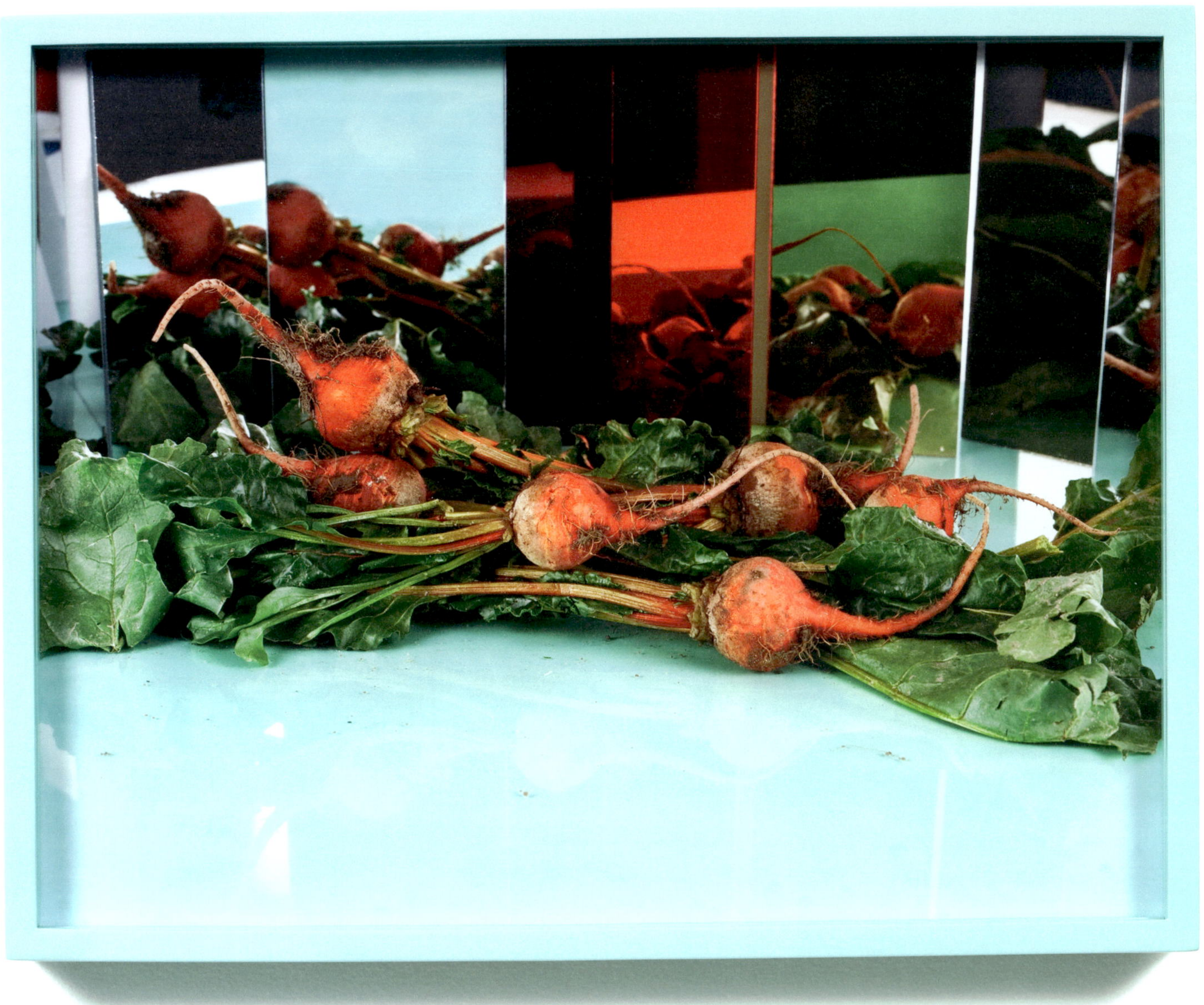

Beets, 2010, *C-print, framed, 29.2 x 36.8*

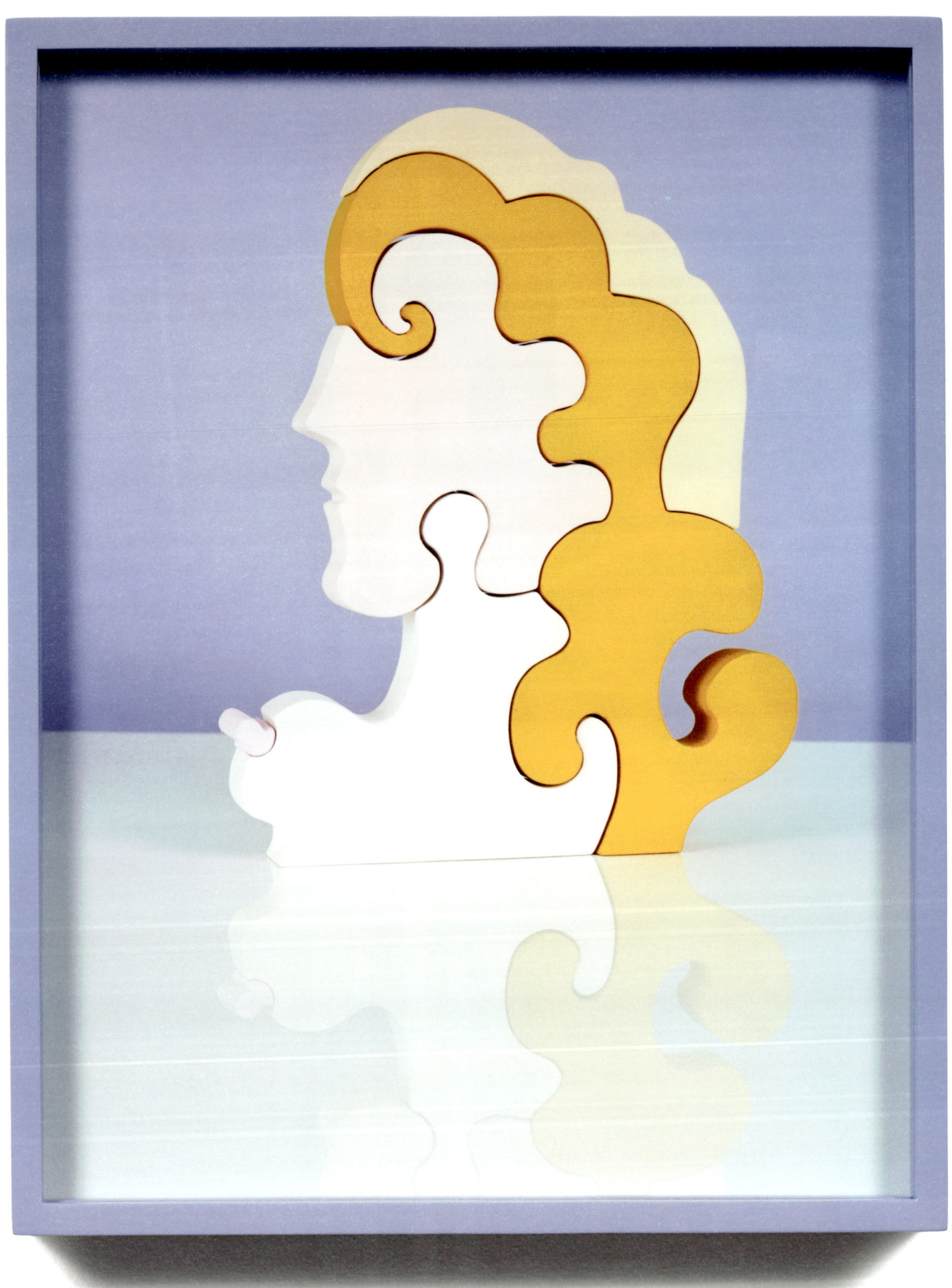

Woman (Puzzle), 2010, *C-print, framed, 36.8 x 29.2*

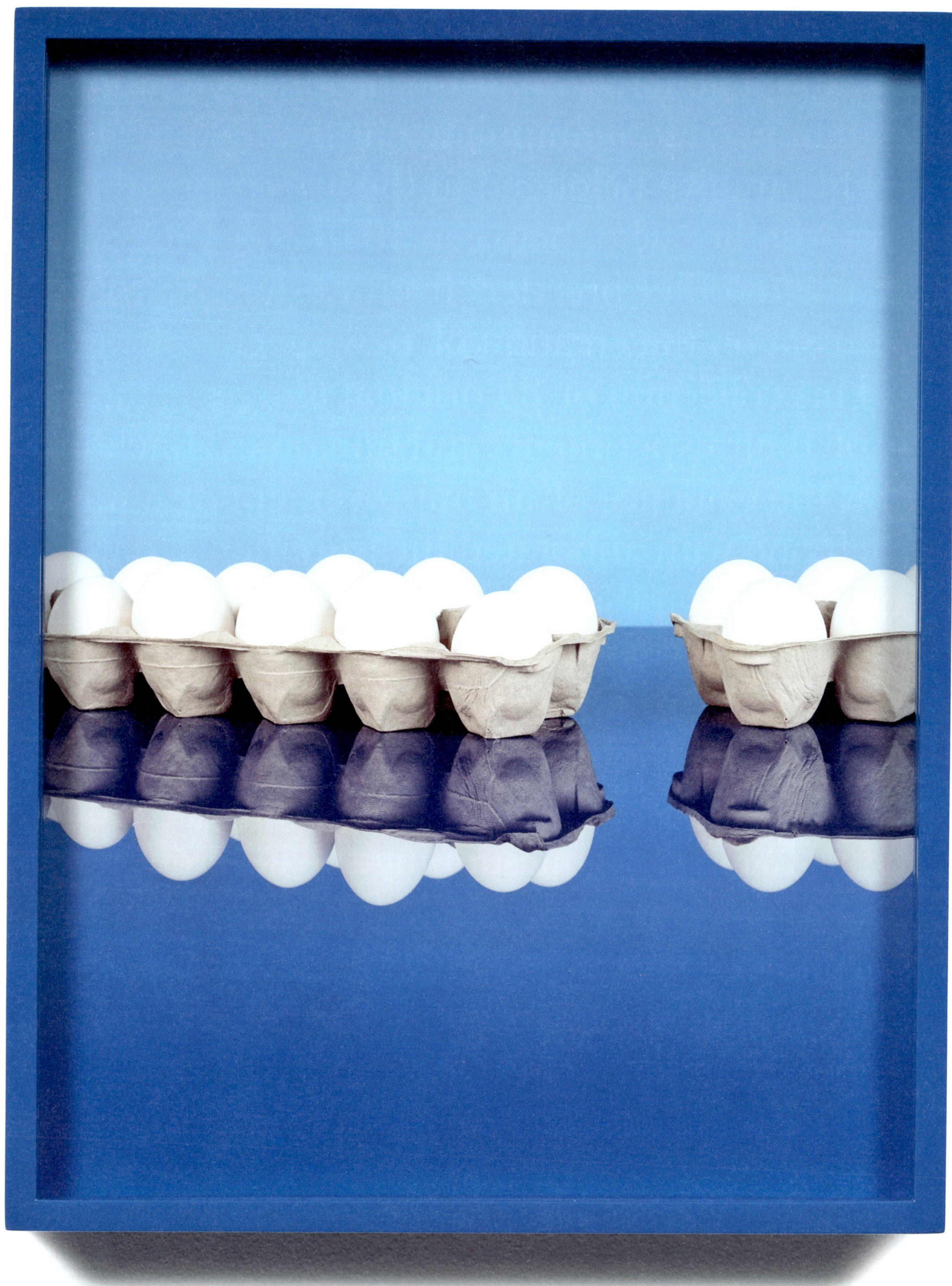

Eggs, 2010, *C-print, framed, 36.8 x 29.2*

PETRA FERIANCOVA Creator is a subtle work about generation and appropriation, about the human need to manipulate nature, beauty and life. This archive belonged to the artist's ornithologist grandfather who, between 1948 and 1962 worked with other breeders from Eastern Europe and Russia on the creation of new species of pigeons. This collection of 85 original images is the result of their experiments and outcomes. Each image is the evidence of an improvement or a mistake, each one with annotated measurements, dates and comments on the developments of the tests. What fascinated Feriancova is the breeders' utopian desire to deceive natural evolution, having the illusion of being in charge of someone else's life themselves. As she says, "*Creator* is about a human intervention into Natural Selection, questioning the inherent features of the evolution - gradual changes of hereditary characteristics within generations. It is about an effort to create new species in a short time span (during one human life) thus being in contradiction with the evolution itself. Despite many possibilities of real time, the creator can manifest a human desire to survive or to live forever". - Petra Feriancova was born in 1977 in Bratislava, where she lives and works.

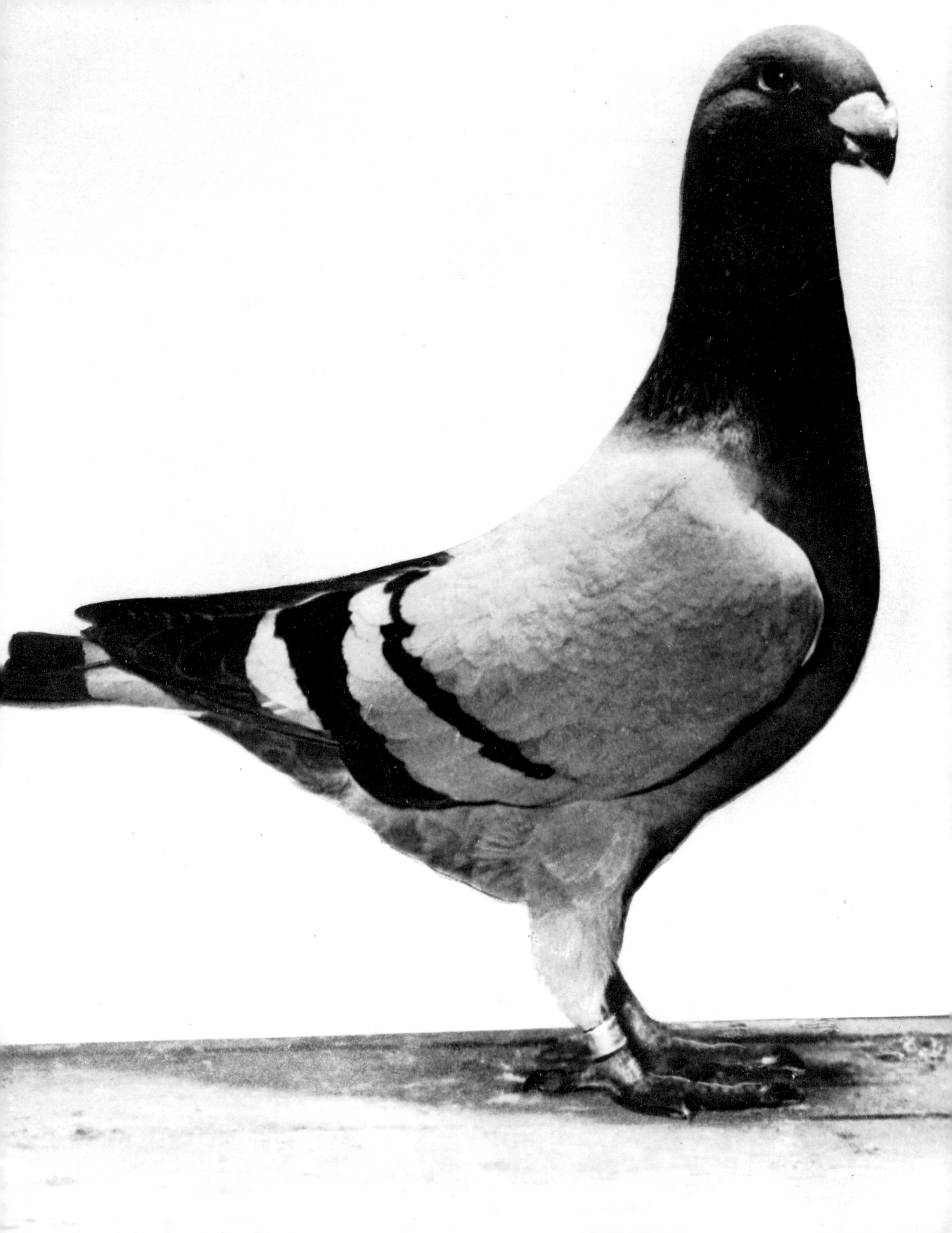

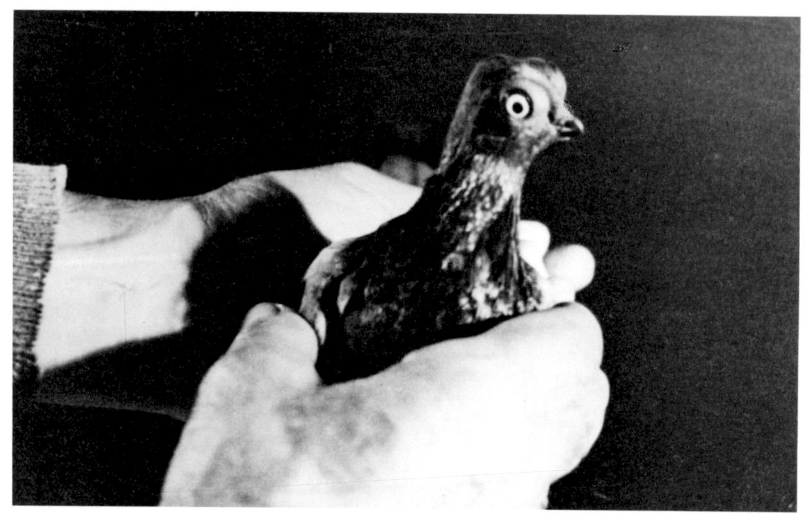
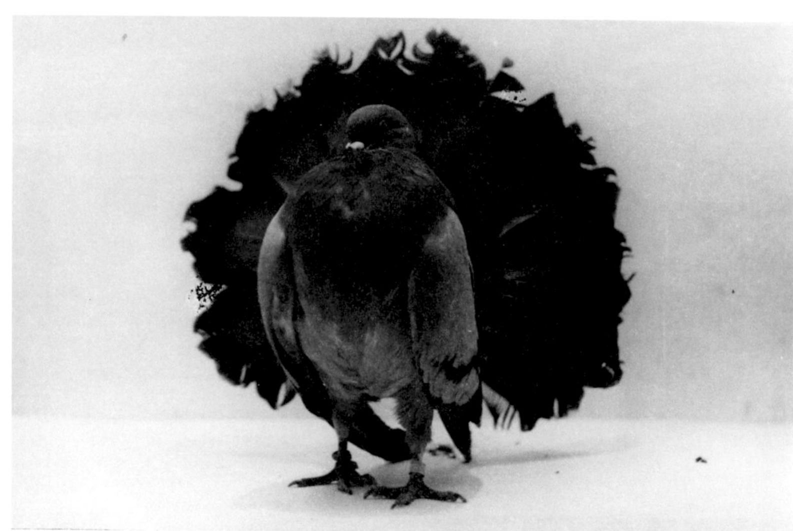
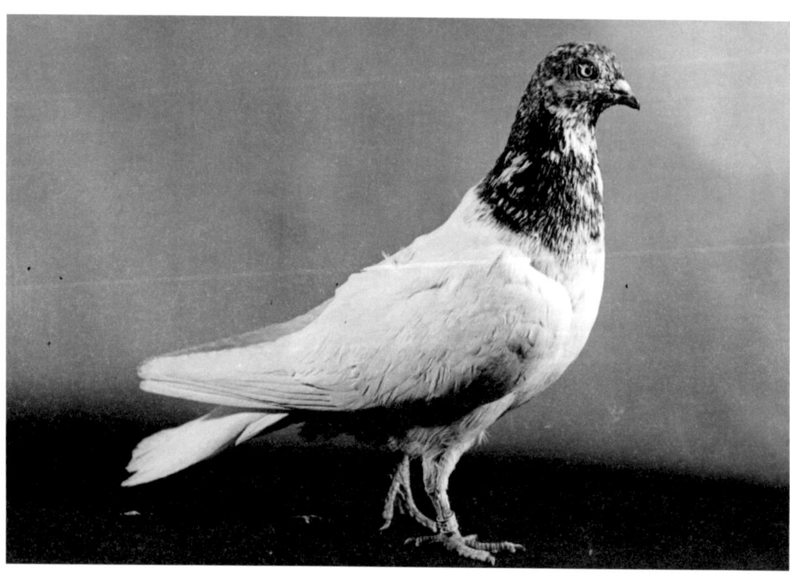
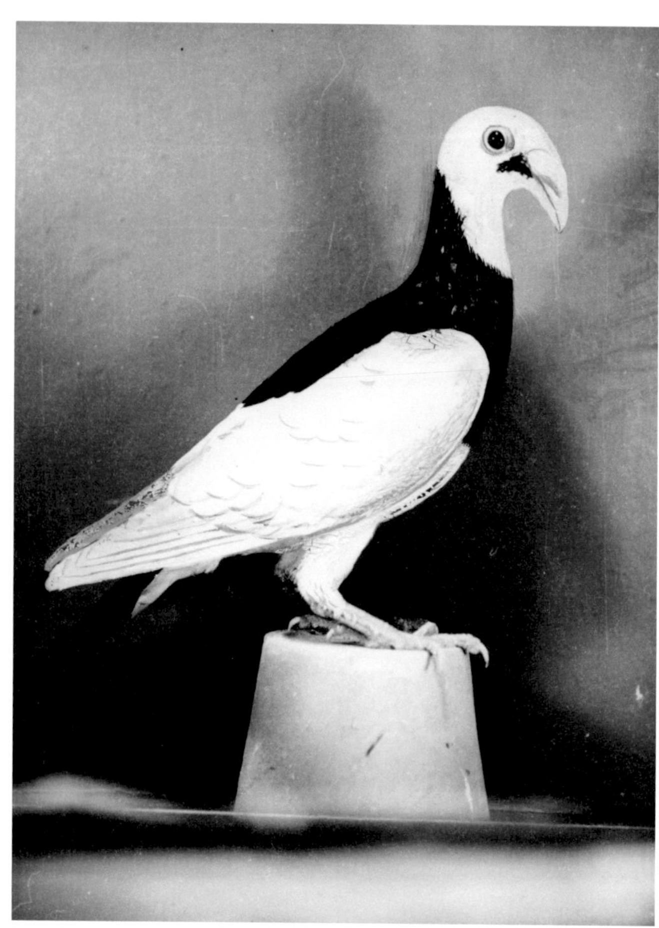
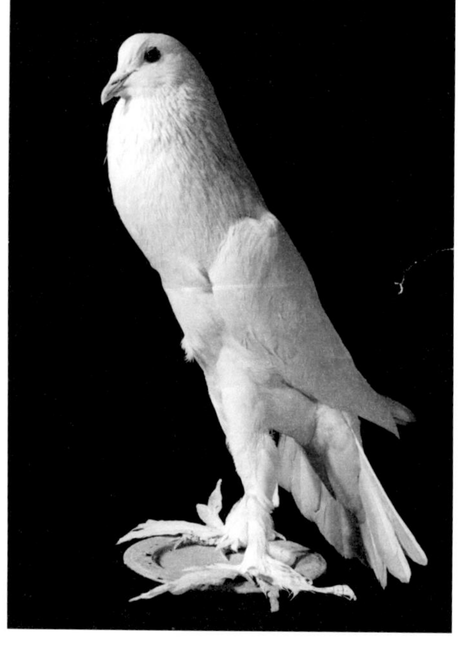

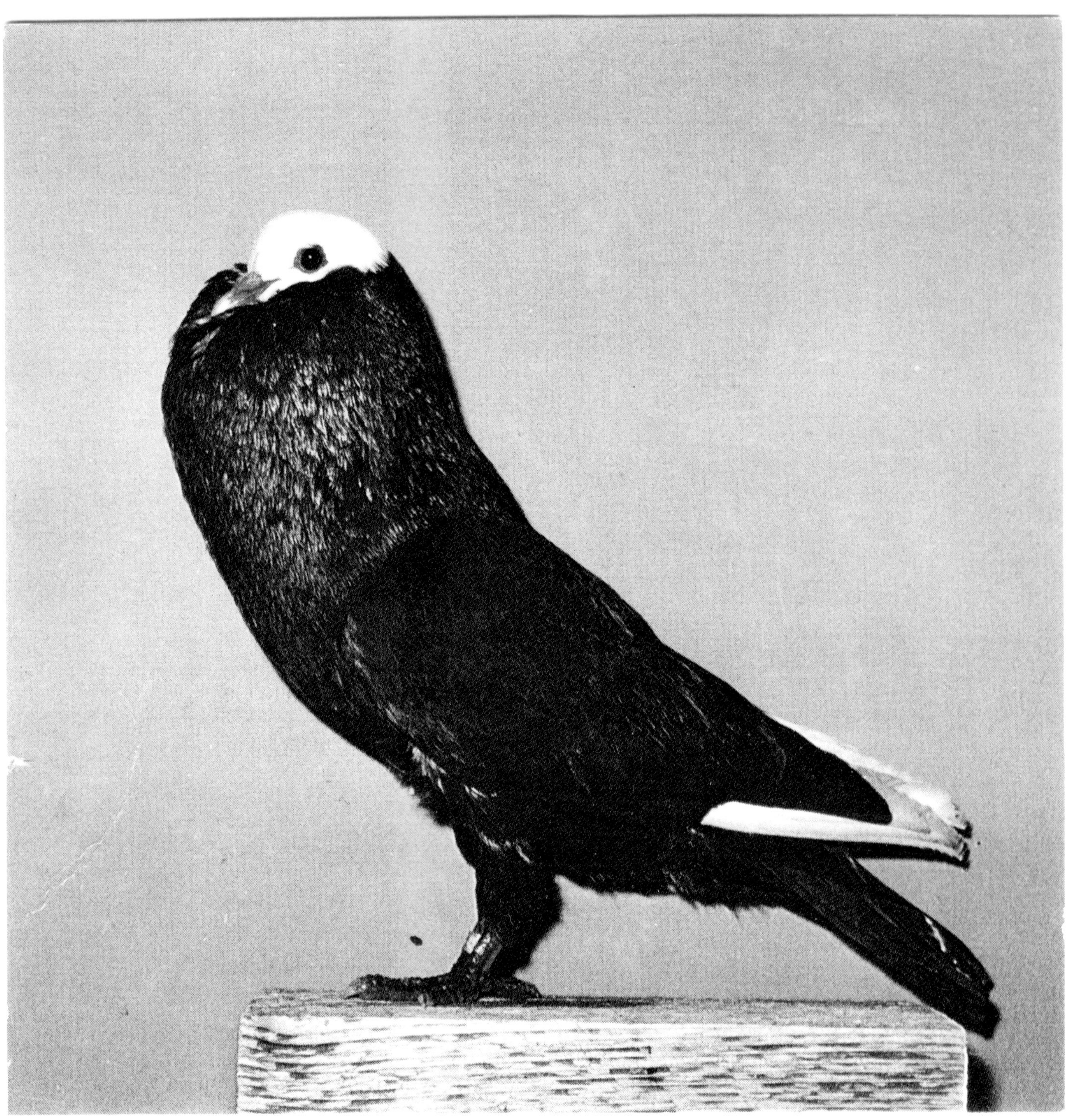

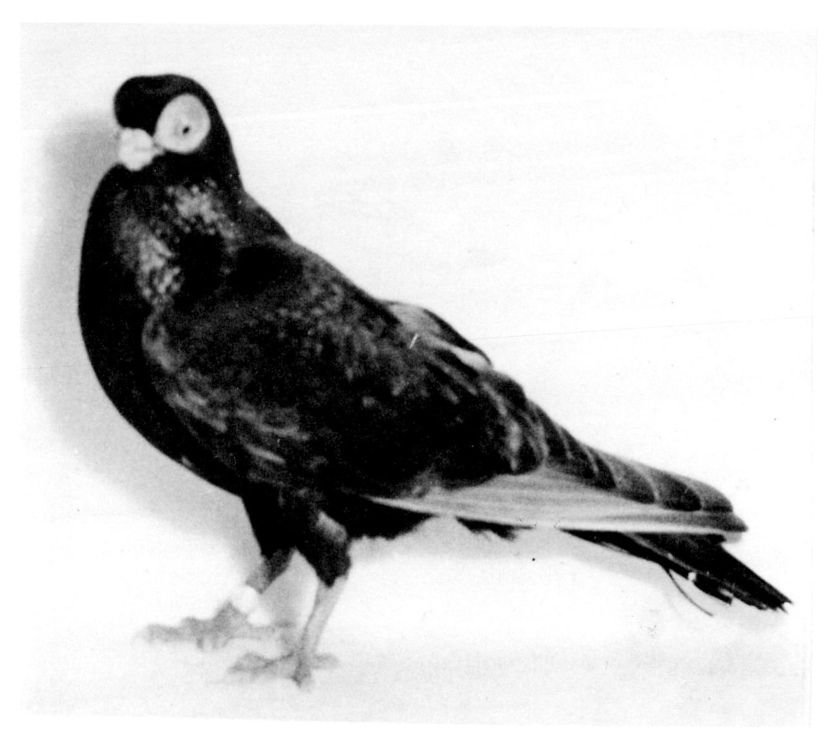

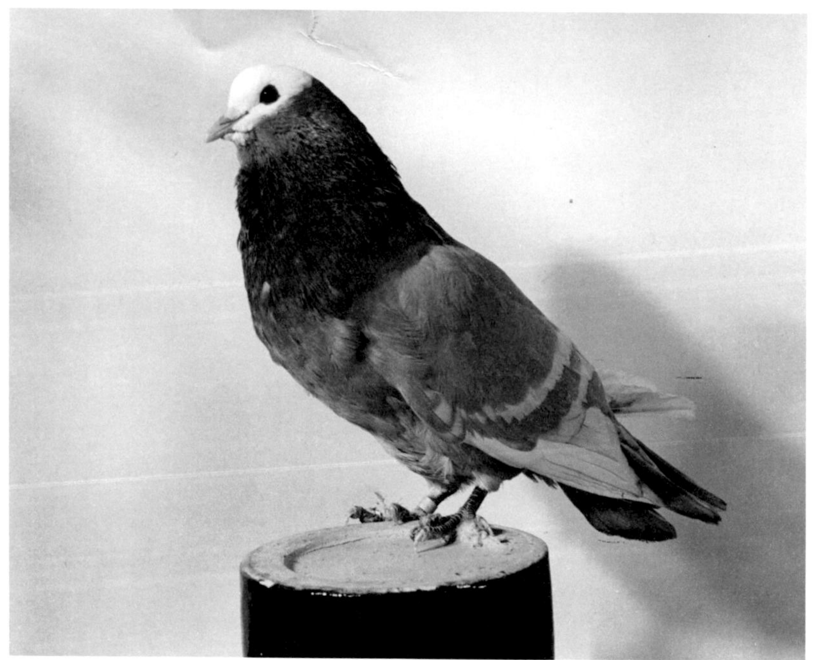

Глубокоуважаемый проф. Feriancz,

с новым годом – с новым счастьем!
Я уже имею Ваше превосходния
"Chov holubov". У нас в зоопарке
я сделал колекцию 250 голуби
с которых 10 породи турецко белоких.
Мне очень интересуют Ваше откуда
– где можно опубликовать (на нем.
языке) статья о незнакомых бал-
канских породах голубей"?
Попросту Вами есть так любезних
посылать мне Ваши оттиски.
Мне кажеться (а наверное я ошибаюсь)
что Ваши статьи в Sykora – о которой
той горлице есть что-то смешная.
И снимки наверное сделанные на гиб-
ридах –Lachttaube (Streptopelia risoria)
X Turkentaube (Str. decrocto). Не знаю
Всего хорошего – счастья, к нам, здоров
и голубей   Ваш Б.

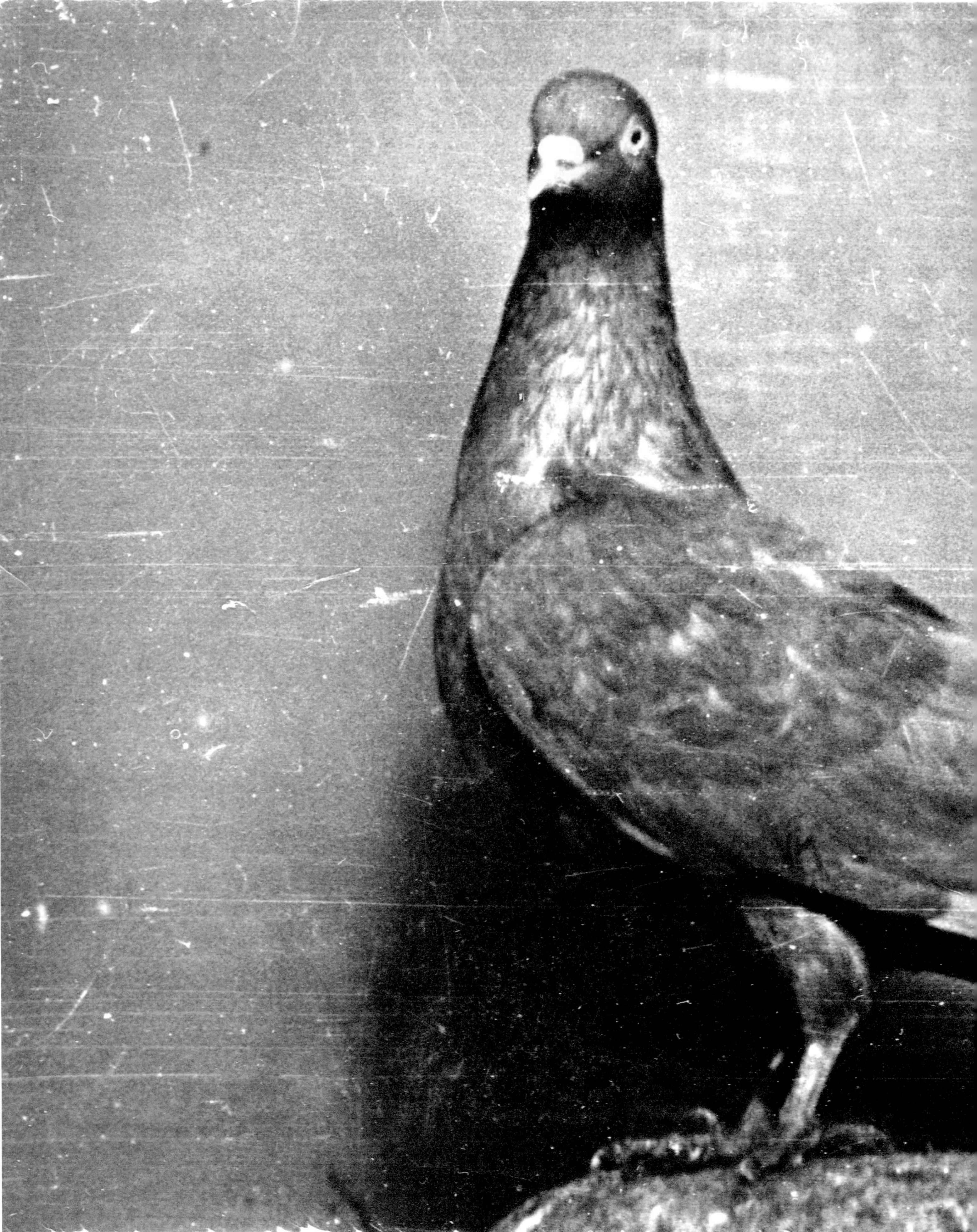

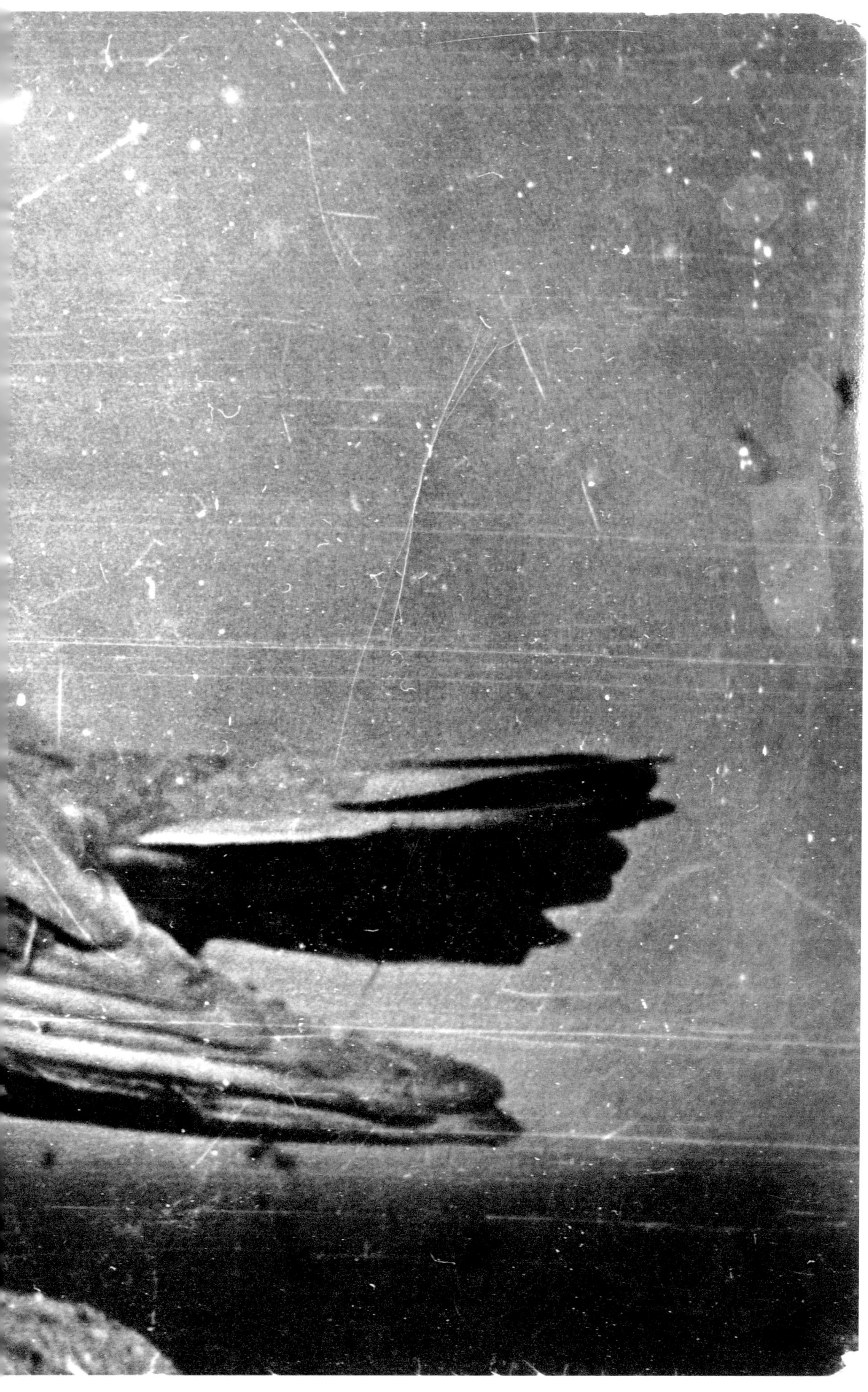

YAO LU New Landscape By mimetically recreating the iconography of traditional Chinese mountain-and-water paintings, Yao Lu deceives the viewer with bucolic landscapes made of digitally assembled pictures of waste; the debris of the persistent development of contemporary China, and of the erasure of the old. "The dumps and rubbish covered with the shield of green net are an ubiquitous view. This is the new face of China, a paradox of confusion and conflicts". Maintaining the balance of traditional framing, composition, line, density and calligraphy, through the use of technology Lu merges pictures he takes with details downloaded from the web, replacing idealized landscapes with a cry for a more thoughtful and ecologically aware development. "Gathering the chrysanthemums, I see the South Mountain in leisure". Quoting Tao Yuanming's description of what he considers the utopian ideal of ancient Chinese painting, Lu invites us all to make the world a more harmonious place - Yao Lu, born in Beijing in 1967, has exhibited throughout the world, won the 2008 BMW Paris Photo Prize and he's an associate professor at The Central Academy of Fine Arts, Beijing.

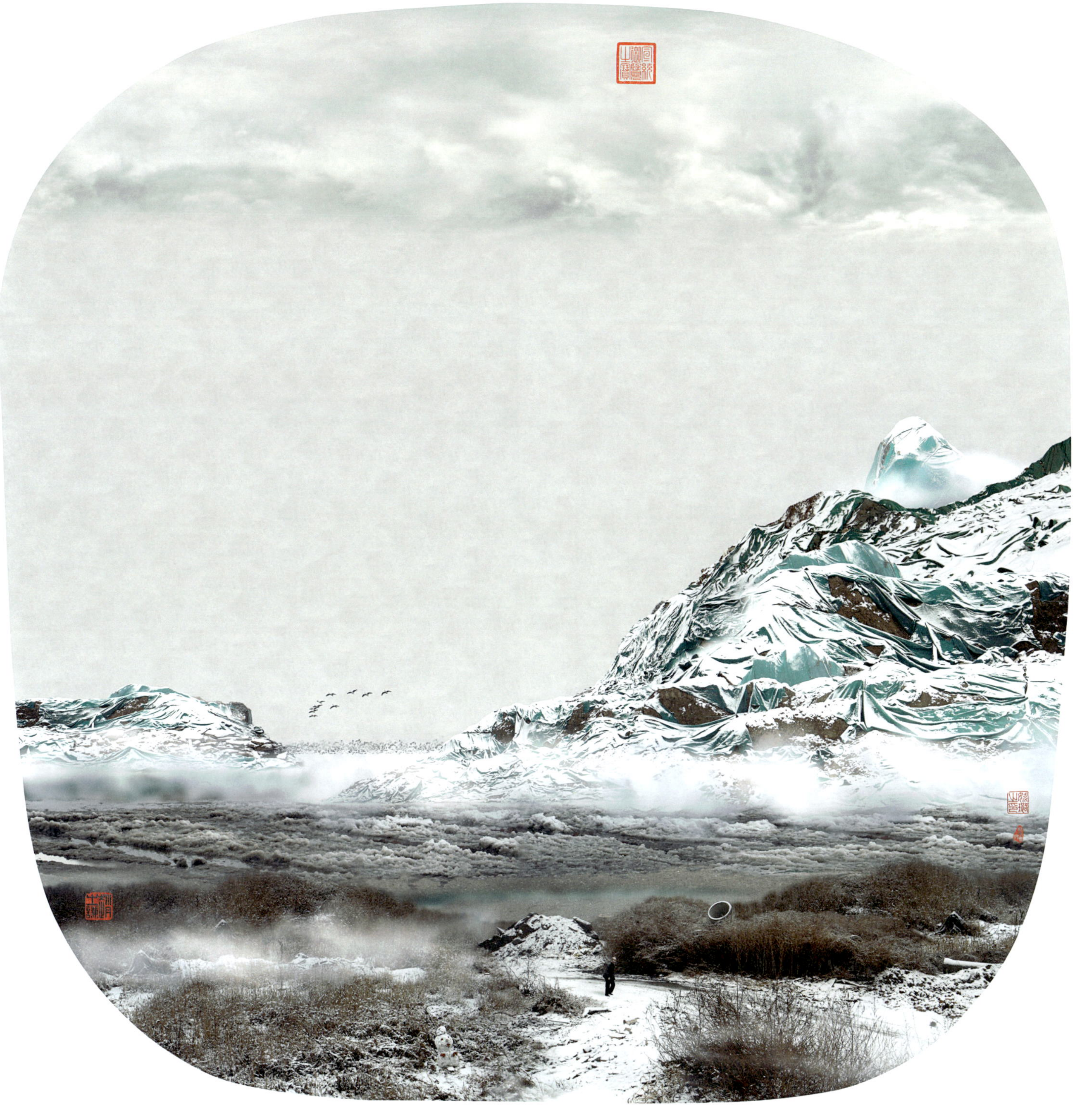

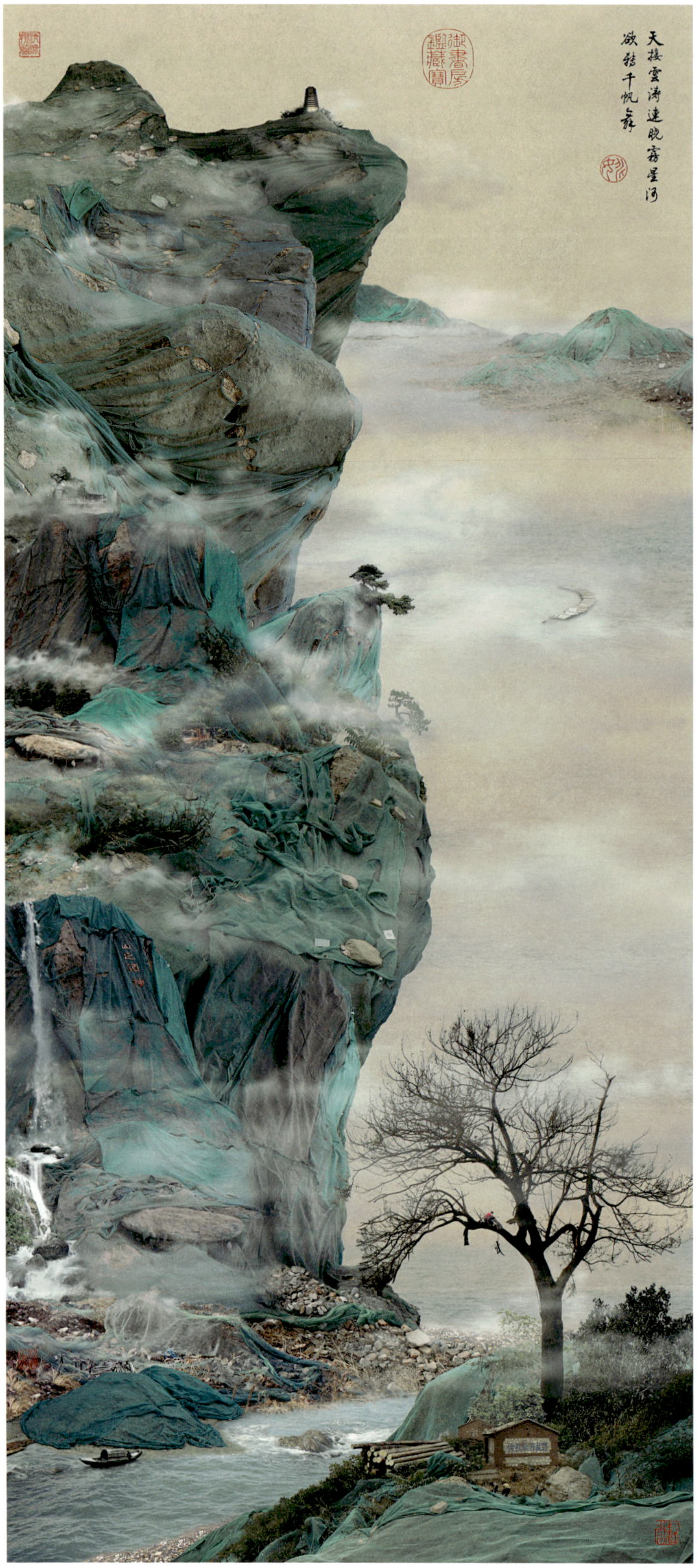

天接雲濤連曉霧星河
欲轉千帆舞

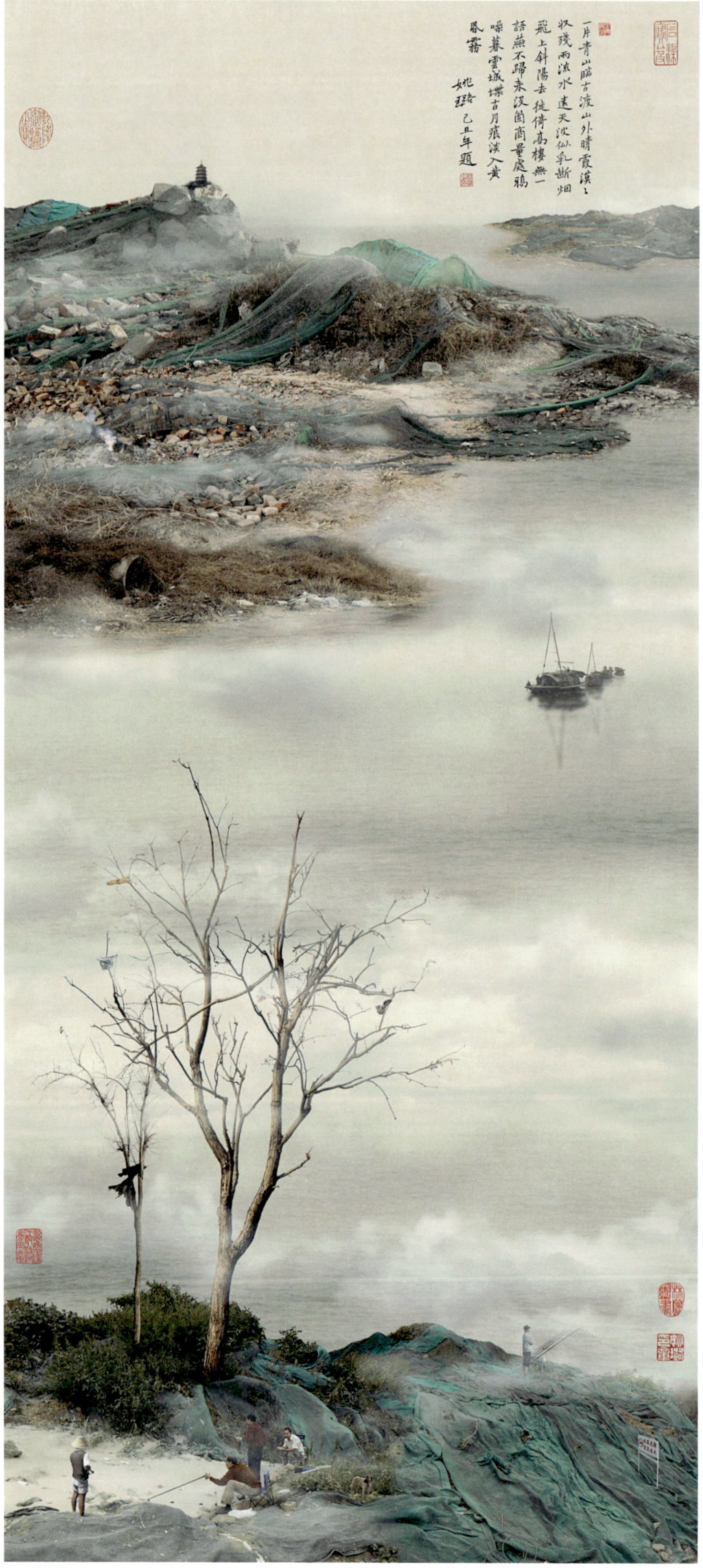

一片青山臨古渡山外晴霞漠漠
收殘雨流水遠天波似乳斷烟
飛上斜陽去徒倚高樓無一
語燕不歸來沒箇商量處鴉
噪暮雲城堞古月痕淡淡入黃
昏霧
姚璐 乙丑年題

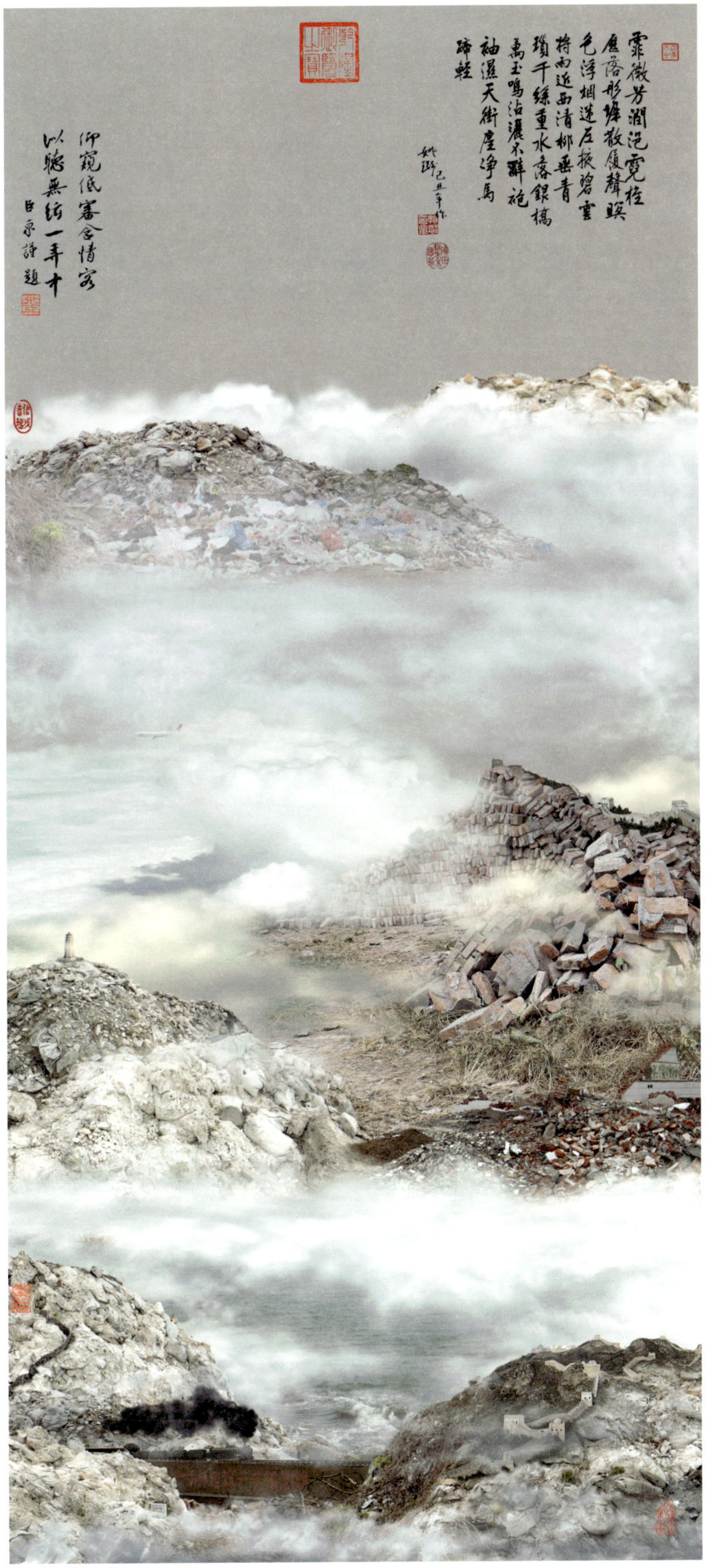

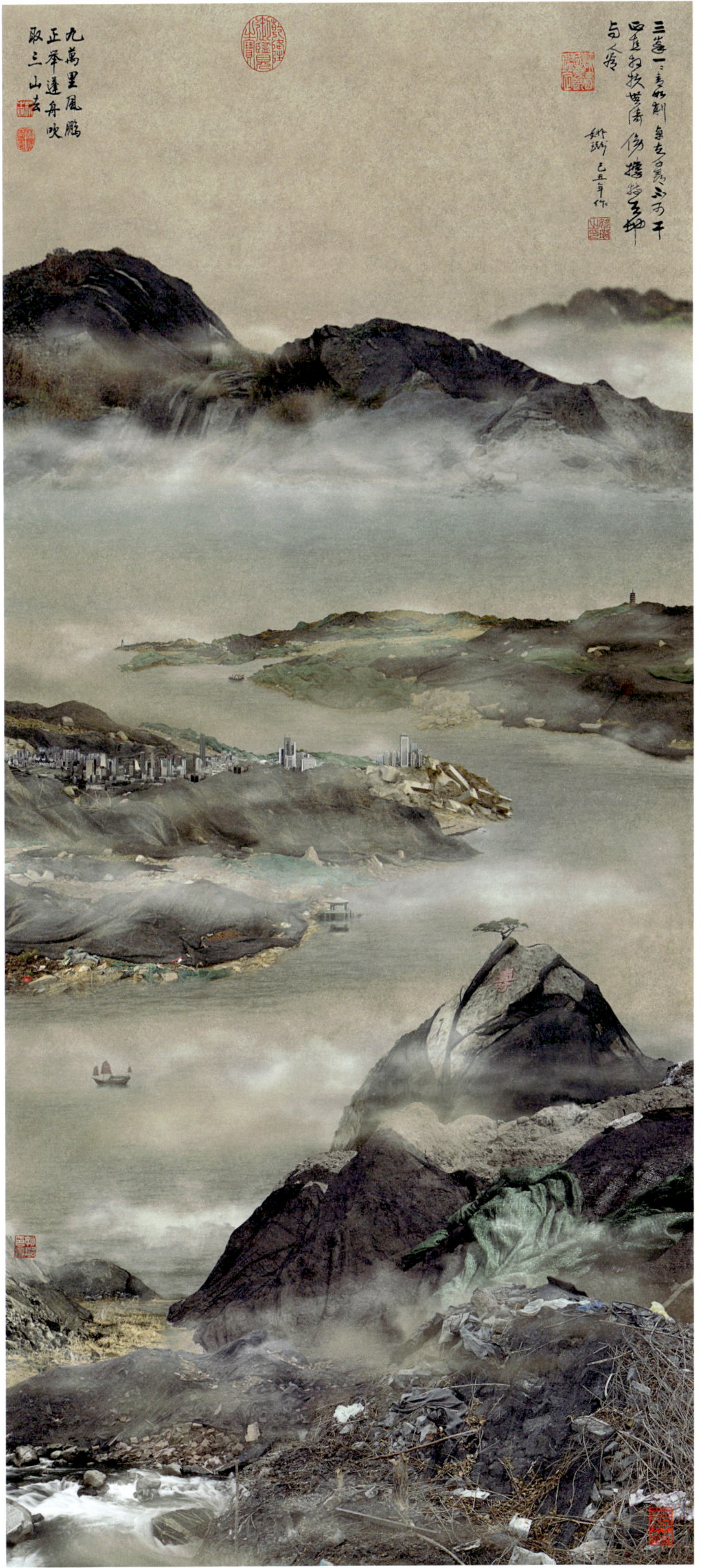

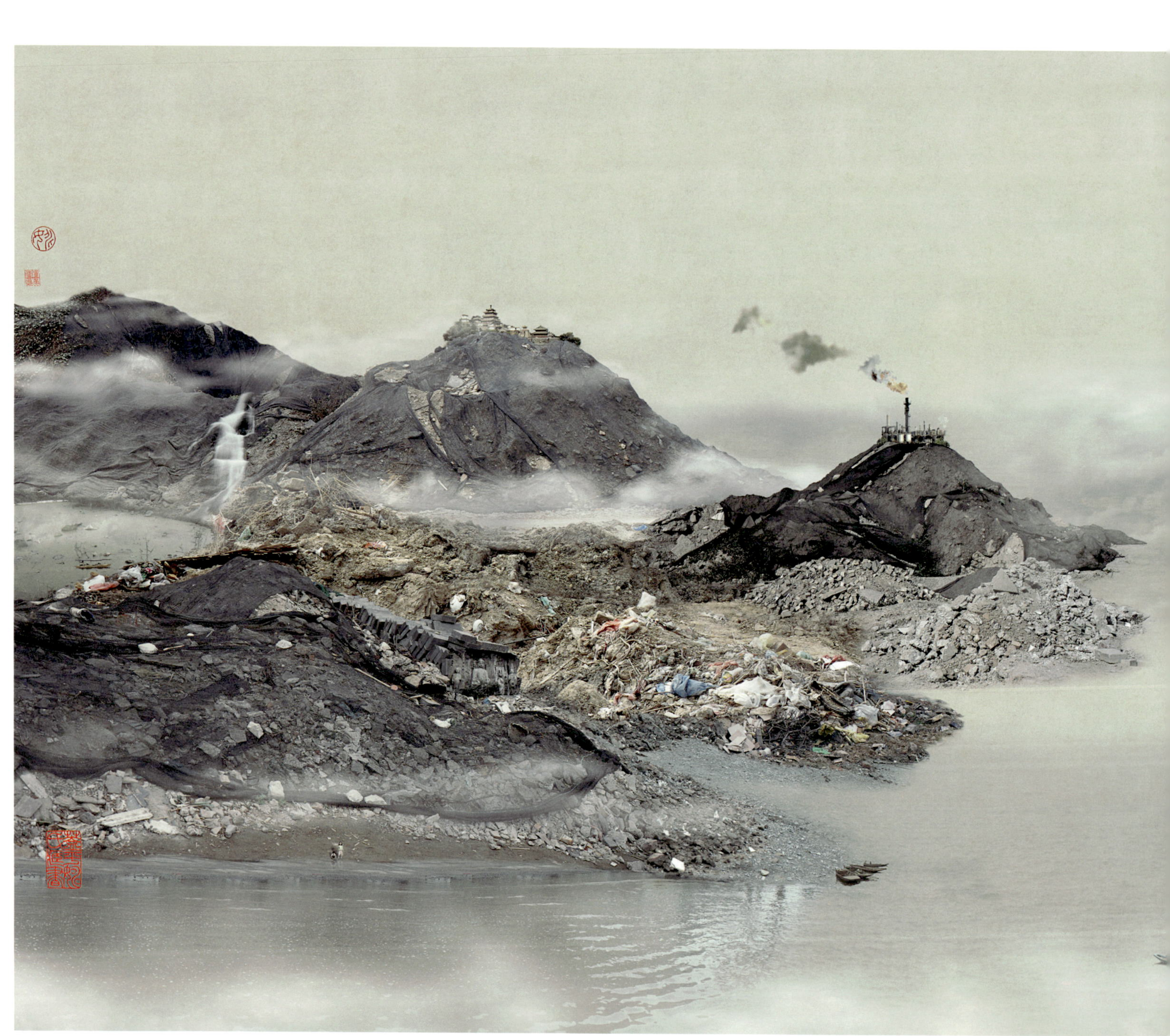

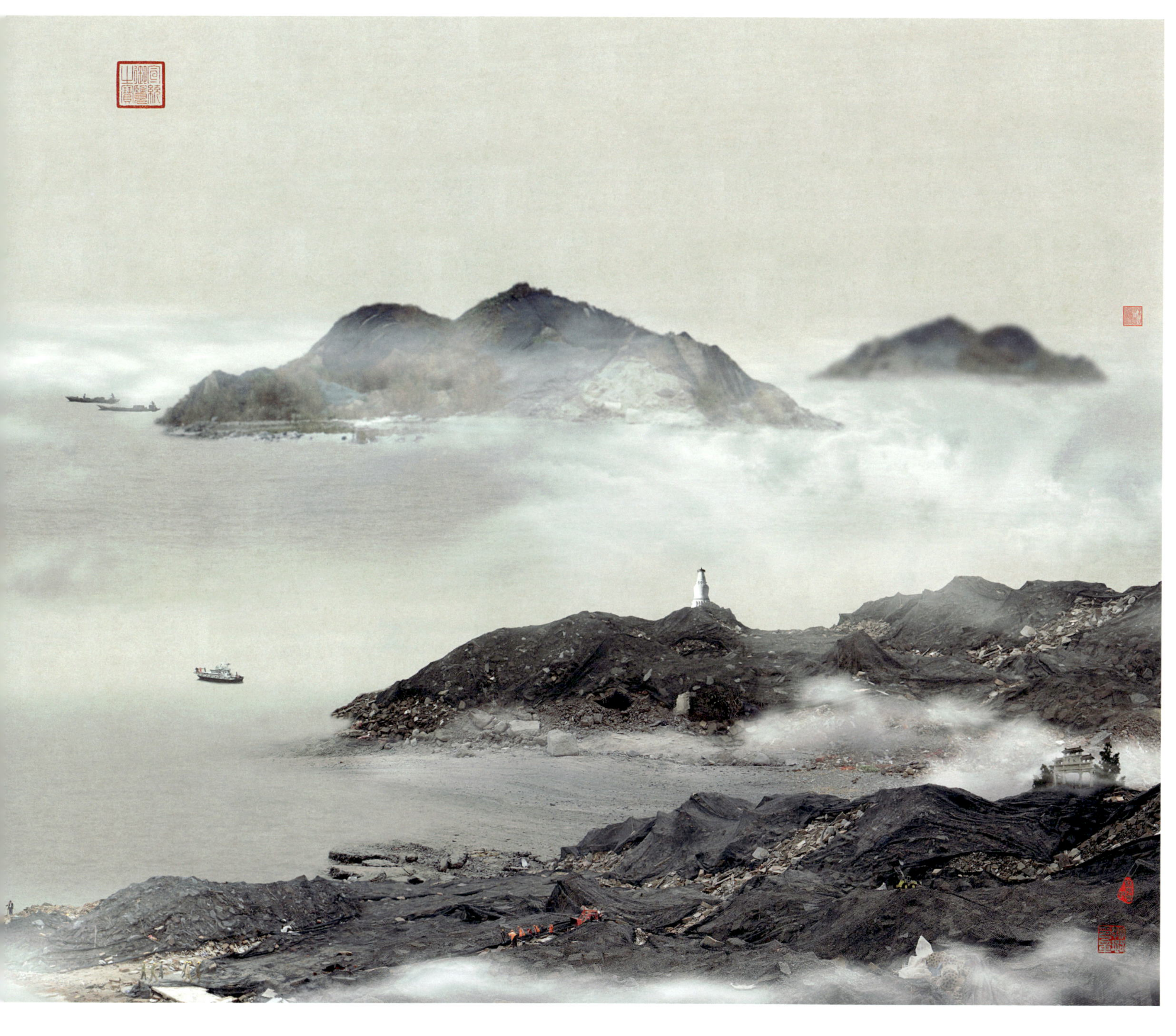

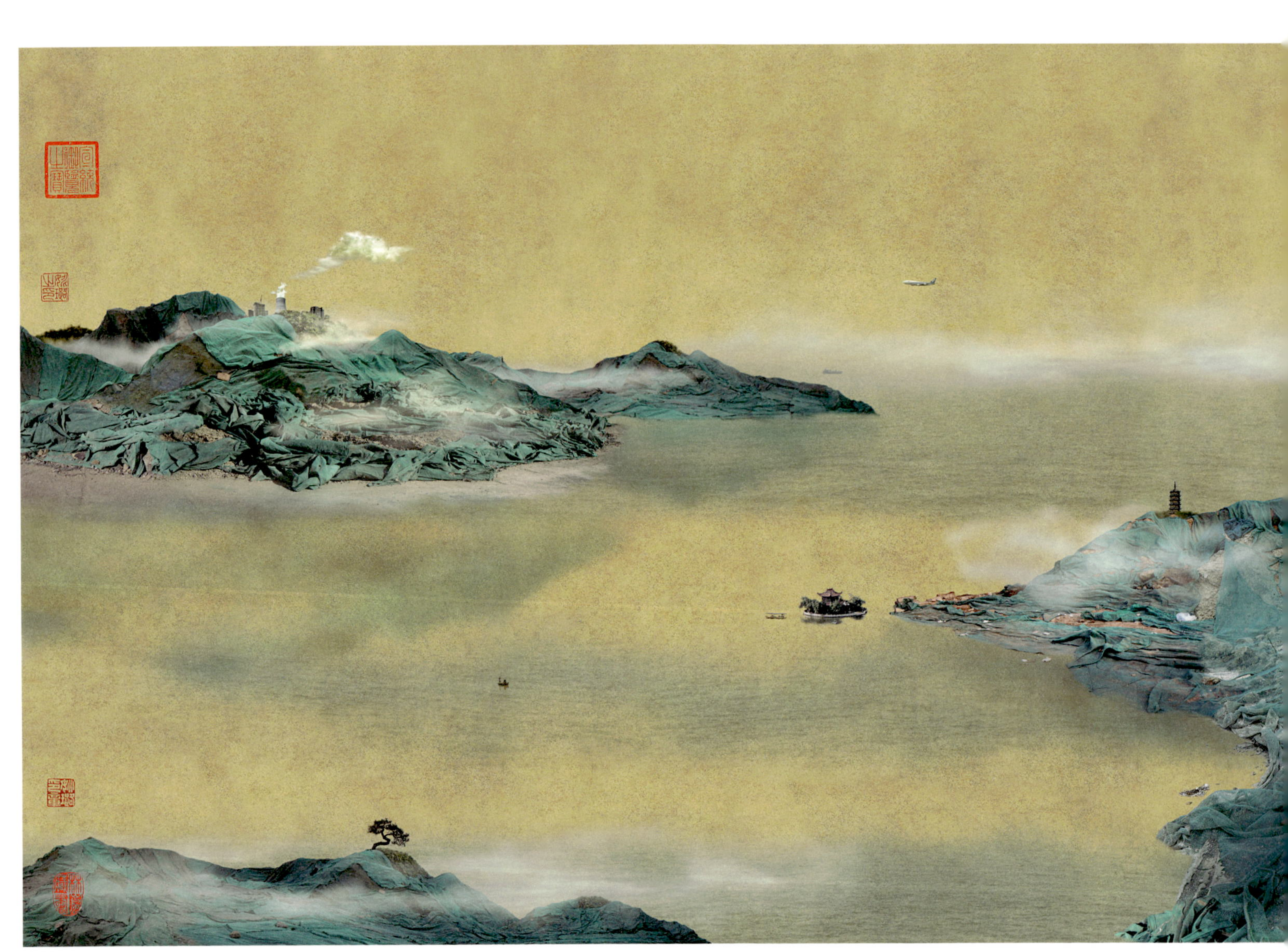

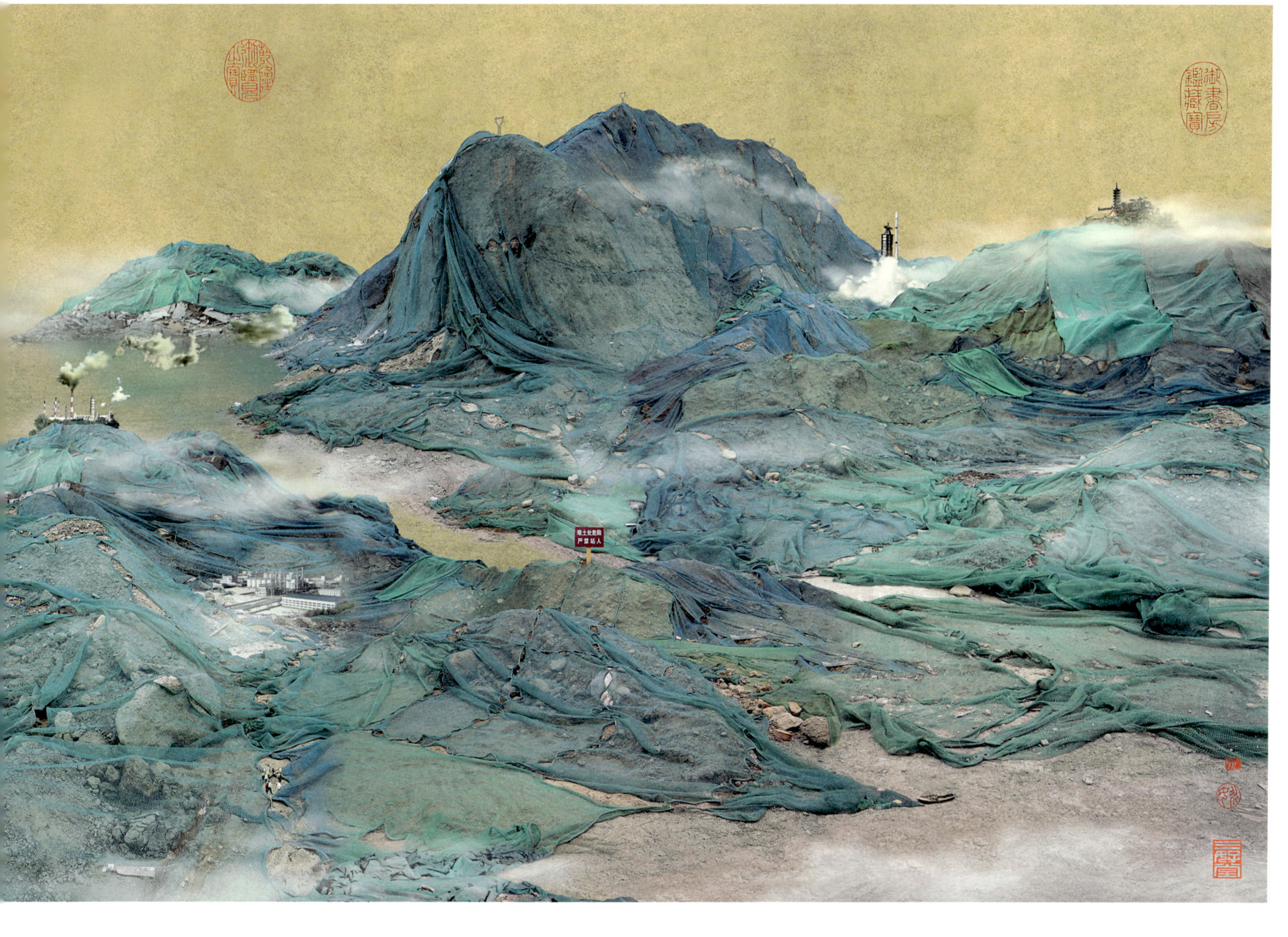

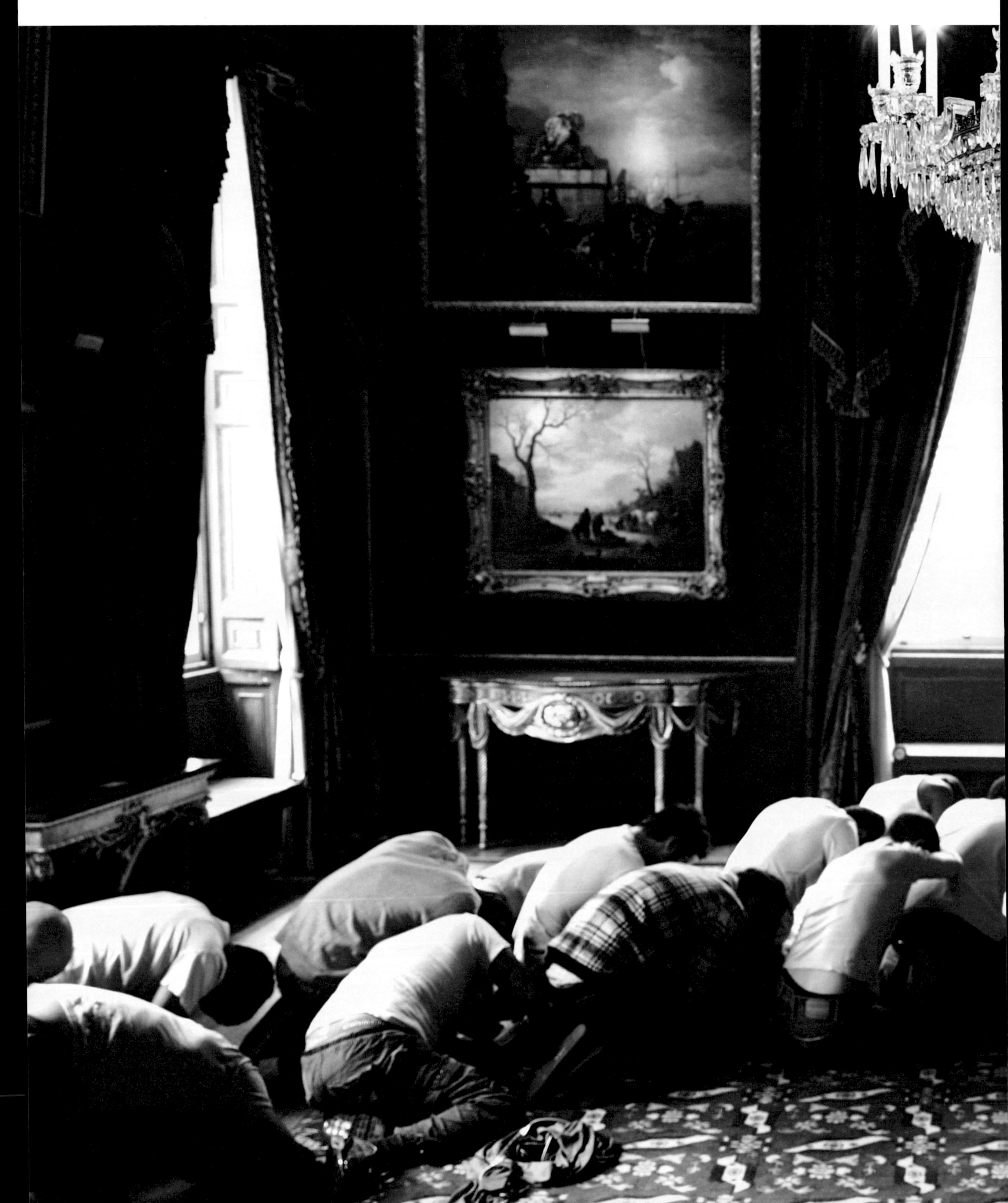

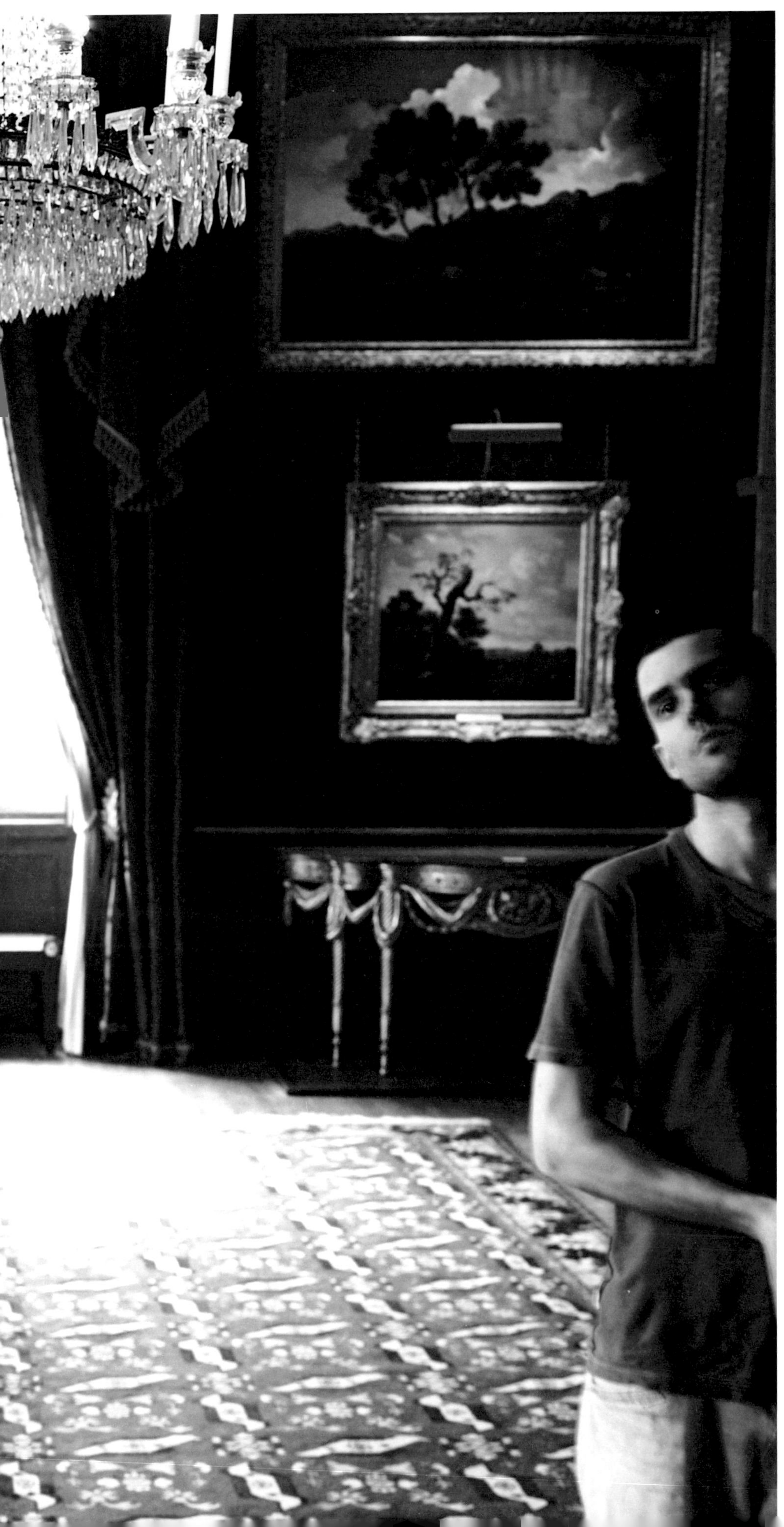

REZA ARAMESH

BETWEEN THE EYE AND THE OBJECT FALLS A SHADOW...

Looking at the work of Reza Aramesh, one inevitably thinks that all styles and approaches to documentary photography have radically changed in relationship with the arts and other media. Aramesh's perfectly executed translations of images taken from the news, merge the opposite ends of the photographic spectrum, reportage and staged photography, illuminating both his subjects and practice. The erasure of arms, and often of those who bear them, renders pictures emblematic, suspended in space and time. Only by reading the titles you actually understand what they stand for. Blurring the boundaries between the most immediate, urgent form of photography and its most constructed counterpart, Aramesh questions the status of both. He reflects on conflicts of meaning, by recreating those among humans. To consider documentary photography as a form of art adds to its significance, and claim as witness to the multiple realities of those who are observed and observe. Pushing the viewer towards a better understanding and towards, possibly, truth, momentary or partial as it might be. The invasion of the media is part of our lives and we know too well that they are devices to create realities rather than to record them. Photography is a protagonist in this comedy of errors. *Aramesh's Between the Eye and the Object Falls a Shadow...* - a title inspired by The Burroughs File of William S. Burroughs - is part of his Actions series. It uses the narrative of Western History, its representations and conflicts, as a point of departure, and by re-contextualizing acts of aggression, it turns our attention away from the description of warfare. Highlighting mechanisms of subjection and submission, it underlines all the suffering human minds are able to inflict and endorse. And the ways we try not to think about it.

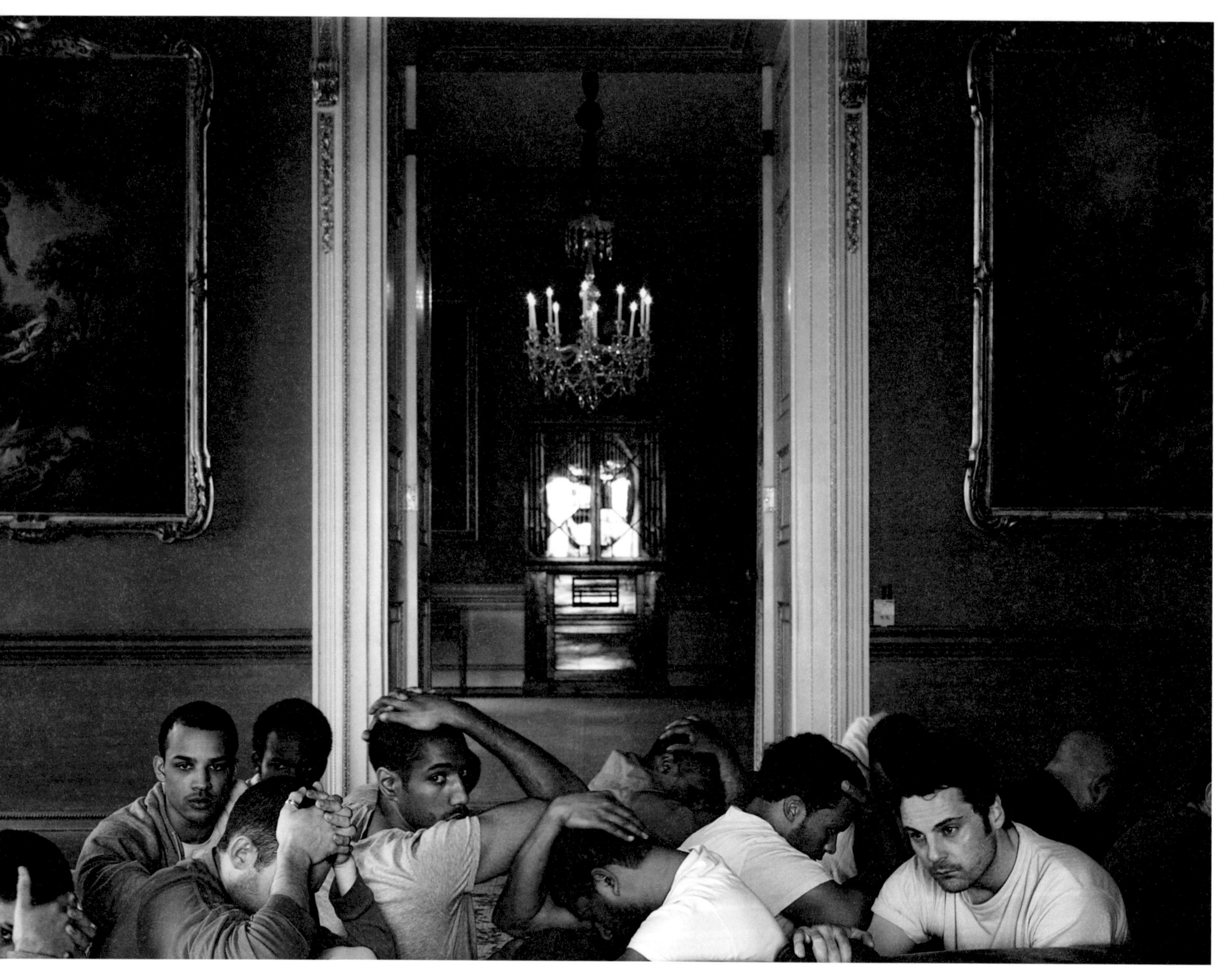

Here Action 65. Egyptian prisoners captured by Israeli troops, during the Six Day War in the Middle East. June 9, 1967. *Silver gelatin print, cm. 124 x 169, 2009. Right* Action 50. Lebanese intelligence agents arrest demonstrators near the justice palace in Beirut, August 9, 2001. *Silver gelatin print, cm. 124 x 157, 2008. Previous spread* Action 72. Korean civilians "suspected of being communist" tied up to poles and blindfolded, with bull's eyes pinned over their hearts, just before being shot by South Korean Military Police firing squad, ten miles northeast of Seoul, April 14, 1950. *Silver gelatin print, cm. 124 x 170, 2009*

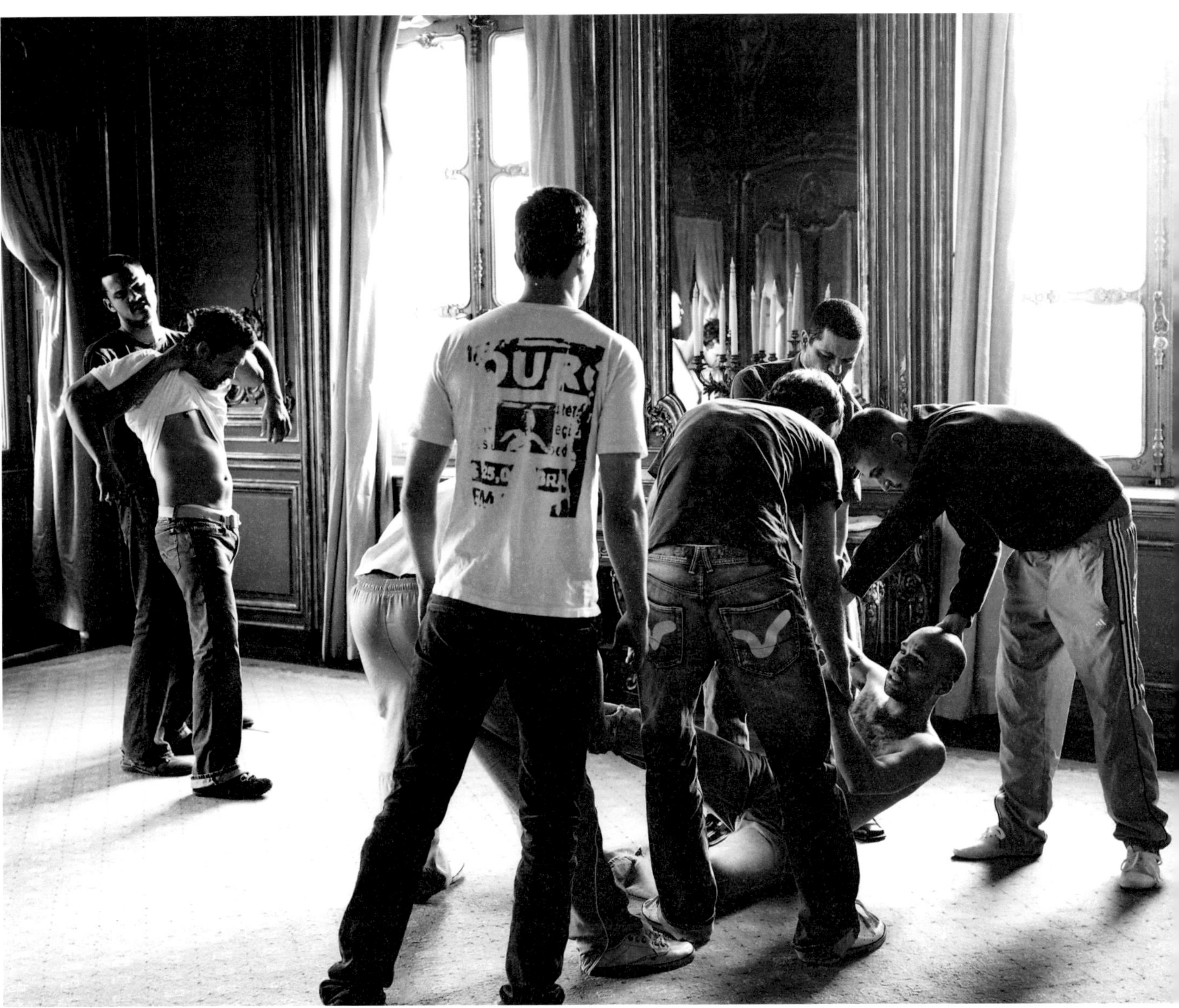

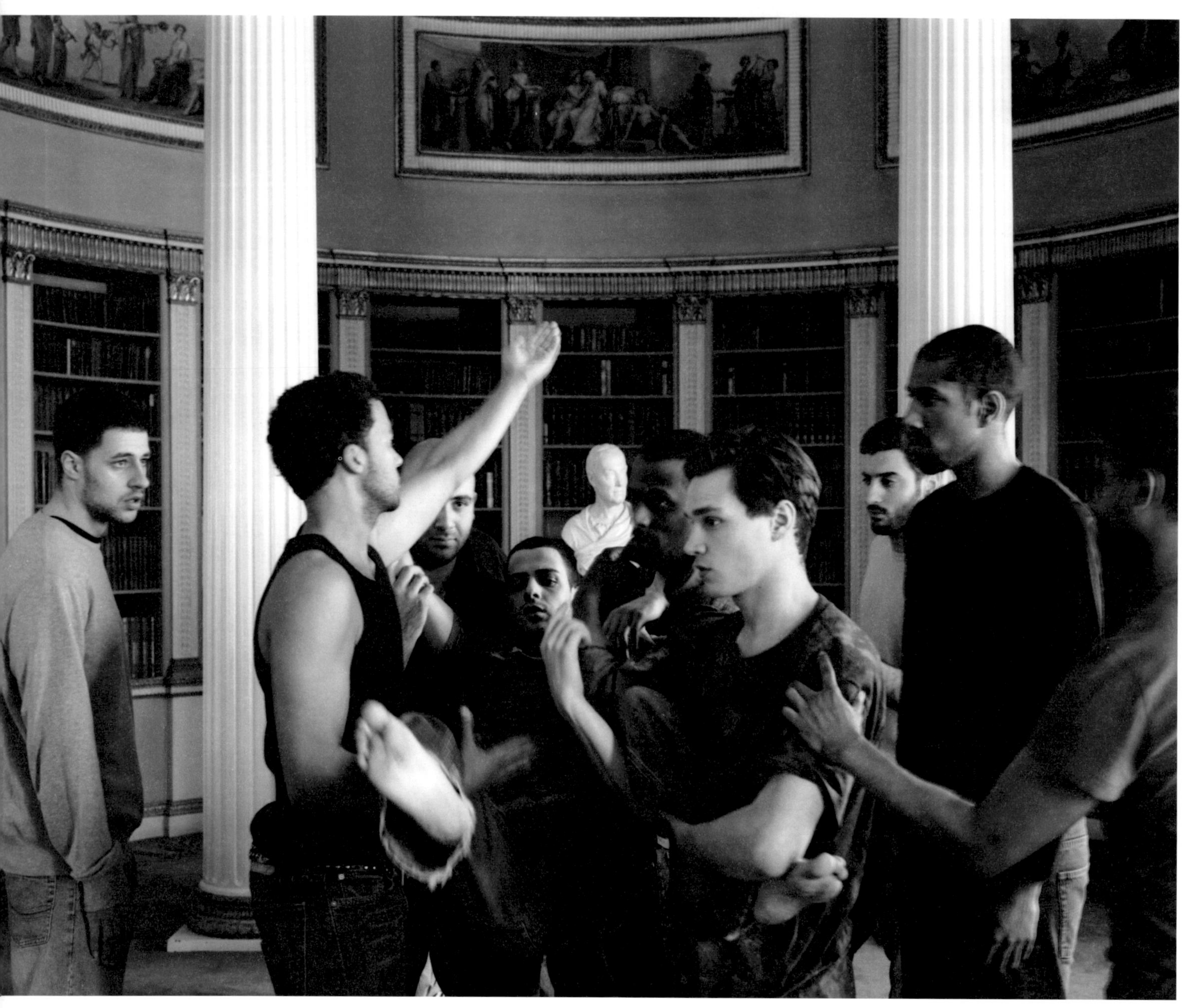

Above Action 70. An injured Palestinian is carried during clashes between security members loyal to President Mahmoud Abbas and members of the security forces controlled by the Hamas-led government. Khan Younis, Gaza Strip - October 1, 2006. *Silver gelatin print, cm. 124 x 158, 2009. Right* Action 67. A Somalian man wounded in mortar attack February 24, 2009 in Mogadishu is assisted to hospital. *Silver gelatin print, cm. 158 x 124, 2009. All images © the artist, courtesy the artist and Gallery Isabelle van den Eynde, Dubai*

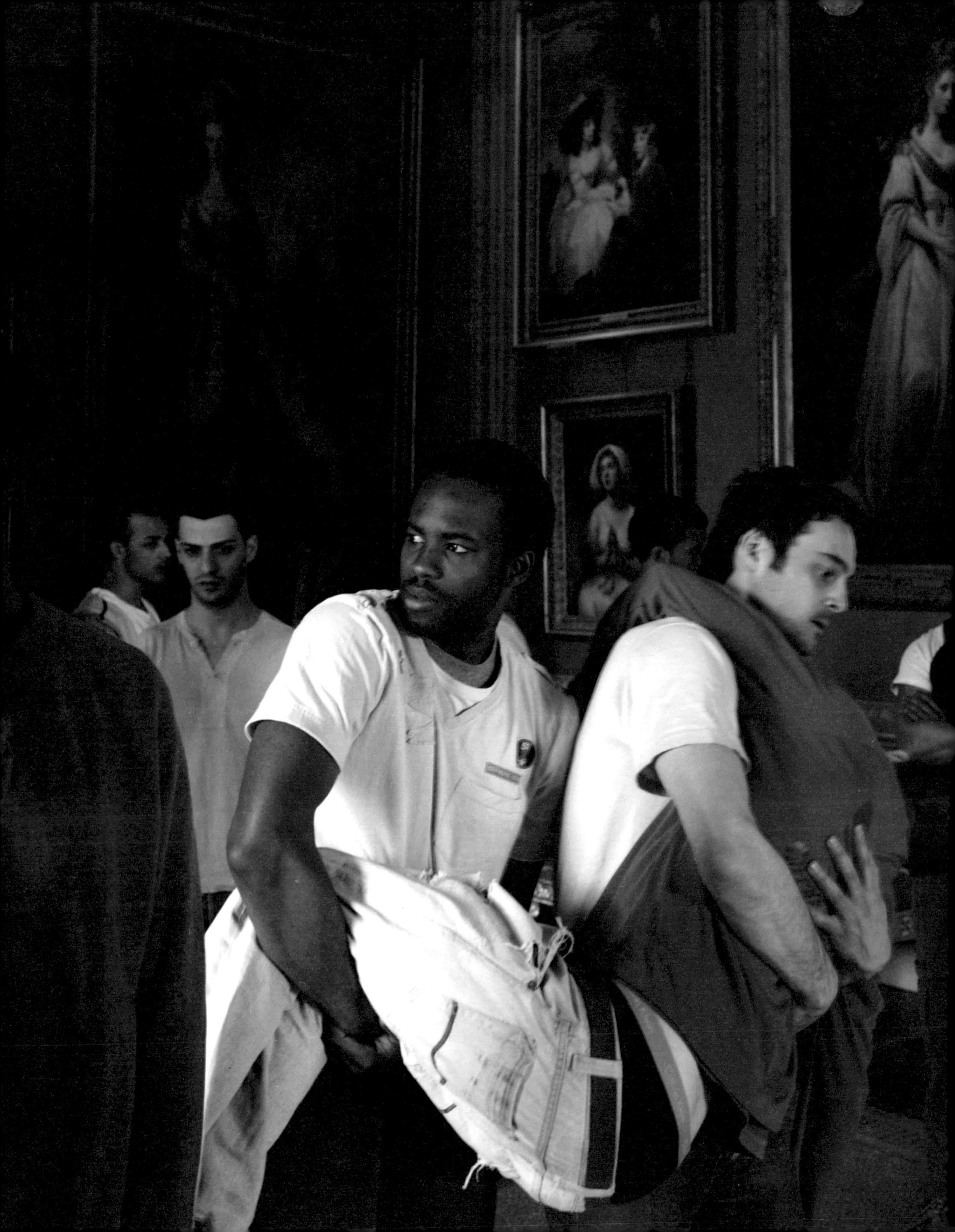

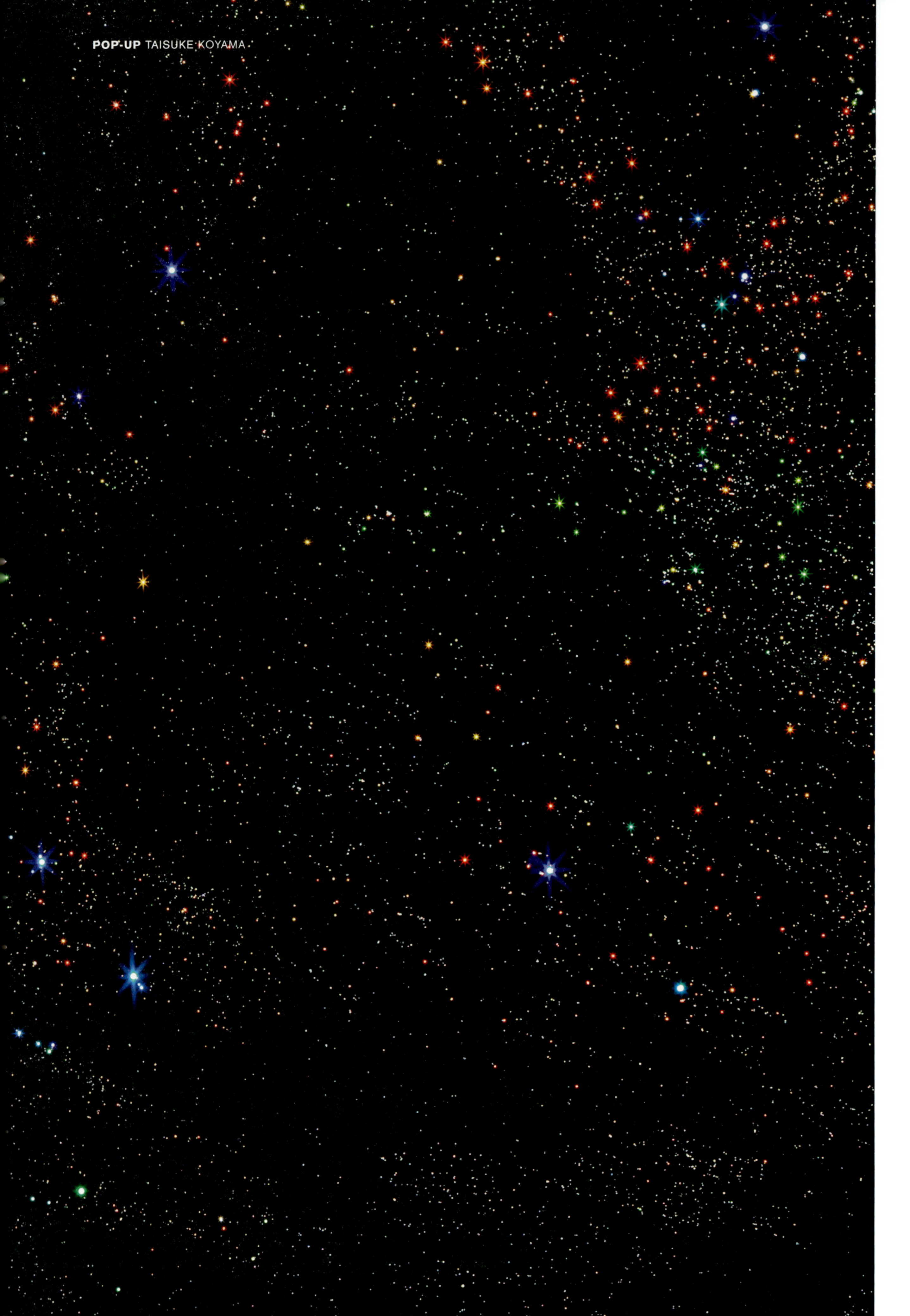

POP-UP TAISUKE KOYAMA
Untitled (Starry 8) 2009

Untitled (Starry 9) 2009 © the artist, courtesy G/P Gallery, Tokyo

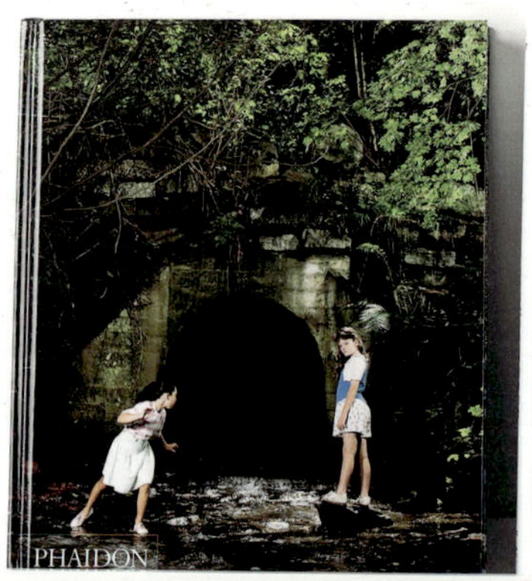
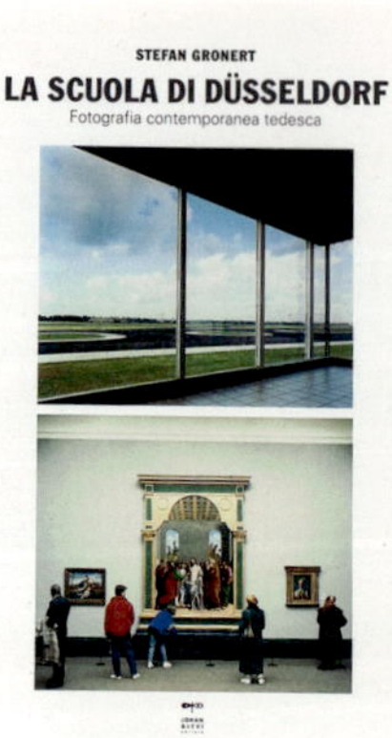

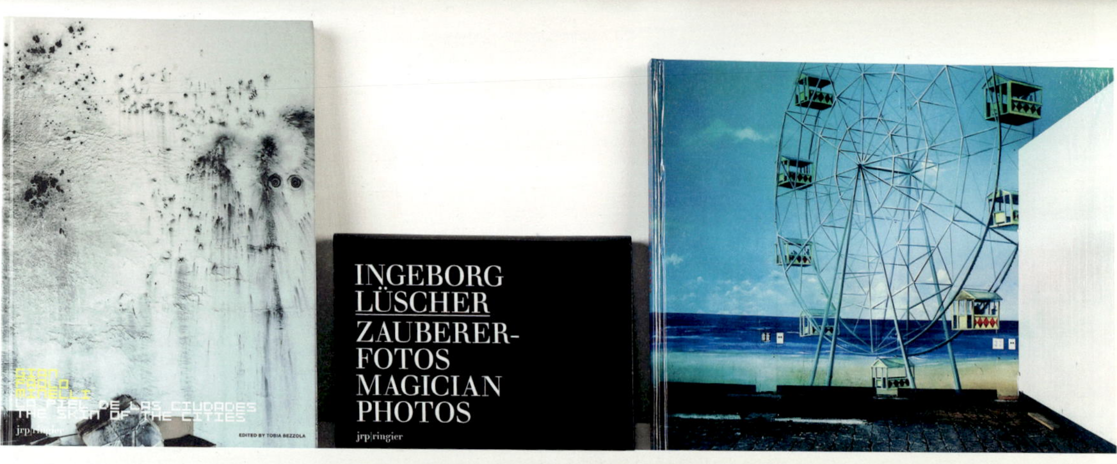

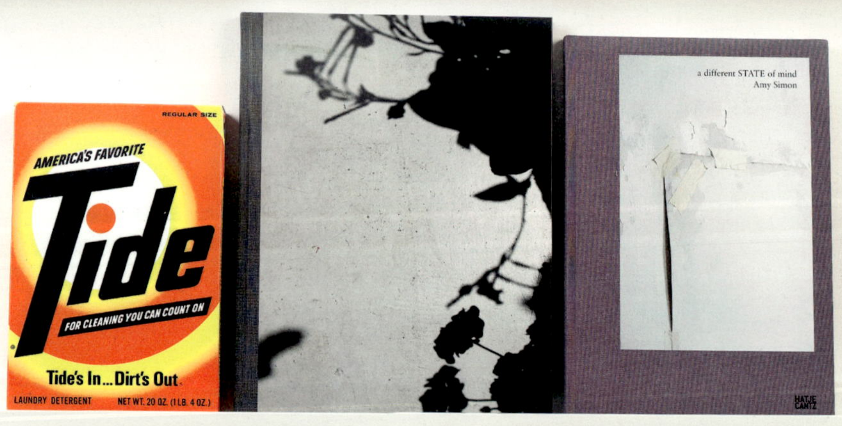

ON OUR SHELVES *Top shelf* Jeff Wall *The Complete Edition*, 280 pages, Phaidon *phaidon.com*; Stefan Gronert *La Scuola di Düsseldorf: Fotografia Contemporanea Tedesca*, 320 pages, Johan & Levi *johanandlevi.com*; *The Museum of Everything*, the collection of James Brett, 296 pages, Pinacoteca Giovanni e Marella Agnelli, Mondadori/Electa *electaweb.com*. *Center shelf* Gian Paolo Minelli *The Skin of the Cities*, edited by Tobia Bezzola, 156 pages, JRP/Ringier *jrp-ringier.com*; Ingeborg Lüscher, *Magician Photos*, 258 pages, JRP/Ringier *jrp-ringier.com*; Liza Kereszi *Fun and Games*, 72 pages, Nazraeli Press *nazraeli.com*. *Bottom shelf* Paul McCarthy *Low Life Slow Life*, edited by Stacen Berg and Jens Hoffmann, 648 pages, Hatje Cantz *hatjecantz.de*; Collier Shorr *Blumen*, 104 pages, Steidl Mack *steidlville.com*; Amy Simon *A Different State of Mind*, 80 pages, Hatje Cantz *hatjecantz.de*

TAISUKE KOYAMA lives and works in Tokyo, where he was born in 1978. With extracts from his series *Entropix* (a focal point of his activity, compound of "entropy", "picture" and "pixel"), *Rainbow Form, Starry* and *Thousand Impacts*, he is the protagonist of this *Fantom* Pop-Up section. "My works can be described as 'organic abstract photography', which depicts the phenomenon and surface of the city by using microlenses. I have studied the two opposing elements, city and nature, and understood that organic and inorganic exist in one intimate circulation. This made me doubt general ideas, opening my attitude to this world with a sense of diversity. So I hope that by looking at my pictures people will see and find something they have missed before, or gain new viewpoints, freely, just like when you listen to music".

REZA ARAMESH was born in Awhaz, Iran, in 1970 and moved to London at the age of sixteen. He studied sciences and then art, eventually earning his MA in Fine Arts at Goldsmith College in 1997. He has exhibited his work in numerous solo and group shows in the UK and abroad. He lives and works in London.

ALEX GARTENFELD is an art critic and Online Editor for *Interview Magazine* and *Art in America*. He is the co-founder of an independent gallery space called Three's Company in New York.

MARCELO KRASILCIC is a Brazilian American artist born in São Paulo into an eastern European Jewish family. He moved to New York in 1990 to study photography at the New York University and yoga at the Jivamukti Center and Patanjali Yoga Shala. Since graduating from NYU, Marcelo started exhibiting his artwork in galleries and museums and contributing to magazines such as *Purple, Dazed & Confused, Interview* and *Visionaire*. Marcelo continues to live in New York, and he travels extensively working in the fields of advertising, portraiture, art and fashion photography. *The Last Decade*, Marcelo's book about the 90's, is set to be out in the fall.

CHRISTIAN RATTEMEYER is an art historian and associate curator for drawings at the Museum of Modern Art in New York.

EMMA REEVES formerly photographic director at London-based Dazed & Confused, Another Magazine and Another Man, is now managing editor of V Magazine and V Man in New York.

FEDERICO SARICA is a journalist and the director of Vice Italy. He is a regular contributor to *D La Repubblica, L'Uomo Vogue, Il Foglio Quotidiano* and *Rolling Stone* with articles on culture and society.

ALEC SOTH is a photographer born and based in Minneapolis, Minnesota. His photographs have been featured in numerous solo and group exhibitions, including Jeu de Paume in Paris, Fotomuseum Winterthur (Switzerland) and the Whitney and São Paulo biennials. In 2010, the Walker Art Center will be exhibiting and touring a large survey of Soth's work in the US. In 2008, Soth started his own publishing company, Little Brown Mushroom.

FABIENNE STEPHAN is a Switzerland-born, New York-based curator. She currently works as a director at the gallery Salon 94 in New York and is the co-founder of Art Since The Summer Of 69, an exhibition space in the Lower East Side. Recent projects include the exhibitions *Early Works* (co-curated with Marilyn Minter and Matthew Higgs) for White Columns, and *New Works, Aloïs Godinat* for Artist Space in New York.

GILDA RACHEL WAJNSZTEJN is a Brazilian creative director, copywriter and strategy planner. She has worked for over 30 years with some of the most important advertising agencies, creating campaigns for a wide variety of clients. She has garnered over 40 awards including Premio Colunista, Globes and Anuario Clube de Criação de São Paulo. She is the aunt of Marcelo Krasilcic, whose work *Just Like The First Time* she introduced for this issue of *Fantom*.

FANTOM *with an F*, is a new international quarterly publication about the uses and abuses of photography. It is about the art of capturing timed effects of light. For practitioners and professionals by professional practitioners, FANTOM enframes its content in sectors: EYE TO EYE where photographers converse; SAMPLE SIZE with ready made discoveries by excellent eyes; BY APPOINTMENT ONLY offered by a collector or about a collection; EYE OF THE BEHOLDER where galler-ists celebrate the time based talents they expose and trade; and MEANS TO AN END surveying the uninten-tional surprises of purposeful image production, i.e. scientific, commercial, surveillance, documentary and the like. Herein the vernacular can take precedence over the artistic and vice versa depending on the value not of a discourse that comes after the image but al-lowing pictures to lead the discussions. A voyage into photography, FANTOM orients readers and viewers in the scaled horizons drawn by photography and those who critique, exhibit, collect, occupy and emulate it. Found, forgotten and not yet discovered, first and fore-most FANTOM features the voice of photographers, in interviews, portfolios, and statements alongside the often silent but rarely without a voice medium of *Fotography.*

GUIDI FIUME GUIDO GUIDI FIUME GUIDO GUIDI FIUME GUIDO GUIDI FIUME
GUIDO GUIDI FIUME GUIDO GUIDI FIUME GUIDO GUIDI FIUME GUIDO GUIDI FIUME
DO GUIDI FIUME GUIDO GUIDI FIUME GUIDO GUIDI FIUME GUIDO GUIDI FIUME
E GUIDO GUIDI FIUME GUIDO GUIDI FIUME GUIDO GUIDI FIUME GUIDO GUIDI FIUME
GUIDI FIUME GUIDO GUIDI FIUME GUIDO GUIDI FIUME GUIDO GUIDI FIUME
UME GUIDO GUIDI FIUME GUIDO GUIDI FIUME GUIDO GUIDI FIUME GUIDO GUIDI FIUME
O GUIDI FIUME GUIDO GUIDI FIUME GUIDO GUIDI FIUME GUIDO GUIDI FIUME
DO GUIDI FIUME GUIDO GUIDI FIUME GUIDO GUIDI FIUME GUIDO GUIDI FIUME
GUIDO GUIDI FIUME GUIDO GUIDI FIUME GUIDO GUIDI FIUME GUIDO GUIDI FIUME
DI FIUME GUIDO GUIDI FIUME GUIDO GUIDI FIUME GUIDO GUIDI FIUME
GUIDO GUIDI FIUME GUIDO GUIDI FIUME GUIDO GUIDI FIUME GUIDO GUIDI FIUME
ME GUIDO GUIDI FIUME GUIDO GUIDI FIUME GUIDO GUIDI FIUME GUIDO GUIDI FIUME
GUIDI FIUME GUIDO GUIDI FIUME GUIDO GUIDI FIUME GUIDO GUIDI FIUME
UIDO GUIDI FIUME GUIDO GUIDI FIUME GUIDO GUIDI FIUME GUIDO GUIDI FIUME
DI FIUME GUIDO GUIDI FIUME GUIDO GUIDI FIUME GUIDO GUIDI FIUME
E GUIDO GUIDI FIUME GUIDO GUIDI FIUME GUIDO GUIDI FIUME GUIDO GUIDI FIUME
IDI FIUME GUIDO GUIDI FIUME GUIDO GUIDI FIUME GUIDO GUIDI FIUME
DO GUIDI FIUME GUIDO GUIDI FIUME GUIDO GUIDI FIUME GUIDO GUIDI FIUME
GUIDI FIUME GUIDO GUIDI FIUME GUIDO GUIDI FIUME GUIDO GUIDI FIUME
O GUIDI FIUME GUIDO GUIDI FIUME GUIDO GUIDI FIUME GUIDO GUIDI FIUME
FIUME GUIDO GUIDI FIUME GUIDO GUIDI FIUME GUIDO GUIDI FIUME
GUIDI FIUME GUIDO GUIDI FIUME GUIDO GUIDI FIUME GUIDO GUIDI FIUME
UIDI FIUME GUIDO GUIDI FIUME GUIDO GUIDI FIUME GUIDO GUIDI FIUME
E GUIDO GUIDI FIUME GUIDO GUIDI FIUME GUIDO GUIDI FIUME GUIDO GUIDI FIUME G
FIUME GUIDO GUIDI FIUME GUIDO GUIDI FIUME GUIDO GUIDI FIUME
GUIDI FIUME GUIDO GUIDI FIUME GUIDO GUIDI FIUME GUIDO GUIDI FIUME
UME GUIDO GUIDI FIUME GUIDO GUIDI FIUME GUIDO GUIDI FIUME
O GUIDI FIUME GUIDO GUIDI FIUME GUIDO GUIDI FIUME GUIDO GUIDI FIUME GUIDO
IDI FIUME GUIDO GUIDI FIUME GUIDO GUIDI FIUME GUIDO GUIDI FIUME
O GUIDI FIUME GUIDO GUIDI FIUME GUIDO GUIDI FIUME GUIDO GUIDI FIUME
FIUME GUIDO GUIDI FIUME GUIDO GUIDI FIUME GUIDO GUIDI FIUME
IDI FIUME GUIDO GUIDI FIUME GUIDO GUIDI FIUME GUIDO GUIDI FIUME
ME GUIDO GUIDI FIUME GUIDO GUIDI FIUME GUIDO GUIDI FIUME
O GUIDI FIUME GUIDO GUIDI FIUME GUIDO GUIDI FIUME GUIDO GUIDI FIUME
IDI FIUME GUIDO GUIDI FIUME GUIDO GUIDI FIUME GUIDO GUIDI FIUME
DI FIUME GUIDO GUIDI FIUME GUIDO GUIDI FIUME GUIDO GUIDI FIUME
E GUIDO GUIDI FIUME GUIDO GUIDI FIUME GUIDO GUIDI FIUME GUIDO GUIDI FIUME
IDO GUIDI FIUME GUIDO GUIDI FIUME GUIDO GUIDI FIUME GUIDO GUIDI FIUME
GUIDI FIUME GUIDO GUIDI FIUME GUIDO GUIDI FIUME GUIDO GUIDI FIUME
I FIUME GUIDO GUIDI FIUME GUIDO GUIDI FIUME GUIDO GUIDI FIUME GUIDO GUIDI F
IDO GUIDI FIUME GUIDO GUIDI FIUME GUIDO GUIDI FIUME GUIDO GUIDI FIUME
UIDI FANTOMBOOKS GUI IDO GUIDI FIUME GUIDO GUIDI FIUME
DI FI ISBN 978-88-96677-04-9 UIDI O GUIDI FIUME GUIDO GUIDI FIUME
IDO GUIDI FIUME GUIDO GUIDI FIUME GUIDO GUIDI FIUME GUIDO GUIDI FIUME

FONDAZIONE MALVINAMENEGAZ
per le Arti e le Culture

FANTOMBOOKS

FIUME BY GUIDO GUIDI
THE SECOND IN OUR SERIES OF PHOTOBOOKS. LIMITED EDITION OF
300 AVAILABLE IN SELECTED BOOKSHOPS WORLDWIDE AND THROUGH
FANTOMEDITIONS.COM *an imprint of Boiler Corporation*

COLOPHON

EDITORS
Cay Sophie Rabinowitz, Selva Barni
editorial@fantomeditions.com

CONTRIBUTING EDITOR
Francesco Zanot
francesco@fantomeditions.com

ART DIRECTOR
Davies Costacurta
sm-work.com

VISUAL EDITOR AT LARGE
Pino Pipoli
pipoli@fantomeditions.com

EDITORIAL ASSISTANT
Didier Falzone
didier@fantomeditions.com

DESIGN ASSISTANT
Pietro Malacarne

INTERN
Erin Tao (New York)

TRANSLATIONS
Judith Mundell

COPY EDITOR
Kyre Chenven

THANKS TO
Agnese Bossi, Alberto Pellegrinet, Angelo Maestroni, Luca Cipelletti, Luciano Cirelli, Martina Scapinello, Mary Skinner, Massimo Mezzavilla, Pasquale Marini, Sean Beolchini, Skype, Sofia Sizzi and Iacopo Falai, Stefano Pitigliani

FANTOM OFFICE MILANO
Via Nicola Palmieri 34, 20141 Milano, Italy

FANTOM OFFICE NEW YORK
137 Grand Street, 10013 New York, NY, USA

ADVERTISING ENQUIRIES
info@fantomeditions.com

WWW.FANTOMEDITIONS.COM

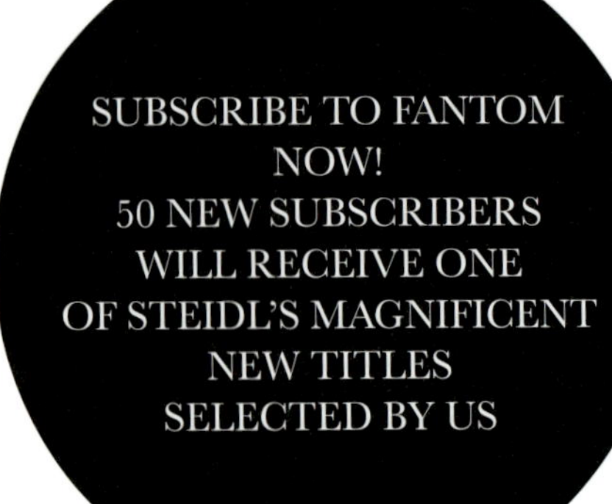

SUBSCRIPTIONS
Bruil & van de Staaij
PO Box 75, 7940 AB Meppel, The Netherlands
T +31 522 261303 - F + 31 522 257827
www.bruil.info/magazine-fantom

DISTRIBUTION
Italia and International: S.I.E.S. Srl
Via Bettola 18, 20092 Cinisello Balsamo (MI), Italy
T +39 02 66030400 - F +39 02 66030269
sies@siesnet.it - www.siesnet.it

North America: D.A.P./Distributed Art Publishers
155 Sixth Avenue, 2nd Floor, 10013 New York, NY, USA
T +1 212 627 1999 - F +1 212 627 9484
www.artbook.com

PUBLISHED BY
Boiler Corporation Srl
Piazza Castello 19, 20121 Milano, Italy

Numero di Iscrizione al R.O.C. 19.061 del 12/10/2009

PUBLISHER & EDITOR AT LARGE
Massimo Torrigiani
m.torrigiani@boilercorporation.com

ASSISTANT PUBLISHER
Pier Mario Simula
p.simula@boilercorporation.com

BOILER INTERN
Gabriele Verratti

Printed in Italy by Grafiche Antiga, Via delle Industrie 1
31035 Crocetta del Montello (TV)
www.graficheantiga.it

Periodico registrato presso il Tribunale di Milano
N° 436 del 07/10/2009
Direttore Responsabile: Selva Barni

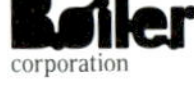

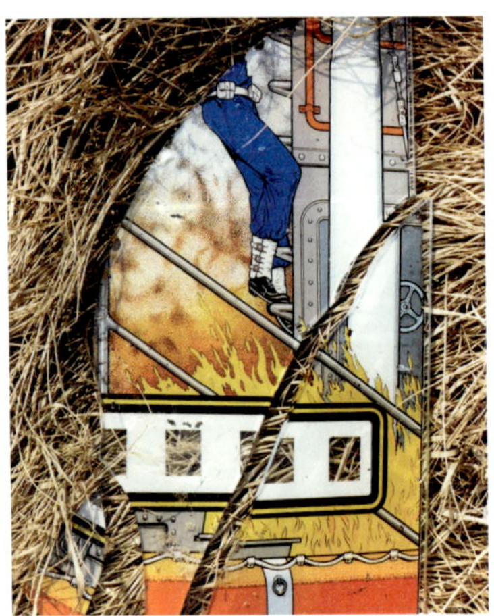

Fantom cover artist Olivo Barbieri will be featured in our next issue out in Summer 2010. On this cover: from the series *Flippers*, 1977-78 © the artist

FANTOM

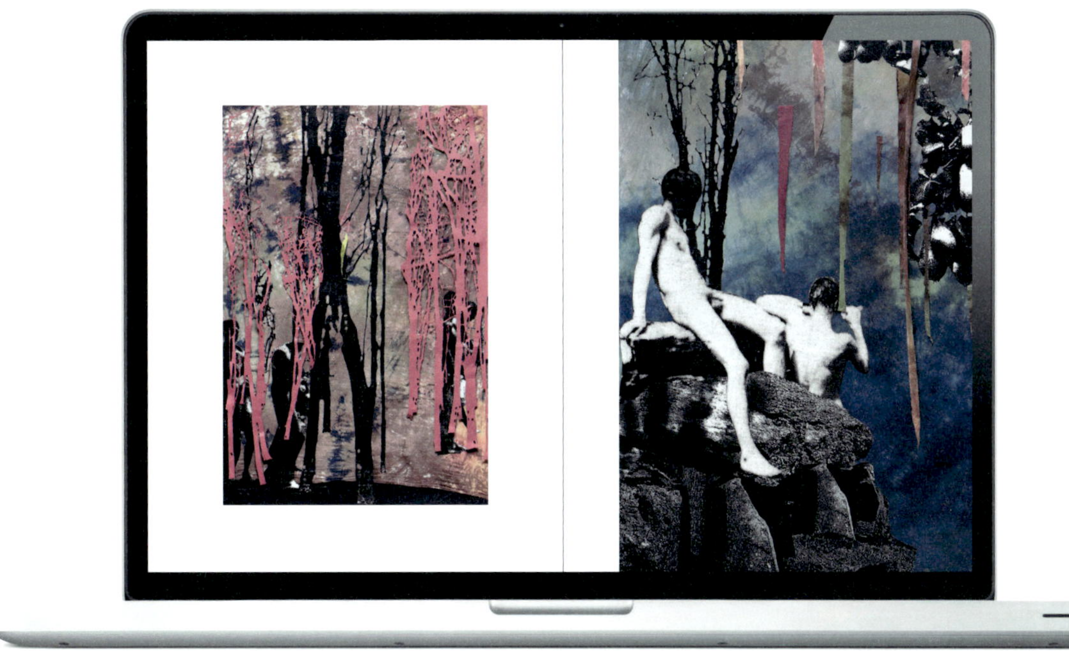

NOW ANYTIME,
ANYWHERE.

Other Edition.com

NYPH
10 New York Photo Festival May 12-16
DUMBOBrooklyn
The Future of Contemporary Photography
Curated by
Vince Aletti
Erik Kessels
Fred Ritchin
Lou Reed
www.newyorkphotofestival.com

Art | 41 | Basel 16–20 | 6 | 10

Vernissage | giugno 15, 2010 | unicamente su invito
Art Basel Conversations | giugno 16 a 20, 2010 | dalle ore 10 alle 11

The International Art Show – La Mostra Internazionale d'Arte
Art 41 Basel, MCH Fiera Svizzera (Basilea) SA, CH-4005 Basel
Fax +41 58 206 26 86, info@artbasel.com, www.artbasel.com

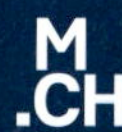

UBS

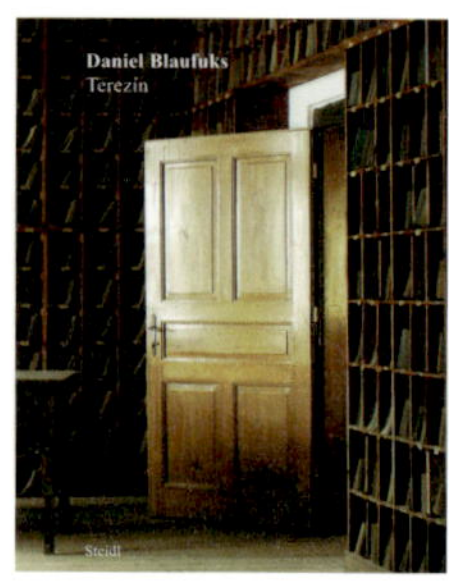

Terezín
Daniel Blaufuks
The book includes a DVD of Daniel
Blaufuks' film "Theresienstadt"
192 pages, 126 tritone plates
ISBN 978-3-86521-699-1

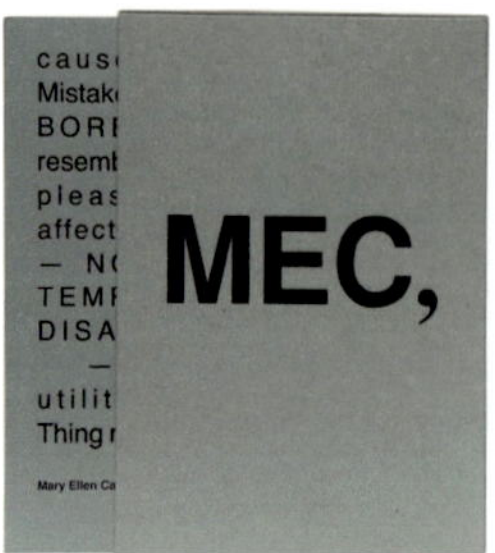

MEC
Mary Ellen Carroll
Essays by Jonathan Flatley
& Hamza Walker
Softcover housed in a slipcase
360 pages, 400 illustrations
ISBN 978-3-86521-618-2

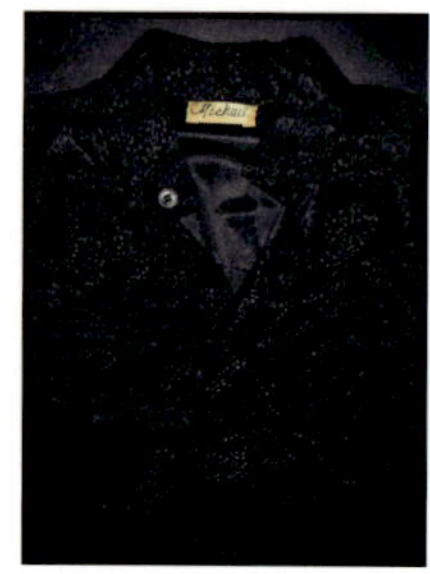

Neverland Lost. A Portrait
of Michael Jackson
by Henry Leutwyler
96 pages, hardcover
ISBN 978-3-86930-050-4

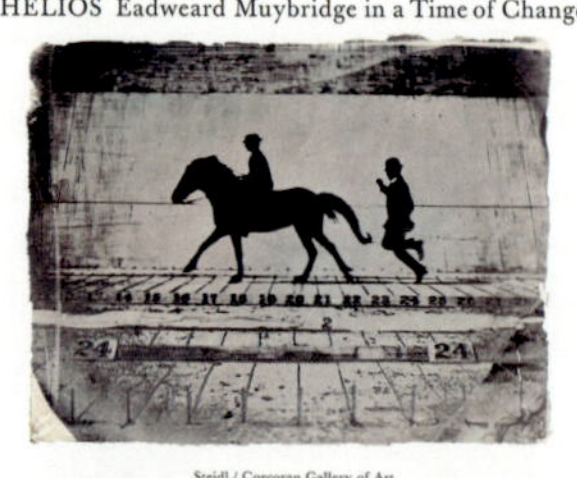

Helios: Eadweard Muybridge
in a Time of Change
Text by Philip Brookman, Rebecca Solnit,
Marta Braun & Corey Keller
360 pages, 389 photographs & illustrations
ISBN 978-3-86521-926-8

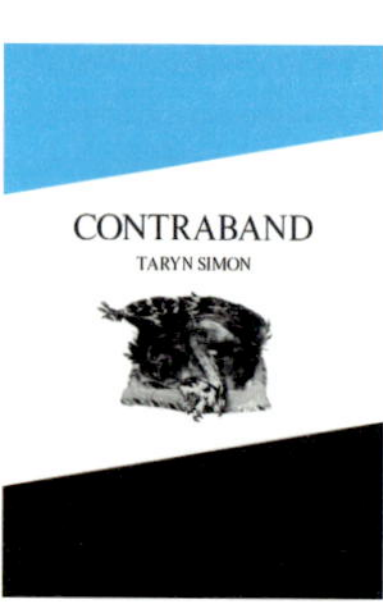

Contraband
Taryn Simon
Text by Hans Ulrich Obrist
224 pages, 200 colour plates
ISBN 978-3-86930-134-1

Dream Villa
Dayanita Singh
136 pages, four colour plates throughout
ISBN 978-3-86521-985-5

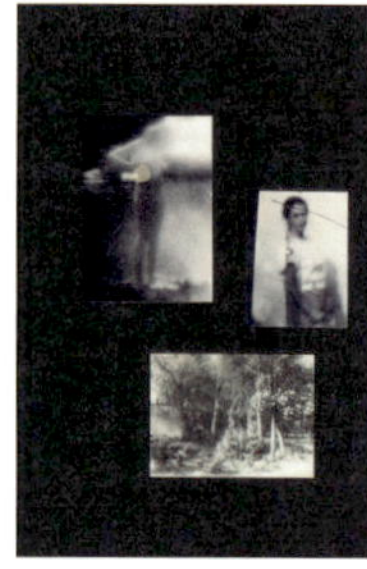

Miroslav Tichý
Texts by Brian Wallis, Roman Buxbaum,
Carolyn Christov-Bakargiev & Richard Prince
328 pages, 364 colour plates
ISBN 978-3-86930-102-0

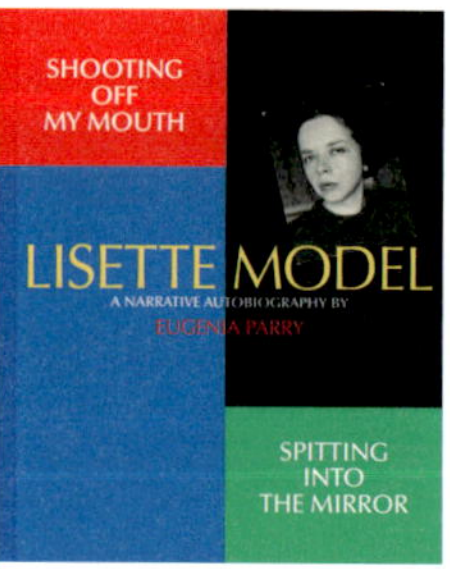

Shooting Off My Mouth.
Spitting Into the Mirror.
Lisette Model - A Narrative
Autobiography by Eugenia Parry
128 pages, hardcover
ISBN 978-3-86521-920-6

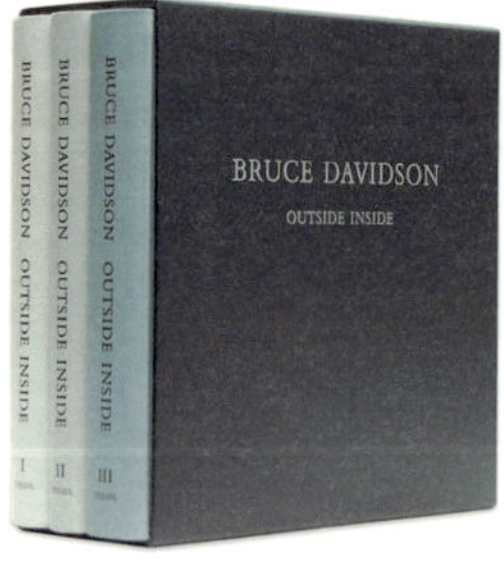

Outside Inside
Bruce Davidson
Three clothbound hardcover volumes
housed in a slipcase
800 pages, tritone plates throughout
ISBN 978-3-86521-908-4

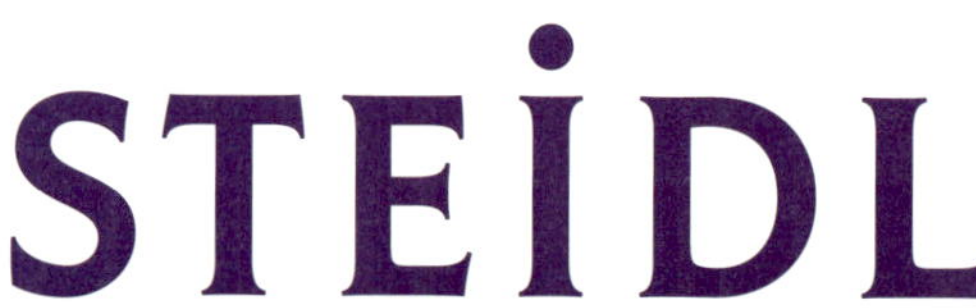

STEIDL

Available at all good bookstores
& online at Steidlville.com

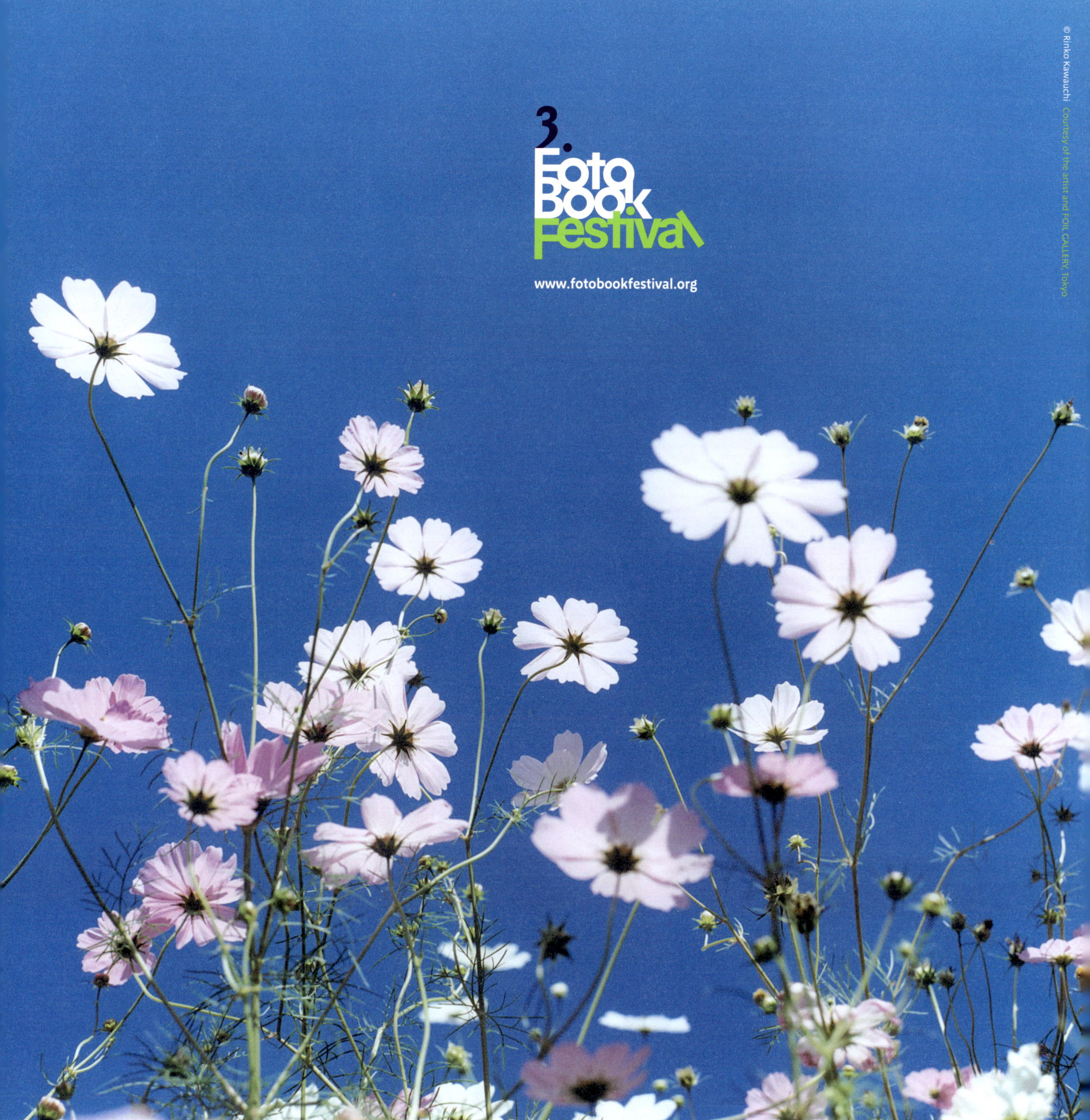

3rd International Photobook Festival
13 to 16 May 2010
documenta-Halle Kassel

From 13 to 16 May 2010 photobook enthusiasts from around the world will once again gather for the 3rd International Photobook Festival Kassel to address recent developments of this fascinating medium. Just like in previous years, internationally renowned practitioners have been invited to present their work with photobooks and to engage in conversations with the festival participants. We invite you to take part in the many talks, exhibitions, workshops, reviews, information and book stalls as well as a range of networking services. And we hope you will also enter our photobook dummy competition or reviewer prize.